149

BEYOND WALL STREET

THE ART OF INVESTING

S. L. Mintz
Dana Dakin
Thomas Willison

JOHN WILEY & SONS, INC.

New York • Chichester • Weinheim • Brisbane • Singapore • Toronto

Published by John Wiley & Sons, Inc.

Published simultaneously in Canada.

This publication is designed to provide accurate and authoritative information in regard to the subject matter covered. It is sold with the understanding that the publisher is not engaged in rendering professional services. If legal advice or other expert assistance is required, the services of a competent professional person should be sought.

Library of Congress Cataloging-in-Publication Data:

Mintz, Steven L.
    Beyond Wall Street : the art of investing / Steven L. Mintz.
       p.   cm.
    ISBN 0-471-24737-5 (cloth : alk. paper)
    1. Investments—United States.   2. Investment analysis—United
States.   I. Title.
    HG4910.M54   1998
    332.67′ 8—dc21   97-45081

Printed in the United States of America

10 9 8 7 6 5 4 3 2 1

To Melissa

Foreword

I'm a big fan of TV and not ashamed to say it. But TV has no index. TV has to be watched on its own schedule. TV can't be paused while we ponder or watched on our towel at the beach.

So if you are one of the 5.8 billion people on the planet who somehow missed much or all of *Beyond Wall Street,* the eight-part PBS documentary I got to host with my colleague Jane Bryant Quinn, this book is for you. Even if you didn't miss it you might be interested, because the authors have so nicely captured the stories, styles, and wisdom of our eight interviewees, often adding material that did not fit within the confines of a 27-minute broadcast.

THE STARS OF *BEYOND WALL STREET*

Foster Friess, whom I interviewed at his huge log cabin in Jackson, Wyoming, elected Jesus Christ chairman of his board some years ago and is as sunny and positive a presence as I've ever encountered. But we didn't select him for this or because he has a pet pig named Wilbur to whom he turns occasionally for 450 pounds of porcine investment advice. Rather, in overseeing upward of $13 billion, Foster embodies a style of investing that shouldn't work, but does. He jumps from one stock to another in hope of catching huge updrafts in growth stocks just before they occur—and kicks out the winners as soon as a more promising prospect comes along, never mind the taxes.

I met John Neff at his home outside Philadelphia. He's my kind of investor, stubbornly buying the stuff others don't want—like Citicorp, once upon a time—knowing that one day the cycle will turn and they'll want it again. I had long "known" Neff from his annual appearances in *Barron's* roundtable. Thanks to *Beyond Wall Street,* I got to know him better.

Barr Rosenberg does it all by computer. Except the one part you might *expect* to be done by computer—the actual trading. At his Orinda,

California firm, that's done by humans. But the computer decides what to buy or sell, and the level of intelligence that goes into its software, along with the billions of bits of data that stream into it every day from around the world, are awesome. When I playfully reached down to one of the cables and asked "what would happen if I unplugged this?" Barr's composure held—but barely. Brilliant, unlikely in some ways (he raises chickens but, being Buddhist, will not kill them), he begs the question: can a computer beat the market?

Bill Sharpe showed me a replica of his 1990 Nobel Prize, the real one being in a safe deposit someplace, and drove me around his Palo Alto neighborhood in a 1965 Citroën Deux Chevaux—and I actually got paid for this. It was Sharpe who pointed out that beating the market is only an achievement *when the risk you took to do it* is factored into the equation. And he wrote the equation. How does he invest much of his own money? Index funds.

Mark Mobius is our man in Thailand. And Singapore. And 40 other emerging markets we *didn't* follow him to. It's a big world out there, and drifting down Bangkok's Chao Praya River at midnight, and then visiting a factory that very likely makes the black nylon fabric in the umbrella that keeps you dry, I learned a good bit about it.

Bill Gross manages $90 billion or so in bonds, which has to be really boring until you realize that he somehow squeezes an extra 1 percent return out of his portfolio year after year—an extra $900 million. But the image that impressed me even more, as we looked out over the Pacific from his Laguna Beach living room, was of a 53-year-old man determined to live to 100, getting it into his mind to run from San Francisco to the Golden Gate Bridge—five back-to-back marathons over five successive days. On the last day of this run, his kidney ruptured. Blood was running down his leg. But he hadn't reached the bridge, so he kept running. Only when he finished did he allow the ambulance to whisk him away.

Gary Brinson, in Chicago, showed me a graph (although my eye did keep wandering to the Monet) which demonstrated something both interesting and important. Even though foreign stocks—Japanese stocks, say—are riskier than U.S. stocks, you can actually *reduce* the risk of your own portfolio, at the same time as you juice up your expected return a bit, by adding them to your mix. And this is a guy who oversees $120 billion, or, we calculated, roughly one quarter of 1 percent of all the world's investible assets. So listen up.

Peter Bernstein, it turned out, went to my high school way back when, had known my dad shortly after World War II, and now here we were in a helicopter off Santa Barbara flying to oil rig Irene to talk about risk. He'd recently published a whole book on the subject, *Against the Gods: The Remarkable Story of Risk,* a bestseller. As we landed on the rig in a stiff wind, hundreds of feet above the rough sea and the sharks below— yes, there were sharks—the setting seemed right. Although a long time horizon helps to reduce the risks, investing is anything but a smooth ride.

I drew three overall lessons from these visits. First: There is more than one way to skin a cat. No single investment style is the "right" one. Second: Each of these people had consistently done his homework, putting far more time and effort and passion into this than you or I would ever be likely to. Third: When we invest, these folks, and others like them, are our competition.

ANDREW TOBIAS

Preface

Any book about eight extraordinary investors in today's markets must cover the entire globe. The title of this book, *Beyond Wall Street,* suggests a world view, but it was by accident, not by design, that seven of the eight investors make their homes far from New York City's financial district. Value man John Neff, an Ohio native, now lives in suburban Philadelphia. Gary Brinson, the asset allocater from Washington State, makes his home in Chicago. Growth stock aficionado Foster Friess hails originally from Wisconsin and now divides his time between Wilmington, Delaware, and Jackson Hole, Wyoming. Nobel laureate William Sharpe, an indexing advocate, and bond guru William Gross are Californians, by way of Boston and Middletown, Ohio. Barr Rosenberg also lives and works in California, his home state. If you can catch up to globe-trotting Mark Mobius, a native of Long Island and now a German citizen based in Hong Kong and Singapore, he'll be en route from one emerging market to another. That leaves Peter Bernstein, a lifelong New Yorker whose proximity to Wall Street has never curtailed his broad historical perspective on markets and investment.

In a profession where distinctions often suffer from fuzziness, these eight investment professionals come through with clarity and confidence. This book provides an opportunity to learn what each of them has discovered in the course of a very prominent career. Don't expect to find one investment style that beats the others in all markets. The choice of a suitable investment strategy always rests with an individual's financial circumstance and risk tolerance. Be wary of efforts to promote bonds over growth stocks, asset allocation models over value stocks, emerging markets over quantitative analysis, or any single investment style over all others. They all have flaws as well as merits. None of these investors expects to be right 100 percent of the time. For every ten stocks Foster Friess picks for the Brandywine fund, four won't pan out. And that ratio tends to be typical for this group.

In a market where every tick of a stock price represents the opinion of thousands of investors, hot tips seldom convey information not present already in the stock price, and short-term strategies generally do more harm than good. An informed investor with a long-term view, however, can sift sound growth stocks from roman candles, or recognize an unpopular value stock poised for a return to favor, or plot an investment strategy that exploits the different ways asset classes interact. These are the skills that individual investors require when embarking on the long-term challenge of building wealth.

Nobel laureate William Sharpe likens this financial challenge to the options facing a driver who wants to travel from Pasadena, California, to Los Angeles. There are many routes, but the Los Angeles freeway is the best way to go, despite the prospects of inevitable traffic jams, occasional flat tires, and the ever-present threat of an earthquake. Side streets and back alleys through the hills and suburbs don't rule out calamities, and they certainly increase the chance of getting lost.

For investors counting on sufficient nest eggs, later in life, when the time comes to build a house, send kids to college, or retire, the biggest risk is to shun risk. As every careful automobile driver knows, pulling out of a driveway entails risk, far more risk, arguably, than careful investing. Yet many individuals who think nothing of driving across town, or across country, tremble at the thought of buying stocks or bonds in an active market.

For reluctant investors, the perilous line between too little risk and too much risk is easy to cross. An investor who squirrels money away in a savings account that doesn't keep up with inflation often tries to catch up at the worst times, when groupthink propels the markets to excess.

Fortunately, investors are getting smarter—with no time to spare. Assets today are accumulating at record levels, and investors are offered more ways than ever to put those assets to work. Just making money is not enough any more. As Woody Allen has said, now we have to worry about our money making money.

A common thread seems to link all eight successful careers that are the subjects of this book: These investors treat investment risk as a friend, not as an adversary. Despite inevitable uncertainty about what will happen in markets tomorrow, they embrace risk in the knowledge that prudent investing improves the odds of a favorable outcome.

Be warned, however. Past performance of investments and investment styles does not guarantee results in the future. Even the most talented investment managers fall off the pace from time to time. If the history of investing proves anything, it is that the pendulum never swings for too long in one direction.

If you want to learn about the art of investing, however, you won't find a more able group of practitioners. Happily, through these pages, those who excel in the art of investing also can teach.

S. L. MINTZ

Montclair, New Jersey
January 1998

Acknowledgments

Thanks are owed first and foremost to Eugene B. Shirley, Jr., the superbly capable producer and director who brought *Beyond Wall Street* to life for PBS audiences. I am deeply indebted to him for welcome encouragement and keen insights.

Without the relentless determination of Dana Dakin and Tom Willison, who dreamed up a great idea and stuck with it, *Beyond Wall Street* would not exist in print or video. I am grateful also to Andy Tobias, whose talents as an interviewer produced the transcripts on which much of this book is based.

Readers who caught errors, added perspective, and repeatedly steered me back to the correct path include Roland Machold, Dean LeBaron, Bill Fouse, and Peter Rubinstein.

As for the editorial crew at John Wiley & Sons, a writer could not ask for more capable or supportive colleagues than Myles Thompson, Jennifer Pincott, and Mary Daniello. Everett Sims is a truly talented editor. Nancy Marcus Land, of Publications Development Company, on the production side, kept life bearable if busy.

Julia Homer, the very able editor-in-chief of *CFO Magazine,* contributed to this book with unwavering encouragement and a flexible workload. I am grateful also to my fellow editors at *CFO:* Lori Calabro, Ed Teach, Roy Harris, and Ron Fink. Mere thanks do not express my gratitude to Sam Newborn for his loyalty and guidance at every step, or to Jim Fraser, a constant reminder that smart investing requires a sense of history and a sense of humor. John Goff, Philip Berry, Chuck Fisher, John Wilcox, Michael O'Loughlin, and Al Ehrbar all took time from their busy days to nudge this project along.

But most of all, I thank my wife, Melissa, and our sons, Ben and Thomas, who make everything worthwhile.

S. L. M.

Contents

1

Growth

FLYING HIGH

On his first foray into the stock market, Foster Friess lost his shirt and found a career. "I was taking a securities analysis course at the University of Wisconsin," says Friess, who was a nineteen-year-old sophomore at the time. "This professor was in love with the company, a great company. He was on the board, and I cashed in a twelve-hundred-dollar insurance policy my father had bought for me from the Lutheran Brotherhood." Such was his ardor that Friess unwittingly paid two dollars more than the published high in the stock guide, he later realized. "I lost so much money. I think I lost about eighty, ninety percent of my money. I was determined to get it back, so I launched off into the investment arena."

Friess's original career itinerary had not included investing. "I was slated to become a lawyer, like my brother," Friess says. "He had gone to business school and then to law school. And so that was the track I was on until I met this family who rescued me from being a lawyer." In the summer between his junior and senior years, a scholarship sponsored by the Brittingham family, of Wilmington, Delaware, paid Friess's fare for a summer in Scandinavia. Eventually, after a stint in the army, Friess went to work in the small investment firm that managed the Brittinghams' far-flung investments. It was a move he doesn't regret. "I have a mission now,"

1

he says. "I try to find young people headed for law school and rescue them and bring them into the investing business."

Since unfurling his own banner in 1974, Friess has posted a superlative record managing growth stocks, a highly volatile investment category. Thanks to the Brittingham connection, The Nobel Foundation became Friess Associates' first customer, and recipients of the prestigious Nobel Prize can thank Friess for a substantial portion of the prize money they take home.

Baron Stig Ramel, a former Nobel Foundation president, still sits on Friess's three-man board of directors. "When I joined The Nobel Foundation in 1972," Ramel recalls, "I went over to the States to visit the Brittingham family, who at the time were responsible for The Nobel Foundation's U.S. investments. I understood immediately that Foster, although a junior member of the staff, was the man who did the job. The next year, I came back and Foster drove me to the airport and said he planned to start his own business. He said, 'Will you give me the responsibility to manage the Nobel Fund in America?'"

Ramel agreed to be supportive, subject to approval by Nobel's directors. "The relationship with the Brittingham institution had lasted for quite some time," Ramel explains, "and my predecessor was a very close friend of the Brittinghams, but the father and the son had died and so it was not the same Brittingham company." Ramel returned to Stockholm and proposed that Friess Associates manage 70 percent of the fund and that the Brittinghams retain 30 percent. Each January, the Foundation would allot one-tenth of the U.S. total to the firm that had managed funds best in the previous year. "For three years, Foster managed his funds substantially better than the Brittinghams, and after three years he controlled 100 percent of the portfolio," says Ramel, "as was the rule of the game."

NO CHAIRS AT THE CONFERENCE TABLE

A lean board of directors reflects Friess's Spartan view of an investment process that demands quick action. "We have a very, very committed notion of avoiding meetings at all costs. We never believe in transferring information in the meeting or making a decision in a meeting. What you have meetings for is to transfer emotion if you want to recognize someone for doing a good job—for exhortation or for brainstorming. Where you get everybody together and say, 'Hey, let's brainstorm.' But in terms of day-to-day operations, we not only want to avoid meetings of four or five people, we want to avoid one-on-one meetings. And so, when we do have the meetings, we have them in a room with no chairs."

"Voiceless communication," or VC, prevails in a virtual office setup with branches in Wilmington, Delaware; Jackson Hole, Wyoming; and Phoenix, Arizona. "We've harnessed the e-mail and the fax and the overnight mail in such a way that all of our internal operations are done in a written format," Friess boasts, offering tangible evidence of the benefits. "We got everybody into a room one time. And we said, 'Ok, here's a page out of *Business Week*. Everybody read it and when you finish, raise your hand.' We timed it when everybody finished. We then said, 'Ok, could you please read this to us out loud.' It took sixty percent longer." Setting aside the extraneous issues that distract business conversations, like last night's basketball game and Michael Jordan's point count, it takes longer for a speaker to articulate a single word and the listener to absorb it than to communicate the same word in writing. "So we've learned that our eyes process information much faster than our ears. And every Friess associate gets to decide if they want to be a 286 chip or a Pentium chip."

To bolster the point that verbal communication wastes time, Friess and his assistant, Debbie Shipee, once communicated only in writing for an entire day. The messages included, at one point, adding 500,000 shares of stock to a position. "The only hitch was a note from Debbie saying 'I can't read your handwriting.' So I had to slow down a little bit." At the end of the nine-hour all-writing day, they counted 177 interchanges. "Now I challenge anybody who's using a telephone to get more than 25 or 30 of those interactions." Friess hastens to add that written communication also discourages distracting expressions of emotional distress and reduces the likelihood that someone will show up at 12:30 for a noon appointment.

METHOD IN THE MADNESS

There is method in this madness, apparently. From its inception in 1985 through November 30, 1997, the Brandywine Fund, managed by Friess Associates, chalked up a stunning 710.2 percent return on investment, or 19.2 percent a year, far outpacing a heady 544.3 percent gain by Standard & Poor's index of 500 stocks, or 16.9 percent a year. The difference in outcomes, in dollar terms, amounts to more than one and a half times the original stake. A $100,000 investment in Brandywine at its outset grew to

$810,200 in a dozen years, while the same stake, if invested across the S&P 500, would have produced only $644,300.

On the strength of ten-year returns through March 1997, the Lipper Analytical Survey, widely followed by investment professionals, christened Brandywine the nation's number-one no-load growth fund still available to new investors. In February 1997, Brandywine topped *Money* magazine's list of eleven superior funds. Brandywine led the pack in one-year, five-year, and ten-year intervals by racking up a 24.9 percent return for calendar year 1986, and 19.2 percent annual returns for both five-year and ten-year intervals.

After naming Brandywine to the list of Superstar mutual funds in 1993, 1994, and 1996, the editors of *SmartMoney* magazine expressed regret for omitting Brandywine in 1995 in the mistaken belief that it had grown too large. "The fact is," *SmartMoney's* editors apologized, "we never should have turned away."[1]

PICKING WINNERS

What Foster Friess usually does better than just about anyone else is pick winners. He finds the stocks that are primed to grow fast, buys them before other investors wake up, then sells them again before gravity reclaims them. Three rules guide his investment policy:

1. Never invest in the stock market; invest in individual companies.
2. Once you own a stock, never look where it has been; look only where it is going.
3. If it's not going up faster and farther than an alternative, sell it and buy the alternative.

Friess summed up his strategy for *Money* magazine in February 1997: "We are searching for companies that will somehow surprise the investment community."[2] How does he find them? With bottom–up research by a crew of relentless analysts who keep their eyes trained on lists of stocks reaching new price levels and posting earnings records.

High turnover goes with this territory. A seasoned stock is three months old. An average stock in the Brandywine Fund lasts about six months; turnover approaches 200 percent a year. How fast is that? In March 1997, Brandywine owned fifteen stocks in the communications sector with market value, as a group, that was 5.3 percent above cost. Six months later, ten of those stocks were out, twelve new stocks were in, and the communications sector's market value was up 41 percent over cost. Of fourteen stocks in the apparel and shoes sector in March, up 17.6 percent as a group, only three remained six months later among nine stocks in the apparel and shoes sector, which was up nearly 60 percent above Brandywine's cost.

Top-heavy organizations can't compete effectively in this climate, where a five-minute delay can cost investors millions of dollars. Friess, who carries a beeper everywhere, has three minutes—literally, 180 seconds—to veto a portfolio manager's investment decision. Otherwise, the stock moves. That's the reaction speed needed to keep a step ahead of the competition. Daunting pressure accompanies success. "You might think it's a stressless environment sitting here in the hot tub with a Coor's," says Friess. "But in this business, you're never stress-free. It's really tension-packed."

Momentum is critical. Blink, and the outlook can change. "You can pick up the *Wall Street Journal* every day and the paper will say they missed their estimate by three cents—and the stock's down 35 percent," observes Ted Kellner, a former Friess protégé who extols his mentor's exceptional ability to size up investment opportunities.

A KEEN INSTINCT

"There are people who can understand the inner workings of a company and of an industry better than others," says Kellner, now chairman of Fiduciary Management, a Milwaukee-based money management firm. "Picking apart a balance sheet—a CPA can do that. To really get into a company and to take a look at all the variables, to see and understand where the leverage really comes from—that isn't just an accounting function, and I think Foster does that better than any others. He has an intuitive sense that I can't put a finger on or give a neat narrative as to why he understands more, maybe, than others—why the market will pay for a Cisco Systems versus Ascend Communications—but he's got a real knack for that."

There's no denying that Friess has a keen instinct. Average earnings of companies in Brandywine's portfolio grew by almost 50 percent during the 12 months through March 1997. That's four times the average growth in the S&P 500. In the preceding quarter, Brandywine posted an average growth rate of 51 percent versus 17 percent for the market. Laggards were companies like Kellstrom Industries, Burlington Coat Factories, and Hollywood Entertainment. These three increased their value by only a third.

Competition for top honors in the growth category is fierce. Morningstar Inc. tracked 771 large, medium, and small growth funds in mid-1997, and the ranks were growing as fast as the torrid Dow Jones Industrial Average. Such proliferation reflects the perennial allure of investing for growth. Every investor who hopes for a killing—and who doesn't?—dreams of picking what will become the hottest stock on Wall Street *before* it heats up, and then riding it to a tenfold gain.

Beyond the notion that growth stocks are stocks that go up and up and up, however, the term "growth stock" loses focus. Discussions of growth investment at cocktail parties and around water coolers, and even among professional money managers, spark differences of opinion.

GROWTH DEFINED

Growth companies can be large or small. They can be in any industry. They can be service companies or manufacturers. A quick trigger finger is not part of every definition. Some growth investors intend to own stock for years, a legacy of the generation that filled portfolios in the 1950s with industrial giants like IBM, Eastman Kodak, and Union Carbide, and watched their value increase for two generations, notwithstanding a few jolts along the way.

To some investors, a favorable change in market sentiment is sufficient to bestow growth status on an otherwise lackluster share of stock. Settling a lawsuit, firing an ill-equipped CEO, or the bankruptcy of a main rival can cause a stock's price to spurt. Great windfalls have been collected on no more substance than this.

Ordinarily, though, more material developments are needed. "A growth stock is one of a company whose sales, earnings and share of the market are expanding faster than the general economy and faster than average for the industry," according to Jerome Cohen, Edward Zinbarg, and Arthur Zeikel, authors of *Investment Analysis and Portfolio Management*. Growth companies, according to their textbook definition, tend to be aggressive and research-minded, and they prefer to reinvest earnings in the business rather than pay dividends. "Although there is a great variety of growth companies, several key characteristics can be identified. Normally, the company has a solidly entrenched position in an expanding market. Its products or services are distinctive or unique. The company achieves high profitability in most cases by pre-empting a special part of the market."[3]

In the 1950s, growth stocks regained favor with investors for the first time since the 1929 Crash instilled a preference for income and safety of principal. This revived appetite for growth spurred efforts to define the category. Author, editor, and investment adviser Peter L. Bernstein observed, in a 1956 issue of *Harvard Business Review:*

> Growth stocks are a happy and haphazard category of investments which, curiously enough, have little or nothing to do with growth companies. Perhaps the most important conclusion of this analysis is that the term "growth stock" is meaningless; a growth stock can be identified only with hindsight—it is simply a stock which went way up. But the concept of "growth company" can be used to identify the most creative, most imaginative management groups; and if, in addition, their stocks are valued at a reasonable ratio to their increase in earnings power over a period of time, the odds are favorable for appreciation in the future.[4]

COFFEE CANS, GARP, AND MOMENTUM

Growth is one of the more difficult concepts to define, declares Warren Shaw, former chief executive, Chancellor LGT, a money-management firm based in New York City. Several distinct styles fall under the growth rubric. "Depending on what style of growth you choose in managing your portfolio, it makes a great deal of difference what attributes you need to have present," Shaw observes. "So, for example, there's the coffee can approach, otherwise known as buy-and-hold investing. That's a style that involves identifying very, very high-quality companies, outstanding franchises where the companies are able to produce above-average growth on a reliable basis over the very long term. This style of investing requires that the investor be very attuned to the longer term, that the investor have a great deal of patience, and that the investor be very, very interested and concerned about long-term wealth building."

There are other approaches, Shaw says, including GARP, an acronym for "growth at a reasonable price." In that approach, the investor is looking for undervalued growth stocks, a.k.a. cheap growth stocks. And the GARP approach requires sensitivity to near-term valuation anomalies in trends and the ability to identify companies that begin to sell at discounts to their growth rates, or have price–earnings ratios lower than normal for their class of company.

Shaw also names a third growth characteristic: momentum. This calls for identifying companies that have above-average trends in terms of earnings acceleration, earnings revision, or earnings surprises. The focus for those companies is decidedly short-term, and access to high-quality, real-time information is paramount. Notwithstanding Friess's aversion to the term, *momentum investing* is an apt description of his style.

"We like to be classified as growth investors who implement our approach in a very intense, aggressive way," Friess says, "but we think we're being conservative by demanding that the accounting be clean, that the marketing program be in place, that companies have good distribution systems. And we go through the entire business as if we're going to own it and take it private."

He won't invest in a company with, say, a new drug that promises to pay off in five years. "We're not buying dreams and hopes," Friess says. "We want to see the whites of the eyes of the profits."

MAGICAL MULTIPLES

The legendary Benjamin Graham stressed attention to the price–earnings (PE) multiple, or ratio, a measure of value equal to the stock price divided by the earnings per share. "The term 'growth stock' is applied to one which has increased its per-share earnings in the past at well above the rate for common stocks generally and is expected to do so in the future."[5]

A supermarket analogy helps Friess explain price–earnings multiples, a concept central to his investment process. "If you go into a grocery store and buy a quantity of hamburger," Friess explains, "you pay five dollars for it, but what do you get? You get a certain amount of weight. Let's say you get one pound. So the ratio of price to weight is five to one. It's the same with stocks. You have a five-dollar stock and it has one dollar's worth of earnings power. Instead of talking about dollars worth of hamburger, you're talking about dollars worth of earnings power. So you could have a high PE stock, one selling at $50 a share that only earns $1. A stock selling for $100 with $20 of earnings power, with a PE of 5, is cheaper than the $50 stock that earns $1, for a PE of 50. So when people talk about a stock being expensive, they shouldn't talk about the selling price, they should be talking about the PE ratio. The whole idea is that a $20 stock is cheaper than a $5 stock if it has more earnings."

BIGGER, BETTER, HIGHER, FASTER

If investors have confidence that earnings will grow, they will bid a multiple of the earnings per share they expect eventually to collect. The bigger the expected growth, the bigger the multiple and the higher the price. By buying into a company early and staying with it over time, investors reap benefits of expanding earnings *plus* an expanding PE multiple.

Savvy investors must always distinguish *trailing* PEs from *prospective* PEs. A trailing PE highlights the ratio of the current stock price to earnings for the previous 12 months. A prospective PE highlights the ratio of the current stock price to expected earnings in the year ahead. Say, for example, the trailing PE for a company is 30 times earnings, a little too pricey for Friess. If careful research suggests that earnings will double in the next 12 months, however, the prospective PE is only fifteen times earnings.

Historically, shares listed on the New York Stock Exchange have posted an average trailing PE ratio of about 12 to 15. In hot markets, the average ratio can go much higher. It was 22 in the summer of 1997, when Securities and Exchange Commission (SEC) Chairman Alan Greenspan pronounced the economy in fine shape six years into an exceptional bull market. At that point, an average PE of 22 meant that stock of an average company expecting to earn $1 a share changed hands for $22 a share.

Companies growing faster than average warrant higher PEs simply because investors eager to own shares of fast-growing companies bid up prices. Take an average company earning $1 a share. News circulates that earnings are likely to grow 30 percent in the coming year—a rather modest increase by Brandywine's standards. Say the PE goes from 22 to 30, a multiple in line with the expected growth. When the stock begins to change hands because of an expected increase in earnings, investors who anticipated the increase will enjoy a 77 percent gain on their investment. Therein lies the magic of growth investing:

Magical Multiples

Current Market Price	Original PE	Expanded PE
Current earnings	$1	$1
Current market price	$22	$22
Expected earnings	$1.30	$1.30
PE multiple	22	30
New market price	$28.60	$39
Percent gain	30%	77%

During the first six months of 1997, the PE for Microsoft, this era's most glamorous growth stock, jumped by 24 percent, to 54.6 times earnings. For the 18-month stretch starting in December 1995, the PE increased by 80 percent. Dell Computer illustrates an even more spectacular example of PE expansion. Between July 1996 and July 1997, its PE rose a dizzying 144 percent, to 42.2 times earnings.

YES (SADLY), THERE'S A DOWNSIDE

The hitch, alas, is that price–earnings ratios can also contract just as dramatically. "Investors often project recent earnings trends too far into the future, failing to realize how quickly circumstances can—and do—change," warns Jeremy Siegel, author of *Stocks for the Long Run*. "When earnings growth slows, as it invariably does, this deflates the price–earnings multiple and causes a dramatic drop in the price for a stock," Siegel says.[6]

Noting such risks, Benjamin Graham urged caution before pinning an investment strategy to hopes of rapid growth. "[W]e regard growth stocks as a whole as too uncertain and risky a vehicle for the defensive investor. Of course, wonders can be accomplished with the right individual selections, bought at the right levels, and later sold after a huge rise and before the probable decline. But the average investor can no more expect to accomplish this than to find money growing on trees."[7]

Friess parries assertions that Brandywine courts too much risk. "Our fund is risky," he allows. "I think any fund that invests in common stocks is risky, but people know it because they know the stock market is risky." So is the bond market, for that matter, where inflation can ravage a portfolio. The question, in his mind, is how investors define risk. Most, in his view, get it wrong. "There's a wonderful tie in most people's minds between risk and volatility. Our argument is that risk is defined by a myriad of other things. Just saying volatility is risk is making it too simplistic. We measure risk by the ease of entry, the rate of profit margins, the ability to introduce new products, the quality of the management, and the quality of the balance sheet," Friess declares. "We could find forty different parameters for measuring risk in a given company."

The market's erratic behavior in late 1997 tested Friess's conviction. Consistent with the fate usually accorded to volatile growth funds, upheaval suffered by Brandywine exceeded declines in the major indices. Friess tried to reassure shareholders afterwards. "In the 33 years I have been responsible for shepherding other people's hard-earned assets, I have seen the world 'come to an end' seven times," he wrote Brandywine shareholders in November 1997. "During those times it was always comforting to embrace an investment philosophy that focused on the reality of a company's individual progress."

Don't confuse holding stocks in these companies for short periods with excessive volatility, Friess warns. "If I buy a stock at 24 and it goes to 36 in two years, would I be a long-term investor? If it goes from 24 to 36 in two months and I sell it, why am I suddenly worse?"

GROWTH: AN OLD FRIEND *AND* ADVERSARY

Long before the twentieth century, investors were lured by prospects of growth. Frenzies dating back to the Renaissance are well documented; a media favorite is the tulip-mania in seventeenth-century Holland, when exotic tulip bulbs rocketed in value—and later plummeted.

In the United States in this century, growth caught the popular imagination in the months leading up to the 1929 Crash. So eager were investors to participate in a raging bull market that they flocked in large numbers not just to common stocks, but to investment trusts marketed on the flaky claims of still more spectacular growth. "The virtue of the investment trust," wrote Professor John Kenneth Galbraith in *The Great Crash,* "was that it brought about an almost complete divorce of the volume of corporate securities outstanding from the volume of corporate assets in existence."[8]

Common stocks languished in disfavor for the next two decades. In the 1930s, if a stock could meet its dividend, capital gains were not to be expected. Until the mid-1950s, strange as it may seem to legions of growth-hungry 401(k) participants today, few pension funds were allowed to own common stocks. And, in retrospect, what a time it was to invest!

As fears spawned by the Crash finally began to recede, Donaldson Lufkin & Jenrette, then a fledgling Wall Street investment firm, published four guidelines for growth investing, in a 1958 letter to its customers:

1. A steadily improving record of sales (recognizing unit as well as dollar sales), per-share earnings and, to a lesser extent, profit margins.
2. A good record of new product or process development and/or old product or process improvement resulting in sales volume generated

in new markets or through a steadily growing share of existing old markets.

3. Management . . . The successful growth stock investor cannot solely rely on the past to judge the future. He (sic) must make judgments as to the policies management is pursuing to achieve comparable future growth.

4. Operating presence in a market characterized by rapid development of new applications and new products within an expanding market.[9]

HOOKED ON TRONICS

Reintroduced to growth investing, investors went hog-wild by 1961. Sound guidelines went by the wayside as they embraced the so-called "Tronics" boom, a post-Sputnik mania for anything that sounded electronic. Companies named Astron, Dutron, Vulcatron, Circuitronics, Supronics, and Powertron Ultrasonics lured investors. Growth became a magic word. In his popular book, *A Random Walk Down Wall Street,* Princeton economics professor Burton Malkiel caught the drunken mood of that era in a comment by Jack Dreyfus, then CEO of Dreyfus & Company:

> Take a nice little company that's been making shoelaces for 40 years and sells at a respectable six times earnings ratio. Change the name from Shoelaces, Inc., to Electronics and Silicon Furth Burners. In today's market, the words "electronics" and "silicon" are worth 15 times earnings. However, the real play comes from the word "furth burners," which no one understands. A word that no one understands entitles you to double your entire score. Therefore, we have six times earnings for the shoelace business and 15 times earnings for "electronic" and "silicon," or a total of 21 times earnings. Multiply this by two for "furth burners" and we now have a score of 42 times earnings for the new company.[10]

Caveats printed on prospectuses in bold letters could not shake investors' enthusiasm. With astonishing impunity, they snapped up shares of companies with no assets, no earnings, and no foreseeable prospects of paying dividends. Big stocks comprising the Dow Jones Industrial Average rode the crest of the wave. But after motoring up to a 734.34 close in November 1961, the Dow Jones Industrial Average began to sputter. A 7 percent drop on May 28, 1962, was steep by historical standards but the worst it got was closing at 535.76 a month later, 27 percent off the November peak.[11]

GROWTH AT ANY PRICE

The 1962 slump restored investors to their senses only for a brief time. Growth came back into fashion again less than five years later as investors fell under the spell of "story stocks"—stocks that substituted promising stories for earnings. Swami-like "go-go" fund managers took credit for doubling investments in thirty days by catching fledgling stocks with big futures. Smitten by exuberant prospects for companies that made leather boots and assorted gizmos, investors bid up stock prices to spectacular levels. Once more, the Dow industrials rode the crest, closing above 900 for the first time in January 1965. One year later, the average flirted for the first time with the 1,000 mark but after touching 1,000.50 on January 8, failed to close above 1,000 that day—or for the next 6½ years. Beginning in December 1968 and for the next 18 nail-biting months, the Dow Jones Industrials tumbled again, erasing in the process most traces of hundreds of once-hot "story stocks."

Disappointed twice in a decade by flaky growth stocks with, ultimately, little or no underlying value, investors soon focused on a short list of sturdy companies with enviable earnings records. Drug companies like Merck, Bristol Myers, and Pfizer, along with McDonald's, Xerox, JC Penney, Texas Instruments, IBM, and Dow Chemical, and their peers, comprised the "Nifty Fifty." Widespread belief in limitless earnings growth at a 20 percent annual clip, coupled with a limited supply of shares, appeared to guarantee perpetual appreciation. These were "one decision" growth stocks—buy them and hold them forever.

The Nifty-Fifty balloon carried stock prices to unprecedented heights. At the peak, top blue-chip companies changed hands at prices exceeding 60 times earnings. One sage quipped that the PE for Xerox contemplated not only the future, but the hereafter also. This was GAAP—Growth At Any Price. And then the air came out. In 1973 and 1974, the S&P average tumbled, ushering in a prolonged bear market that would eventually prompt *Business Week* to ask, on its cover, whether equities were dead.

In the very year that the Nifty Fifty lost their hold on investors, Friess hung out his shingle. It seemed an inauspicious time. But while most investors rued the market's grim state, Friess beamed with confidence. Such moxie comes naturally to the grandson of a spirited Wisconsin cattle rancher, Herman F. Friess, who sold supply beef to the Sioux Line Railroad in the late 1800s. "My grandfather was a pretty tough hombre," Friess recalls. Once, after a thief stole his horse, Herman Friess tracked him for three days and took his horse back. As he was riding off, the thief shot him in the wrist. "And I remember as a young man seeing the purple mark of the bullet. You did not want to argue with him. When he was 77, he broke the jaw of a 55-year-old businessman who cheated him in a deal."

MANY FACES OF GROWTH

Trim and handsome at 57, and inclined to wear pressed jeans and a cowboy hat, Friess cuts the swath of a Marlboro man. In truth, he's earned the part. Raised in a small northern Wisconsin town where the richest citizen ran the local Mobil station and owned the funeral home, Friess grew up on horseback and, in his teens, had charge of 120 head of cattle. A painting in his Jackson Hole, Wyoming, home depicts a rampaging herd. "I took care of Herefords or Angus and sometimes Holsteins. I'd get on my horse and round them up and I'd doctor them up. In those days the way you'd doctor hoof rot was pretty awful. You'd pour turpentine on it."

As it turned out, herding cattle supplied incentive for his investment career. "I used to feed calves that my father would transport from Wisconsin out to Dakota. It was a fairly smelly job. It would be 2 o'clock in the morning, getting them ready to load on trucks. And I said, 'Dad, why can't I get a job with an accounting firm or at the bank or the newspaper so I can learn something?' He said, 'You get back in the calf pen and you're gonna learn the value of a dollar.'" That wasn't the only lesson that paid off later. "With all the kicks to my shins," Friess says, "I can take the kicks in the stock market easily."

Growth stocks, to Friess, have many faces. "It could be an airline where fuel prices have dropped and their load factors have gone up and they've got a new marketing guy who's opened up the Dallas-to-Houston market," says Friess. "It's not a growth stock in terms of a company that's going to grow year after year after year at the same rate, but it's a growth stock in that the earnings are growing."

In an ideal sense, Friess suggests, growth comes from more unit sales—putting more widgets into customers' hands this year than last year. "Now, if that's not growing rapidly, you might still be able to get growth because the prices at which they're selling the widgets are higher than a year ago. So there's all different ways you can get growth, and we're willing to buy growth even realizing that it might be a catch-up from past lethargy, where they've written off some divisions and now they're going to grow for a couple of years."

GLAMOROUS BUT ARDUOUS

"Never invest in the stock market," Friess warns. "Invest in individual companies." That's easier said than done. Singling out individual companies takes endless legwork and an eye for change.

Friess got an early lesson in legwork as a reporter for his hometown newspaper, the *Rice Lake* [Wisconsin] *Chronotype*. Besides covering weddings and writing all the obituaries for a weekly newspaper with 5,000 subscribers, "I had these major stories," Friess recalls. "John Jones sold his Guernsey to Gomer Johnson." A subsequent stint in Army Intelligence, which he dismisses as an administrative post with security clearance, acquainted him with the level of rigorous scrutiny that investing in growth stocks routinely demands.

That's not all the army taught him. Now and then, there was a lesson in humility, which he admits is not his long suit. "I was taught how to remember a whole list of things, and I showed off to my sergeant and his young corporals. We were sitting around in the office. I said, 'OK, list off a few things.' So they listed off a few things: a giraffe, a pocket knife, a glass. They listed 21 things. And so I said, 'OK, call them out.' Now I could do them bang, bang, bang, bang. They were getting very irritated at this brash young lieutenant. But then I enumerated all 21 just from memory, using a mnemonic device I'd learned in intelligence school. So they were pretty irritated. But they got their very exciting reward. The next day, I forgot the combination to the [company] safe. So I had to go down to headquarters. It's a nightmare when you forget the combination to a safe."

DON'T BE SHY: QUIZ FELLOW TRAVELERS

These days, legwork is instinctive to the former reporter. Friess pleads guilty to interrogating fellow passengers on long airplane flights, in search of fresh investment ideas. "As soon as the seatbelt light goes out, I go up and down the aisles, sort of casually strolling, looking for what I think are hard-hitting business types. And if a fellow's reading the latest Clancy novel in a golf shirt, he's maybe not gonna be as likely a candidate for me as some guy pounding on a laptop." Such is his fervor that friends kid him about neglecting the fellow reading the Clancy book.

"I'll introduce myself and I'll say, 'Where you headed for? Do you live in Phoenix?' And they say, 'Yeah,' so I'll find out he works for Motorola, and then a whole series of questions can ensue." Friess might press for news, say, of Motorola's reaction to a competing product from Nokia. "What we're doing is trying to find, at a grass-roots level, what is taking place in the marketplace."

Among acquaintances, Friess's tenacious pursuit of growth stocks is legendary. Ted Kellner recalls introducing Friess to the CEO of a regional airline company—at a funeral, no less. "Within literally 30 seconds, Foster was asking about load factors, fuel costs—just digging into the company," Kellner recalls. "And [the CEO] is kind of a low-key guy. I later saw him and he said, 'Who was that barracuda you introduced me to?' That's just Foster. He digs very hard. He's relentless. He will talk to whoever he thinks can give him an edge in terms of learning more about a company and learning why and how that company might exceed Wall Street's expectation. And so he has a better edge on earnings growth. He's really a momentum player to the *n*th degree."

Relentless pursuit pays off. In the universe of some 5,000 stocks that Friess's analysts follow, something is always popping—and seldom the obvious suspects. "All of our money has not been made in gee-whiz companies like Cisco making switches for the Internet. We can make it in shoes, we can make it in food. The key thing is that there's something we can perceive that's changing within that company."

LOOK FOR NEW HIGHS

Companies posting new highs in earnings and stock prices are primary targets. Every day, research teams peruse the *Wall Street Journal*'s stock columns and earnings reports. What companies are hitting new highs in the stock market, and why? Which ones are recording record earnings, and why? "If a company reports good earnings, a 30 percent increase following a 25 percent sales increase, we call up, find out why. What's driving those earnings? A new division? A new product? A new management? Something happening internally at that company as opposed to interest rate changes or currency changes or commodity price changes? The more we can find something internal to that company, we've increased our chances exceedingly, because it's so much more difficult to make calls on these big macro issues that other people spend an inordinate amount of time trying to call."

"We're looking for companies that are going to do better than expected," says Friess Associates analyst John Fenn, who prowls shoe conventions in search of hot products. Legions of analysts for institutions that buy stocks and firms that sell stocks supply stiff competition. "We need to go a step farther than they are going, to get to information they don't have. If all we're doing is what the next guy is doing, we're not going to come across new information. We're not going to have insights that are truly different than the rest of the Street has. So what we try to do is go a step farther, talk to more customers, talk to more competitors, talk to more suppliers, talk to more retailers, really understand the details that other investors may be missing. I mean, we need a situation where there's a misperception and expectations are low. We need to find a situation where the market is missing something and the only way to do that is to go a step farther than your competitors. It is intense. You need to be out there talking to people on the phone, making the extra call your competitors may not be making. And by doing that, you get information that Wall Street may not have."

Information this good can look suspicious at times. "We just had a situation where we sold a stock and we sold it actually too well," says Friess, "because it dropped out right afterward. And then people said, 'Well, did you have inside information?' I called our analyst to review the circumstances and, basically, it was a company that had a particular toy. And as we went through the stores, we couldn't find the toy in inventory. And, second, when we called two or three of the supposedly biggest purchasers of that toy, they didn't give it particularly glowing remarks as to how it was moving. So, we spend time walking through stores finding products." This kind of investment research, in Friess's lexicon, is "bottom-up investing."

A visit to Gart Brothers, the local Jackson Hole sporting goods store, alerted Fenn to prospects for Nike, the athletic shoe manufacturer whose stock price sprinted 183 percent from the time Brandywine bought the first shares in August 1995 to the sale of the last shares in February 1997. Not only was the latest shipment of running shoes already sold out, the store manager explained, but they always sell out within a few hours of delivery.

SCRUTINIZE EARNINGS

Investigating financial performance starts with financial statements and earnings estimates. First, Fenn checks databases that supply earnings estimates on companies he is pursuing. Meanwhile, he pores over financial reports. If it all checks out, he phones the company to speak with the investor relations person or the chief financial officer. At Nike, he called investor relations. His questions: What were analysts expecting—what were they looking for in terms of earnings estimates? Then he asked for the names of the largest retailers. "They were the people I really wanted to talk to," says Fenn. "They were the ones that were going to buy product from Nike."

Fenn's assistant, Andrea Paul, got on the phone and called up the buyers at Foot Action, Foot Locker, Sports Authority, Sport Mart. The list ultimately included all the large retailers in the country that handle the bulk of Nike's business. It was largely a domestic running shoe business when Fenn started poking around, though it soon became international. Fenn talked to the buyers. Were Nike products selling well? Were discounts necessary? Was promotion required? The feedback indicated that Nike shoes were selling extremely well. Buyers were not taking markdowns, and they were going to order significantly more product.

DON'T BE GULLED BY GOOD NEWS

Friess insists on quantifying. In general, he finds, people like to be subjective. They like to say good things about a company. Nike's business is great, but that doesn't really mean much. What Fenn must find out is how much more Nike product will retailers buy over the next six months versus the same period a year earlier. Fenn became convinced that their future purchases of Nike products were going to outpace past sales significantly, and that's why Brandywine bought the shares. "Wall Street was looking for, say, 20 percent growth," Fenn says, "and we started to hear back from these retailers that they were going to buy 30, 40, maybe even 50 percent more product over the next six months. So Wall Street was clearly missing something in terms of the growth rate in Nike's business. And that was really the determining factor."

Fenn credits Brandywine's impressive edge to this exhaustive investigative process. Too many analysts take a strictly quantitative approach. They look at charts. They look at models developed by firms that sell stocks and then look at PE ratios. "We basically go out and do grunt work," says Fenn. "We don't spend a lot of time running through spreadsheets. We find out what is selling well, what is not selling well, instead of trying to figure out, is this price–earnings to growth rate better than this [other] company. We're always comparing one investment to another, but we're getting into the details on what is driving the business. What is going to cause it to do better than expected or worse than expected?"

Out in the field, Fenn's high-flying colleague Diane Hakala—the country's fourth-ranked woman stunt pilot—meets with Mike Yonkers, the chief financial officer of In Focus Systems. "What we're trying to accomplish is [to learn] where they're going to be in the coming quarter. They're in the middle of a product transition, and we're trying to get a feel for how well that transition is going." She wants to know how pricing is holding up in different parts of the business in light of growing competition and increased advertising, with obvious implications for profit margins.

Hakala has met many times with Yonkers. "We know him pretty well," she says. Besides listening to what he has to say, Hakala listens for changes in the tone of his voice—signs of confidence or lack of it. She checks his expectations against Wall Street's expectations and, ultimately, against her own appraisal. If there is any reason for doubt, Hakala springs Friess's "post mortem" question: If you were to miss one of the analysts' expectations, what would the reason be?

"If he says something like, 'Well, the whole world has to go into economic recession,' then I'm not very worried," says Hakala. But if he equivocates with an answer that sounds like, "Gee, you know, if I don't get enough components for that particular system to produce that particular product . . . ," Hakala would tune in even more closely. "We're trying to engage the company officer," she says, "and get him to teach us about what's going on."

POBODY'S NERFECT

Picking growth stocks calls for excellence, not perfection. There's a vast difference, according to Friess. "Perfectionism abhors error, hates mistakes," he says. "Perfection tries to eradicate error and destroy it. Excellence embraces error, builds on it, transforms it. Every time we make a mistake, we call it an adjustment opportunity. And we look at it as an opportunity to get better."

The goal is to be right most of the time, not all of the time. "In our business," Friess declares, "if we can be right sixty percent of the time and have stocks go down forty percent of the time, we'll actually come up with fairly good numbers. The studies that we've run show that the top five stocks can offset all the losses." Still, losers hold an indelible place in memory.

Six notable disappointments cost Brandywine $136 million on paper during the first quarter of 1997: 3Com Corp., Toys 'R Us, Staples, Chesapeake Energy, CompUSA, and Seagate Technology. Of 27 stock sectors, five were trading for less than Brandywine's cost. Six months later, however, all 27 sectors were in the black including pharmaceuticals, which went from a 13.4 percent deficit to a 16.7 percent gain after dropping three of four stocks from the sector and adding five new ones.

WATCH FOR UNDERLYING CHANGE

Besides relentless digging, successful growth investing requires an inborn talent for recognizing broad change in early stages and figuring out how it is likely to affect companies. Any time an industry experiences change that affects how people perceive it, says Friess, that's where market opportunities arise. "What are the changes taking place and which are the companies that are not only participating in those changes but may be actually orchestrating those changes?" Friess asks. "It's very much like being a detective rather than a [securities] analyst.

"Basically, our job is just to perceive how a society changes. Think of all of the things that are being spawned from the growth in the Internet. Now, a lot of the Internet companies you know don't fit our criteria, because they're selling fifty, sixty, seventy times earnings. But there's a company making switches that might be selling at sixteen or seventeen times earnings. There might be companies that have all kinds of products that relate to the Internet growth, that you can buy at a reasonable price."

Investing poses an intellectual puzzle. "You are trying to piece together all the marketing news, all the accounting nuances," says Friess. "Can these people lead and organize and build a new plant, develop a new product? But I think it's very do-able because it just analyzes information, and the market is just an average."

Now and then, this way of thinking fosters serendipity. Chance favors the prepared mind, Louis Pasteur said many years ago. It's equally true today in investing. A few years ago, Lynn Friess, Foster's wife, spotted an ad in a women's magazine. The Gap, a specialty clothing retailer, had shifted from sweatsuits and low-end clothing into trendier, more fashion-oriented clothing. "That transforms a company," says Friess. He caught the Gap before an upswing—but later got out before another change in consumer tastes caused growth to stall.

Being attuned to change led Friess Associates to the world's leading but little-known distributor of cellular phones made by Nokia, Ericsson, Motorola, and NEC. Friess researchers learned that the distributor was the first company to be authorized by the Chinese government to sell wireless products in that country. Purchased for $14 in January 1997, the shares approached $50 by September, a 227 percent increase.

A SHORT-TERM KIND OF GUY

Because society changes so fast, it's always possible to find a company that some investors feel will grow at a 30 percent rate for the next five years. But Friess does not attach a whole lot of credence to long-term projections. "I don't think there's any management that honestly knows what their earnings are going to be eighteen months out. And so we're very cautious to keep in that time frame where we have a good feel as to what reality is, rather than more of a conceptual, long-term growth." Remember, he wants to see the whites of the eyes of the profits.

Although momentum investing appears to fit his short-term horizon, Friess resists the label. "To me, a momentum investor is one who sees a stock going up and so he's investing because of the momentum of the price action itself." Someone who just jumps on a bandwagon that is rolling along, in Friess's opinion, is a momentum investor. "You could have a momentum investor who is characterized as one who's investing because earnings are beginning to increase at an increasing rate. We would gladly invest in a company that had a 40 percent earnings increase in one quarter and then it's about ready to have a 30 percent earnings increase. The momentum investor might not like that but we would maybe buy that if we felt it was part of a longer-term growth trend and that the 30 percent was better than people were acknowledging because they thought it was going to be 25 percent. So we don't like to be classified as momentum investors."

WHAT HE'S NOT

Selling stocks short, where an investor sells borrowed stock in the expectation that he or she can buy the shares later for less, does not fit Friess's strategy. "There's something about our psychology. We like to be part of building something and we don't like to be betting against people. And it might have something to do with my own experience: the very first time I went short, I got killed."

You certainly won't find Friess trawling for beat-up stocks that lure value investors like John Neff (the subject of Chapter 2). "We don't want to be bottom fishermen," he says. "Show me a stock selling for less than book value and I'll show you a dog," Friess told Kiplinger's *Personal Finance* magazine.[12] Companies don't look like bargains to Friess just because of low PE multiples, an earmark of battered stocks. "That's the last thing we would do," Friess says. Stocks that have doubled in price aren't necessarily more expensive, in his view. "Maybe it's selling at eight, ten, twelve times next year's earnings because their earnings are exploding. Typically, companies that are hitting new lows are hitting new lows for a reason. They've had a bad turn of events, they're losing money, their momentum is slowing."

Friess is no fan of efficient markets theories, either. As someone who has consistently beaten the market, he's Exhibit A in the case against such theories. "We do not relate to most of those tenets of modern portfolio theory," he told Peter Tannous, author of *Investment Gurus*. "Asking us about standard deviation would be like asking a plumber how many kilowatts he wanted to plug into a lamp. It just doesn't compute with us." How can he ignore tools that have become staples of investment management? "Because I don't think Andrew Carnegie, when he created his steel mill empire, thought about those. I don't think Christopher Columbus, when he came here to look for gold and treasure, thought about them either. We're that traditional."[13]

Look at utility stocks. "Some of these utility companies had unbelievably low betas, low volatility. They'd chug, chug, chug along, chug along, then suddenly their nuclear plant blows up, and their stock goes down 40 percent. Would you rather be in something that had that stability, or low volatility, or be in a Compaq Computer or Dell Computer, which had high volatility, but you're on a long-term growth pattern?"

A CREW OF RISK TAKERS

Friess attributes much of his success to a cast of extremely competitive researchers who embrace risk. Every week, Diane Hakala logs dozens of hours in the cockpit of her single-engine stunt plane. John Fenn was a top downhill skier at the University of Colorado. His specialty was "bump" skiing over moguls at high speeds. "If you look at Diana or any researcher at Friess Associates," says Fenn, "they're going to try to go out there and get that piece of information before somebody else does. They're going to go the extra mile, make the extra phone calls. And that's really the connection. If it's Diana, a stunt pilot, or myself, a freestyle skier, there's just an intensity to what we do. That goes both with our personal activities as well as professional duties to our clients."

A winning strategy can survive mistakes, but it can't survive frail, insecure personalities. Besides intelligence and the ability to pluck telling information from corporate executives, self-assurance is essential. Says Friess: "I've noted that people who are secure about who they are have a lot easier job of admitting when they've made a mistake. And so if you have bought a stock and it's down five points you can say, 'OK, I can sell it; I made a mistake.' Instead of having your whole self-esteem linked into how you perform. So if you have to perform in order to prove that you're of value, you're going to hang on to that stock rather than admit that you're less of a person."

SPIRIT OF COOPERATION

Adds Friess, "We want to create sort of a family structure, where every one of us during our lifetimes are going to have peaks and valleys, and we want to be a firm with the capacity to take them through the valleys by reassigning them to different projects. I don't want to be a firm that's insensitive to the needs of people. That's one of the reasons our culture has been so much fun, because we're pulling for one another.

The bonus system was designed to foster cooperation. Like good investing techniques that pluck great ideas from the commonplace, the bonus plan took its inspiration from a restaurant in Cancun, Mexico, where Friess was impressed by the way waiters covered for each other. "They pool the tips at the end of the night, and they give a certain amount to the busboys, a certain amount to the kitchen help, and a certain amount to the waiters," Friess says. "So if anyone isn't pulling his weight, everyone else is on his case."

At Friess Associates, everyone in the whole firm gets to vote on bonuses for all of their coworkers. "They give me a sheet of paper and they say, 'Well, he's had a good year, we'll give him 8 percent of the bonus pool. Someone else didn't have such a good year, but he helped me get out of two stocks, let's give him 6 percent.' I get all these inputs and averages, so what that means during the course of the year, everybody is trying to help one another because they know they're being evaluated by every one of their peers."

In an environment that often pits participants against each other where bonuses are concerned, the plan encourages teamwork instead. "The last thing you want in a firm like this is people competing against each other. We're all competing against the market. You want a spirit of cooperativeness. So we have an enormous amount of cooperation, where someone might be in 3Com and someone who's in Cisco can pass along something they heard about Intel dropping the price of a certain [computer component]. That might hurt 3Com or it might not hurt Cisco. So by sharing this information, we're all generalists, you could have one team following Dell, one following Compaq, another following Gateway, and they're all pulling for each other."

NO SHORT CUTS

The right idea, good people, and attractive compensation can't prevent stock prices from going down, however. "This investing in companies—there's a lot of things that can go wrong," Friess says. "You have to have the ability to say, 'OK, I've checked this, this, this, and this,' *but you never ever have complete full information.*"

There are no shortcuts. Friess dismisses the rule of thumb that equates an attractive PE with a number that approximates the expected growth rate. "Instead, we would take a company that's growing 16 percent and we would say, 'How do we compare that to our company over here that we're [already] paying sixteen times earnings for, that's growing 8, 9, or 10 percent?'" Friess applies a premium to reflect the new stock's additional growth, and sixteen times earnings moves up, over time, to the twenty-two to twenty-five times earnings range.

A reasonable price, to Friess, is sixteen times earnings. That's roughly equal to a 6 percent rate of interest. (If you put $100 in the bank, an interest rate of 6 percent returns $\frac{1}{16}$ of your capital each year.) Friess doesn't adjust this benchmark when other investors lose sight of underlying value. A reasonable purchase price won't jump to twenty-five times earnings just because the market zooms ahead. Friess: "Many investors have the concept of relative price–earnings ratios. We don't embrace that notion. When stocks were selling for forty and fifty times earnings, I remember someone saying, 'Look at McDonald's at fifty times earnings. You can buy Church's Fried Chicken for twenty-eight times earnings and what a relative bargain.' And then, two years later, when McDonald's went to eighteen times earnings, Church's went to six times."

ON MISSED OPPORTUNITIES

"It is very important," Friess says, "to underscore that we have missed many great opportunities—the Home Depots, the Wal-Marts—because we weren't willing to pay that high price–earnings ratio." If you look at Brandywine's holdings on any given year, it would be very unusual to find more than 10 percent of the portfolio selling for more than twenty-two or twenty-three times earnings for the current year. Which raises another important issue: What time frame should earnings be applied to? The previous year? The current year? Next year? Five years from now? "I usually will go out twelve months, and if the PE ratio is thirty times earnings, I'll say, you know, that's a little bit on the edge. Let's not do it. Had I been willing to go out one more year, my PE ratio would drop dramatically. The problem with this process is, it's hard to know how well a company's going to do eighteen months, two years out."

LOOK AHEAD, NOT BACK

Knowing when to buy a growth stock is easy, compared to knowing when to sell. The qualities that lure investors in the first place make divorce difficult.

"When you buy a stock," Friess counsels, "forget what you paid for it and when you bought it. How often do you hear someone say, 'Well, we're at year end, let's nail down some gains; or, we need some losses.' We cover up the part of the cost sheet that shows what we paid and when. We only want to look at where the stock is going. It doesn't matter where it's been."

"By blocking that out of our mind it allows us, number one, to sell a stock that we bought three weeks ago that's down four points. Ordinarily, you have a mental attitude that says, 'Gee, I can't do that, I'll admit I'm wrong and so therefore let's wait till it gets back up to where it [was] or my clients will think I'm an idiot, and that I didn't do my work properly because here, just three weeks ago, I bought it.' And, secondly, it allows us to look at a company that's doubled and say, 'Gee, maybe we ought to add to it.'"

He warns against the inclination to sell half of an investment that has doubled, just to guarantee against loss. "That could be one of the biggest mistakes that lay investors make. They always look at where the stock has been without collecting information to make an assessment as to where it is going from here. I think that's one of the most important things an everyday investor should focus on."

Friess readily admits that it's easy to fall in love with a stock and outstay one's welcome. He did it himself early in his career, with the worst investment he ever made while a professional investor. It was a company called Four Phase Systems. "I had maybe a double or a triple, but I was skiing and I remember calling in the office to see how it was doing. And I had all my money in it. I had maybe $45,000 invested—my entire life's savings—in the stock. And it went down something like 35 percent, 40 percent because of a bad earnings report. There are plenty in which I got my head handed to me. There's plenty of scars here."

A PIG IN TIME SAVES NINE

A rigorous sell discipline guards against more serious injury to Friess and his customers. It's called the "pig-on-the-trough" theory. "Growing up in northern Wisconsin, I visited my friends on a farm and they'd have fifteen pigs on a trough. From across the barnyard would come the sixteenth, who is hungrier than another pig, who gets displaced and wanders off across the barn. He didn't roll over and die. The new pig, because he's hungrier, will enjoy being on the trough more than the one that got displaced. And we think that's a very important approach to take to investing. Lay investors don't have to deal with the 250-stock universe, so in a way it's easier for them. If they have fifteen stocks, when they find a sixteenth, they should force themselves to sell one other that's not likely to appreciate as fast or as far."

As homage to the firm's sell discipline, Friess is now the proud owner of a 600-pound sow given him—as a piglet—by his coworkers. Now known as Wilbur, the piglet won Friess over by nuzzling his chin the first time they met. Wilbur lives in the front yard of Friess's home in Delaware, probably the best-groomed pig in the United States.

Brandywine analysts maintain lists of stocks that are candidates for displacement if something better comes along. That way, they can move swiftly when opportunity knocks.

Here's how forced displacement worked after researcher David Harrington saw a chance in early 1996 to catch shares of Dell Computer Corporation just before they popped. Delays in production and some product transition issues had caused Dell to miss Wall Street's earnings estimates. The stock tumbled, and analysts lowered their future earnings estimates.

Sensing an overreaction, Harrington launched an analysis of Dell's growth prospects. He conferred at length with Dell's management and with other Friess Associates researchers. His conclusion: Falling component prices would help boost Dell's sales volume and operating margins.

Meanwhile, back at the trough, forced displacement took its course. "In order to buy Dell," Friess says, "we sold Cabletron Systems for $77 a share and General Nutrition for $22." Over the ensuing sixteen months, Cabletron sank to $72 a share while General Nutrition, which gained $5, only kept up with the market. "We started buying Dell in February 1996 at a split-adjusted price of $8.70 a share," Friess recalls. Assumptions proved correct. Lower prices fueled revenue growth and gains in market share, and, in subsequent quarters, Dell exceeded expectations. In August 1997, Dell shares changed hands for around $82 and, still on a hot streak, a gain of $390 million for Brandywine investors.

As a practical matter, Friess researchers re-examine a stock's potential if it falls 18 percent from the purchase price. If another company looks like a faster grower, the first one is history. But if the stock that has lost 18 percent is more promising than alternatives, Friess won't sell it just because it's off to a poor start.

On the upside there are limits, too. "We get very nervous once we get above, let's say, thirty times earnings on a stock." Even that is high, by Friess standards. In any given year, it's unusual to find more than 10 percent of Brandywine's portfolio in stocks selling for more than twenty-three times the following year's earnings.

SELL STOCKS WHILE THEY'RE HOT

The idea is to sell stocks when they are still appealing. "We only want to be selling good stocks," says Friess. "With our displacement theory, if we're selling a bad stock, then we're not doing our job of finding good stocks. A lot of times we'll go to—let's say we'll go to you and say, 'You know, you have to sell your XYZ stock.' And you say, 'Look, I just bought it seven months ago. I've still got 30 percent upside.' But we found something we think will have a 70 percent upside. So the trick is, we want to be selling good stocks. If we're selling stocks and have only 5 or 10 percent upside, we're not going to do as well as if we're selling stocks with 30 percent upside."

At times, economic influences larger than a company's prospects warn Friess to lighten up on stocks. "He's amazing because he has gone liquid at certain times when the fundamentals were really bad," says Stig Ramel. "He sold off a lot of shares just after Kuwait [was invaded by Iraq]. He reacted very quickly and very decisively, and his clients really were rescued by his very quick instincts."

Friess's unnerving talent for buying and selling stocks that achieve attractive long-term gains in a couple of months defies the rules that condemn most investors, including professionals, to subaverage performance. Observers liken Friess to the honey bee, which is not supposed to be able to fly, but it does. For his part, Friess is grateful. "Well," he says, "the nice thing is that many of these companies that are out working to produce new products just provide so much honey that I'm in business."

2

Value

BUYING INTO WEAKNESS

John Neff inhabits down-and-out regions of the stock market where most investors tread warily, if at all. It's a long way, philosophically, from the high-flying region of investors like Foster Friess, who treat new highs as buy signals.

Record stock prices and earnings don't inspire Neff, the celebrated apostle of value investing. He prefers "woebegone" companies that once enjoyed popularity but, for shortsighted reasons, have fallen from favor. Whether earnings are down, or just off a hot pace, or reverberating because a prominent competitor has stumbled and jolted the market, or for any number of other causes, Neff's kind of company bangs pots and pans in the dim, dusty, and foreboding bargain basement. To Neff—steward, for thirty-one years, of the Windsor Fund—that cacophony sounds like great investments calling for attention.

At one time or another, most "solid citizens" visit Neff's domain. Some of his biggest moneymakers are household names: Chrysler, Atlantic Richfield, IBM, Tandy, and Citicorp, to name five favorites that weren't favorites when added to Windsor's portfolio. Neff bought all five in the dumps; in retrospect, other investors wish they had, too. The investment in Citicorp, a saga that took five long and painful years to pan out, underscores why value investing is easier to preach than to practice.

Many investors do pluck winners now and then from the market's nether regions. Still more fancy themselves as being shrewdly attuned to the stocks that brokers have a hard time selling. But when it comes to outpacing the stock market over three bruising decades, through market peaks, troughs, and plateaus, Neff stands unchallenged. In the eyes of fellow professional money managers and securities analysts who comprise the Association for Investment Management and Research, Neff owns "a record that is essentially unmatched by his peers in the mutual fund industry."

TROUNCING THE MARKET

Just to say Windsor beat the market during Neff's tenure understates the record. Windsor trounced the market with gains of 13.8 percent a year, compounded, versus 10.7 percent for the market. The advantage, over time, is awesome. A $10,000 investment when Neff took over the reins at Windsor, in June 1964, had grown to $564,000 by the time he retired in December 1995. That's more than twice the $251,000 produced by an equal investment in the benchmark S&P 500, a proxy for the market. Under Neff, Windsor blossomed from a stumbling $75 million fund into an $11 billion mutual-fund powerhouse, notwithstanding the fact that it closed the doors to new investors in 1985.

In a business where eight of ten professionals routinely fall below average, outperforming the market once is sufficient cause for jubilation. At Windsor, it happened often. In baseball terms, if beating the market is a base hit, then Neff is a career .710 hitter. In thirty-one times at bat against the S&P 500, he reached base no fewer than twenty-two times, with plenty of extra base hits and a few home runs to boot. Total return on investment exceeded 20 percent in thirteen years. One year, it fell just shy of that mark, though its 19.1 percent return still dwarfed the 9.8 percent etched by the market. In 1975, Neff hit a grand slam, with a 54.5 percent return against the exuberant market's 37.1 percent return. The next year, Windsor's 46.4 percent return outpaced the S&P industrials by two to one.

THE ROAD TO A WINNING STRATEGY

Neff multiplied investors' wealth with a formula that stresses rigorous fundamental analysis of financial strength and earnings power, robust dividends, low prices relative to earnings per share, and hefty commitments to stocks or sectors with the right stuff. His bottom line, or total return, reflects the rate at which earnings are growing plus dividend yield, divided by the price–earnings (PE) ratio—the stock price divided by earnings per share. "What you get," says Neff, "versus what you pay for it."

Unlike investors who follow the crowd, Neff buys stocks when demand is weak and sells when demand is strong. "*Keep it simple* is a phrase with some validity in the investment business," Neff declares.

That goes for his view of risk. Instead of assuming more of it, Neff outpaced the stock market by avoiding foolish risks and refusing to succumb to fashion trends. Trendy, high-tech measures of risk don't carry much weight with him, although he's as conversant as any other money manager with modern portfolio theory. "Risk's always hard to define," he says. "I usually qualified it in the pit of my stomach."

Computers never played a central role. "We didn't use them," says Neff. "We're judgment. Judgment pure and simple." He points to his head. "Here was my computer, in effect."

His command of facts is far-reaching. "He just has knowledge about an incredible number of things, and not just superficial knowledge, a deep knowledge," says Burton G. Malkiel, Chemical Bank chairman's professor of economics at Princeton University and the author of *A Random Walk Down Wall Street,* which introduced many investors to modern portfolio theory. "If it's a situation I know particularly well, I ask him a question and he amazes me."

Computers are critical for quantitative analysts relying on subtle relative changes in price relationships, Neff concedes. But that's not his style. "You try to cover the waterfront with your own competence," he explains. "My whole life has been made up of being aware of price changes. You just can't be a student of the marketplace without being aware of price changes." To this backdrop of ever-changing prices, Neff applies an investment strategy that boils down to four basic principles:

1. Low price–earnings ratio.
2. High dividend yield.
3. Strong company fundamentals.
4. An eye on the big picture.

There is an informal but critical fifth principle: "You've got to keep an open mind," Neff warns. "You have to be a student of history, but you can't be a captive of history. I've found people in the investment game who can give you chapter and verse on what happened at similar points in the economy, what industries and companies were featured, and whether they should be featured or not featured again. But what they overlook is that no two points in history are the same. There are always differences. The market adjusts. Marketplaces adjust and you've got to adjust. You've got to stay flexible."

Neff buys downtrodden stocks with confidence that eventually the pendulum will swing back for sound companies that have fallen from grace. And so he is prepared to stick with the companies he believes in. An average company in the Windsor portfolio during his tenure was held two years; a few stayed as long as eight or nine years. Sooner or later, the pay-off usually arrives, because behind dull, beaten-up façades, sizzle lurks. "This sounds arrogant to say," Neff declares, "but other institutional investors are going to need these stocks or want them at some point in time, but don't know it yet."

SWEAT, TOIL, AND EARNINGS

The heart of Windsor's investment analysis lies in accurate earnings forecasts, which, in turn, depend on a thorough combing of financial statements and interviews with company managers. Because the companies in Neff's sights tend to be at or near cyclical troughs, the trick is to use all these sources to determine "normalized earnings"—what the company can be expected to earn near the cycle's peak, when it's back in favor. There are no shortcuts. "You've got to do the work," says Neff, "and it's the sweat and toil that determine how realistic the growth rate is."

While guiding Windsor, Neff's approach also had a magical effect on the University of Pennsylvania's endowment fund. Since taking on that assignment in 1980, he has nursed the endowment to $2 billion from just $132 million—a fifteenfold increase in sixteen years, with just $100 million of net cash inflow after withdrawals by the University.

Not bad for an investment manager who is as different from the elite Wall Street mold as his modest Midwestern roots, and whose career is already becoming a legend. Neff's education did not follow the private-school-to-Ivy-League path. He "basically grubbed it out" as a boy in Corpus Christi, Texas, with his mother and stepfather after his parents divorced. Not "to the manor born," he likes to say, he caddied and delivered newspapers, and, he claims, from the age of eleven, he bought his own clothes.

Windsor's fee schedule embodies the notion that you have to work for your money, and you have to succeed most of the time. It rewards exceptional performance and penalizes poor performance. That makes Windsor one of the few funds these days with built-in performance incentive; most funds merely take a percentage of asset values. Neff proposed the arrangement soon after arriving. The base investment management fee is low to begin with, sixteen one hundredths of a percentage point. If Windsor outpaces the S&P 500 on a trailing three-year basis by four percentage points a year, management collects an extra fee equal to one-tenth of one percent of total assets; if results suffer by an equal amount, management gives back one-tenth of one percent. For a fund with $10 billion, the twenty basis-point difference between best and worst performance amounts to $20 million in fees over and above a positive or negative change in asset values. "So the difference is very, very significant in our investment health," Neff observes. "And very significant to the shareholders."

Stubborn conviction is critical to value investors, who often walk a lonely path, and Neff has displayed plenty of it from his earliest days. "My mother used to always say, 'John, you should be a lawyer. You'd argue with a signpost.' And she was essentially right," Neff recalls. "I have a close friend who says, 'You tell John black and he'll say white.' But I did the better thing. I argued with the stock market."

For anyone other than Neff, who brims with self-confidence, his success would have been hard to predict. His high school years passed in a blur of lackluster performance—except on the rare occasions when he was pushed to perform by any suggestion that he wasn't up to it. After high school, he couldn't get away from Texas fast enough. He went north to a series of blue-collar jobs in Michigan. A job in a juke-box factory was interrupted when his father reentered his life. John F. Neff, who owned a small business in Ohio that distributed automotive equipment, offered John a career. But working for his father, an energetic and very successful salesman, didn't pan out, so the younger Neff went his separate way again. This time, it led to the U.S. Navy. As a parting gesture, his father suggested a risk-free investment. He guaranteed his son against losses stemming from an investment in Aero Equipment, the publicly held company that manufactured the automotive equipment that John F. distributed. Neff accepted the offer and his father never had to prove as good as his word, because the shares went up.

A LITTLE NIGHT SCHOOL

The Navy was not an ideal fit for this sailor with a keen intellect and no love for arbitrary authority. "I've always been enthusiastic, I've always run off at the mouth and I've always been reasonably articulate," Neff says. In the Navy, "One guy took me aside and said 'You just don't curse enough.'

Not that I was namby-pamby or anything, but every inanimate object in the service always was preceded by a four-letter word." Besides colorful language, the stint in the Navy taught Neff the value of further education. "As soon as I got in the Navy," Neff recalls, "the bosun's mate just kind of bossed me around. I figured out that if that wasn't going to continue to happen the rest of my life, maybe I ought to go to school."

He finished his tour of duty and enrolled in an undergraduate program at the University of Toledo. Thanks to service credits and correspondence courses, Neff completed his undergraduate program in 24 months. But it was a fateful experience that introduced him to Professor Sidney Robbins, a disciple of Benjamin Graham and fundamental, value investing. "It was a good dove-tailing of professors, both from the academic world but also from the real world, and you could kind of fit it into your work experience." Under Robbins' skilled tutelage, Neff discovered an interest in, and a knack for, finance. "I was fascinated," says Neff. Motivated for the first time, he finished college with a summa cum laude and a special award usually reserved for students who concentrate in finance, not someone who took only two courses.

Just before graduation in a particularly frigid January 1955, Neff hitchhiked to New York City in hopes of becoming a stock broker. No one picked up his expenses or treated him to expensive dinners. Neff camped at the YMCA and checked out four training programs he had learned about in an issue of *Barron's*. Smith Barney, Merrill Lynch, and Blythe Eastman Dillon turned him down flat. The fourth, Bache (later absorbed by Prudential Securities), offered to make him a securities analyst, a position in which, Bache decided, his rusty voice, which lacked authority, would cause no damage. But securities analysis didn't fit in with Neff's determination to buy and sell stocks. So he headed back to Ohio, where a job in a bank trust department awaited and so did his young wife, Lilli, a Midwesterner who was pleased to stay put.

BORN LIKE THE BUDDHA

Neff joined Cleveland's National City Bank "and had a great eight-and-a-half embryonic training years." Meanwhile, he attended an MBA program nights at Western Reserve (now Case Western Reserve).

At the bank, Neff soon met a young portfolio manager named Bill Roe, who still joins Neff for an annual golf outing. According to Roe, Neff arrived at the bank with essentially the same investment ideas he espouses today. He would ponder whether the price–earnings ratio for Eastman Kodak, for example, was too high. Today, says Roe, Neff the celebrity is no different in character or outlook from the Neff who owned a $10,000 attached house and a $500 stock portfolio in 1957. "John was born like the Buddha," Roe says, "fully clothed and a grown man."

Art Boanas, another friend and colleague from the bank, remembers an ebullient Neff who arrived "more full of himself than full of ideas." In Boanas, Neff found a kindred spirit and a mentor who once tried to persuade the bank's staid investment committee to invest in titanium—about as far from the bank's risk-averse practice as was imaginable in those days. The suggestion didn't fly, of course. To Neff, though, the recollection shows how he and Boanas "really went back to kind of basics—usually with a more practical bent than the titanium example."

Boanas, an economist by training, helped shape Neff's grasp of the macroeconomic forces that drive overarching values. "We did kind of go back to the old, basic bottom-up type of analysis," Neff recalls. "I stretched that, I suppose, as I got to be a successful practitioner, to justify Windsor's bold positions in comparatively few industries and companies."

As the bank's assistant research director, Neff rapidly acquired more sway than his junior status ordinarily would permit, according to Roe. Neff was quite a salesman when he saw an opportunity. Normally, research reports ran seven or eight pages in length. Neff produced a one-page research report that persuaded the bank's investment committee to add Polaroid to its list just as color photography was coming on line. The price was $200 a share at the time. Neff predicted that the price would go in several years to a stratospheric $1,680. Adjusted for subsequent splits, Roe says, "That's exactly what happened."

It was not a smooth ride, though. In 1962, the market suffered a wrenching correction, one of many "inflection points" in Neff's career. Polaroid slid to $80 a share, from $240, in a matter of weeks. IBM slumped to $300 a share from almost $600, Roe recalls, accompanied by sharp declines in a long list of blue-chip stocks that suddenly fell out of favor after an extended run. Like subsequent inflection points, this one emerged despite a healthy economy and no obvious sign of a downturn in the business cycle. Perhaps the skittishness engendered thirty-three years earlier, in 1929, still persisted. In any event, the 1962 correction helped set the stage for Neff's future.

Neff and the bank had grown increasingly out of synch. Neff sought growth, even if it meant trading stocks. Polaroid notwithstanding, his most imaginative ideas fell on deaf ears. The bank's buy-and-hold philosophy in those days meant holding stocks for decades, with the expectation that the owner would expire eventually and the heirs would enjoy a step-up in value, avoiding an inheritance tax. "We were not interested in a stock going up 10 and then selling it," Roe says. "John was wise to run his own shop."

Going to Windsor cut Neff loose from a culture that, as he saw it, emphasized "hitting behind the ball." But it plunged him into a situation that was still showing the effects of the previous downturn. Four-year-old Windsor, with its small growth stocks, had lost a quarter of its value in the course of the market's 9 percent decline. Shareholders and brokers were angry, and the reaction of the fund's shell-shocked directors only made bad circumstances worse; fearful of holding onto out-of-favor stocks, they jettisoned blue chips prematurely. Their overreaction left Windsor poorly positioned for a subsequent blue-chip recovery, and it managed to grow at only half the market's pace in 1963. When the directors interviewed Neff, all they were hoping for was a money manager capable of matching the market. In Windsor, ironically, Neff found a mutual fund that exemplified the woebegone qualities that appeal to him.

RESCUING WINDSOR

By October 1964, Neff was in command at Windsor and attuned to the competitive environment. In a lengthy memo to the fund's directors, Neff compared Windsor's investment style with the styles of five other leading mutual funds, including Dreyfus and Putnam Growth—a reasonable cross section in an era when the world was populated by only a few dozen mutual funds of any size.

At that time, Windsor was little more than a small fund dealing in familiar growth stocks that often had large price–earnings multiples. "Like so many portfolio managers," says Neff, "it reacted rather than anticipated." Launched in 1958 under the aegis of Wellington Management, Windsor had performed well enough during its first few years, when growth stocks enjoyed a post-Sputnik heyday driven by a craze for any company that sounded electronic.

Like all crazes, this one eventually faltered. "When it faded, you paid the piper, as inevitably you do," Neff says. "Not only did the price–earnings multiples run down sharply but a lot of those goods were found to be somewhat tawdry. I shouldn't say they were not legitimate companies, but they weren't solid, enduring companies. So you not only lost the earnings, you lost the multiple, and you had all kinds of single-event disasters." Extreme risk aversion gripped the white-shoed directors, who grew conservative at the bottom. "So of course you didn't come back as neatly as you should in the ensuing recovery market. Instead of assuming more risk, you'd grown less risky."

MEASURED PARTICIPATION

In his October 1964 memo to the fund's directors, Neff introduced a notion he called "measured participation." Besides setting the tone for Windsor over the next three decades, whether or not Neff was looking that far into the future, "measured participation" suggests a useful breakdown for investors dealing with portfolio structure and diversification today. Rather than segment the portfolio along industry lines (a conventional approach), Neff introduced five broadly descriptive investment categories:

1. Highly recognized, blue-chip, highly marketable companies.
2. Highly marketable, highly recognized growth companies.
3. Well-recognized growth companies that fail to make the second category because of reduced marketability and an accompanying slight difference in recognition.
4. Less widely recognized growth companies.
5. Special situations, turnarounds, cyclicals, workouts.

Neff couched his conclusions with a caveat typical of his cautious nature: "Like any system of classification," he warned, "this one is not without its weaknesses, depending on the preconceived notions of the observer. It is not a panacea but rather an attempt to peer into the competitive funds with some new perspective."

That said, Neff went on to note that Windsor's relative absence from the blue-chip category would cripple its performance when these "solid citizens" regained favor. In his diplomatic fashion, Windsor's new manager chided his skittish employers:

What is really being said is that we should not feel any apology, for either performance or showcase purposes, for having a Ford or a G.M. in the Windsor Fund. A greater emphasis in this area services several needs. It would aid income, buttress performance both on the upside and downside (assuming capable selection) and might even allow a greater comfort index in respect to liquidity. The joy in operating more aggressively in this area is that there always are opportunities in this sphere because of the marketplace's unwillingness to understand, over the short term, all the cross currents of evaluation, even in the biggest of companies.

The memo expressed Neff's essential ideas about diversification and price–earnings multiples:

One of our past dispositions was to fairly well scatter our shots in [the highly recognized growth] area, and as a result gain both the good performing and the indifferent performing equities, thus diluting the total impact somewhat. To the degree that the universe is fairly permanently defined and the risks of catastrophe are quite small, the principal exposure is that of decline in [price–earnings] multiples rather than severe deterioration in the company's earnings. I would think our representation [in this segment] is about right but that a greater concentration is warranted.

With his explicit guidelines for investing in less widely recognized growth companies, Neff sought to remedy Windsor's historic aversion to a very familiar but poorly understood market sector: out-of-favor stocks poised for recovery. "One possible criticism that can be leveled on past representation in this segment has been our inability to gain positions in 'adrenalin' groups," he informed Windsor's directors:

To the degree these areas or their present-day equivalent are superperformers and we are not represented while the competition is, our relative performance is obviously burdened. I would think that under the new portfolio management divisionalization, more time can be allocated by the portfolio manager toward weighing and assessing potential dramatic gain areas that sometimes involve either greater than ordinary risk or the taking of an "unpopular" or "out-of-favor" position.

A PASSION FOR FUNDAMENTALS

Ten guidelines for picking less recognized growth stocks underscored Neff's passion for thorough fundamental analysis:

1. Price–earnings ratio below that of the general market.
2. Demonstrated or provable fundamental growth of 7 percent or better.
3. Yield protection in about 40 percent of this segment.

4. Quality company in growing field.

5. No more than 5 percent of the floating supply.

6. Clear understanding of the company's franchise and the customer's need for the product.

7. Record of persistent annual increments of earnings, virtually without interruption.

8. Absence of cyclical exposure unless compensated for importantly by low multiple.

9. Easy channel of communication under duress to management.

10. Thorough canvassing of industry information sources.

From a suburban office complex in Valley Forge, Pennsylvania, Neff applied these principles with a steady hand; closer proximity to Wall Street might have caused tremor. "Being somewhat remote probably gives you a little better vantage point," says Neff, "than to be caught up essentially in the emotionalism of the moment."

Instead of being swept up in Wall Street's emotional tide, Neff tapped into it only after completing his exhaustive research. "We essentially did our own work," he says. "Once in a while you might clue Wall Street in, but eventually Wall Street would change its opinion and add coverage. That opinion would educate other institutional investors who don't do their own work, and they would come into the marketplace as buyers."

VALUE MAN

Value investing, to Windsor analyst Jim Mordy, means looking for reasonably attractive companies with attractive prospects, at prices below what investors typically expect to pay. There is a contrarian element to it. "You're, hopefully, buying stocks where not all the news is good news, but you have the upside maybe when news is better, as the prospects improve for your company." The opposite would be true for growth investing, where it is common knowledge among investors that a company like Coca-Cola is a great investment with great prospects.

A value stock does not appeal to rank-and-file investors—except in retrospect, when the outcome is apparent. "You really buy something that's been pummeled, beat up, out of favor, and the chart has been devastated, and pretty well all the proponents are out of it," Neff says. What remains is an attractive core, manifested by the yield and the growth rate together. If perception of the fundamentals is correct, eventually the market warms up to the stock. It will regain favor and "some of the twenty-eight Street

analysts that were against it would start going for it." Their favorable recommendations will influence professional investors and, when enough of
them recommend the stock, others will start to feel pressured into going
along, or at least giving it another look.

Cigna, a large insurance and health care provider, was a case in point.
"We owned that tortuously for four years. It essentially had two businesses. One was managed health care, where they were doing quite an excellent job. Probably the biggest publicly-held HMO company in the
country. But they had a doggy commercial property and casualty insurance businesses. Everybody thought, because of asbestos and toxic wastes,
that the insurance industry was going to have to set aside reserves to satisfy a three- or four-hundred-billion-dollar obligation." Neff believed
that the estimates were far too high, and it turned out that the real liability was lower even than he expected, closer to $50 billion. "When that
became obvious, the managed care business, which was very good all
along, was spotlighted. The Street analysts started to recommend Cigna
and the stock tripled."

It would be nice, of course, if all out-of-favor investments were to
come back in fashion, but that's not always the case. "That's wonderfully
simplistic and they don't all orchestrate quite that way," Neff says. "But
you know you get a honeymoon period in the first year or so of ownership, simply because they've been so beat up and out of favor, that you
will suffer little principal deterioration. You build a model of expectations
of the fundamentals as you perceive them and at that year anniversary, in
three-quarters of the cases, it's fulfilling. The rest of the time you may be
early or you may be wrong."

CRASHING CONGLOMERATES

In the group that went awry, Neff singles out a company called U.S. Industries as his hands-down worst investment. "It was a conglomerate during the period after conglomerates fell out of favor. In the late 1960s, the
Gulf and Westerns and the Ling-Tempco-Voughts ruled the waves. They
fell from favor in the early seventies and we owned up to 16 percent in
conglomerates, one of which was U.S. Industries." The shtick, as Neff
called it, lay in allocating capital wisely. "And what we kind of missed," he
says, "was that you had to have critical mass." Without critical mass, U.S.
Industries lacked economies of scale. By the time Windsor dumped its last
shares, the fund had lost half its investment. Almost two decades later, a

large investment in thrifts—savings and loan and savings banks—proved almost as costly.

During a particularly dispiriting three-year stretch through 1973, Windsor underperformed the market by significant margins. Neff's explanation in Windsor's 1973 annual report sounded a stoic but hopeful note:

> And in this environment, rest assured, your Fund will continue to honor the investment approach so well stated many years ago by Benjamin Franklin: "Be honest; toil constantly; be patient. Have courage and self-reliance. Be ambitious and industrious. Have perseverance, ability and judgment. Cultivate foresight and imagination."
>
> For we view the current devastation in the marketplace, not as a reason for alarm, but rather as one of opportunity. We believe we will look back on this recent period of excessively low evaluations of innovative, accomplishing companies as one not unlike the early 1950s, when stocks of good companies also could be acquired at prices of only four or five times earnings—prices that provided the opportunity for truly remarkable appreciation in ensuing years.

The early 1990s brought back the specter of prolonged subpar performance, in large part because of the disastrous financial services sector. "You had this terrible cathartic in 1989 and 1990, which were two years we underperformed very sharply from the *perception;* and, in some cases, the *reality* of financial intermediaries going over the edge. We're talking about Citicorp, as an example. But there were ones that failed and we owned some of them. Trying to recover from that—and those were great big double-digit poor comparisons—would take a chop out of a period."

Neff contends that his style is better suited to dull and prosaic markets than to adrenalin markets. On a fast track, Windsor tends not to do so well. "We really ask for dull, lackluster, boring markets, and those are the ones where we seem to do best."

As a style, value investing predates Neff. Credit for this enduring approach belongs chiefly to Benjamin Graham and David Dodd, authors of *Security Analysis,* published in 1934. In the aftermath of the Great Crash, they laid out principles that paved the way for John Neff and other value investors, including Warren Buffett, who studied finance under Graham at Columbia University.

Neff willingly acknowledges Dodd and Graham's influence, to which he added his own twist. In Windsor's annual report for 1988—a year in which Windsor's 30.3 percent gain outpaced the S&P 500 by nearly two to one—Vanguard Group chairman John C. Bogle put Neff in proper light: "If the concept of 'value investing' in stocks with relatively low price-to-earnings ratios and with solid book values and above-average dividend yields was not invented by Mr. Neff, certainly he has been a major force in giving it both definition and acceptance."

PE SHOOTIN' MATCH

Neff reportedly once described value investing as buying "stocks that make you twitch." For his part, though, "value investing" sounds too vague. "It's a category consultants use," he says, "but it has always been a bit obtuse to me because it's in the eye of the beholder, and that can mean a lot of things. It can be asset values, it can be cash flow, or whatever. So I've always been a little uncomfortable. Describing ourselves as low PE shooters, that's the way we do it."

Every share of stock has a price and claims a portion of the company's earnings, or earnings per share. Neff typically uses current year earnings forecasts until August, and afterwards switches to forecasts based on the next year's performance. He considers this a middle ground between trailing earnings that reflect actual performance during the past 12 months and prospective earnings that depend on skill, judgment, experience, and some amount of luck.

Once earnings estimates are in place, Neff takes the next step. The price of a share of stock, divided by the earnings per share, gives the crucial price/earnings ratio. Say a share of stock earns $1. If the price is $20, then the PE is 20.

$$\text{Price/earnings ratio} = \text{Price of a share} \div \text{Earnings per share}$$

Instead of doing the arithmetic, investors can find current PE listings daily in most newspaper stock tables, next to prices.

Historically, average PE multiples for well-regarded companies in the S&P 500 range from fifteen to twenty-five times a share. During strong bull markets, PE multiples may reach or even exceed fifty for the most desirable companies. On the strength of their belief that unlimited demand for stock in strong growth companies like McDonald's, Eastman Kodak, and IBM would forever outstrip supply, investors bid prices of the Nifty Fifty as high as ninety times a share in 1973 and 1974—only to see prices and multiples come crashing down again.

CARNAGE AND CANDY SHOPS

The collapse of the Nifty Fifty was carnage to other investors but a candy shop to Neff, who snapped up out-of-favor stocks that produced phenomenal results in 1975, when Windsor gained 54.5 percent, beating the market by more than 17 percentage points. Home runs included McLean Trucking (+100 percent), Pizza Hut (+136 percent), Edison Brother Stores (+137 percent), Jonathan Logan (+143 percent), and White Consolidated Industries (+172 percent), to name but a few.

Just as the Nifty Fifty list was reaching its ill-fated crescendo, Ben Graham depicted the merits of low PE investing in the stock market in his 1973 book, *The Intelligent Investor:*

> If we assume that it is the habit of the market to overvalue common stocks which have been showing excellent growth or are glamorous for some other reason, it is logical to expect that it will undervalue—relatively, at least—companies that are out of favor because of unsatisfactory developments of a temporary nature. This may be set down as a fundamental law of the stock market, and it suggests an investment approach that should prove both conservative and promising.[1]

Graham advised investors to focus on larger companies, for two reasons. "First, they have the resources in capital and brain power to carry them through adversity and back to a satisfactory earnings base. Second, the market is likely to respond with reasonable speed to any improvement shown."[2] As evidence, he tracked the performance by ten stocks in the Dow Jones Industrial Average with the lowest PE ratios. These unpopular stocks were, by Graham's lights, the cheapest available. Although this so-called "Dogs of the Dow" strategy would have been unprofitable in the years 1917 through 1933, in the twenty-five-year stretch from 1937 through 1969, "cheap stocks clearly outperformed the average." In more recent periods, they have generally performed very well.

Contrarian in nature, hunting for low PE ratios invariably turns up woebegone companies with tarnished images. As performance cools off, or just threatens to cool off, PE ratios exhibit an impact even before reported earnings falter. The market gets wind of change, and the stock becomes less attractive. Instead of paying, say, twenty-five times earnings for a stock, new investors pay only twenty times the same earnings. Thus, the price of a stock earning $2 a share can slide, depending on how bad the news is, long before a dip in earnings is recorded.

An expected decline in earnings might appear to cost investors only ten cents a share, but if the PE ratio tumbles from twenty-five to twenty, not an unimaginable scenario when growth falters, shareholders will be looking at a price of $38 a share instead of $50—a 24 percent drop in value.[3] It's not uncommon for the PE ratio to shrink when it is predicted that increased earnings will not meet expectations, even if the company is in strong financial health. You don't have to look far for examples. Says Neff, "It happens everyday."

BETTING ON BETTER DAYS AHEAD

These deflated PE ratios signal stocks that have lost favor with investors— and are worth investigating. "The PE is the ultimate arbitrator," Neff declares. "More than that, a truly low PE." A stock that changed hands formerly at forty times earnings and, subsequently, at twenty times earnings, isn't the stock Neff is looking for. It may be value in a comparative sense, but it's not low enough by Neff's standards. "Low, low PE," says Neff. "That's the driver."

A discount of 40 to 50 percent versus Neff's estimate of the five-year growth rate usually spells opportunity—provided the company is in sound financial condition and is well positioned for a favorable turn of events. In other words, if a company is growing at 16 percent a year, a PE ratio in the vicinity of eight or nine is about right.

The lower the PE ratio at purchase, the higher the total expected return, which Neff calculates as:

$$\text{Total expected return} = (\text{Earnings growth} + \text{Dividend yield}) \div (\text{Price/earnings ratio})$$

Play some realistic numbers into the formula and the effects are quite striking. If Neff pays a PE of ten for shares of a company growing 16 percent a year, the expected total return—if his assumptions are correct— should eventually collect a return in the neighborhood of 60 percent. But if he can lock up the shares at a PE of eight, his expected return leaps to 100 percent over the period of time he holds onto the stock. The economy must perform as expected for these results to materialize—but with Neff they usually do.

The expected growth rate, in Neff's shop, has a ceiling of 20 or 22 percent. "Beyond that is so fraught with additional risk over a five-year period that 22 percent is about as high as we'll go," he says. But even stocks at the top of this range are rare. Neff's strategy usually means combing the bottom quartile of the market, where a growth rate of 19 percent a year is on the high side.

A low PE strategy tends to rule out companies with more enviable growth rates. The average PE ratio in the Windsor Fund when Neff was in charge usually hovered in the vicinity of nine to eleven. (Compare this to stocks managed by Foster Friess, who seldom buys a stock if the PE is less than 16.) "We've never owned Coca-Cola," Neff concedes, "but sooner or later most everything else comes into view on the low PE side. Over 31 years, we only owned two drug stocks; instrumentation stocks probably never came into view, but we owned almost everything else."

Stellar companies have fallen beneath Windsor's PE threshold from time to time, when the market lost favor. In 1994, Windsor bought Intel for the second time, after word circulated that the new Intel computer chip had a bug that affected some calculations. "It was applicable in one tenth of one percent of the cases," Neff says, "and eventually they found it. But it was selling—this miracle company which beat the Japanese in microprocessors—was selling for eight times earnings. It didn't have any yield, but it had a 15 percent growth rate and we loaded up on it."

DIVIDENDS ARE YOUR FRIEND

Unlike investors enamored of sexy earnings growth, Neff often banks on stodgy dividend yields. A dividend yield, or current yield, represents the dividend a company pays out, stated as a percentage of the stock price. Say a company pays a $1 dividend and the price of its stock is $50; the dividend yield is 2 percent.

Dividend yields fluctuate in tandem with the stock price and inversely with the PE ratio. As bull markets drive stock prices and PE ratios up, dividend yields come down. Thus, high yields in bull markets often signal value stocks. Hunting for high yields in bull markets tends to signal candidates for value investments. In December 1997, Philip Morris offered investors the highest dividend yield in the Dow industrials: 3.6 percent. In normal markets, dividend yields at healthy companies fluctuate in the vicinity of 2 to 4 percent. In latter stages of a bull market, when stock prices are highest, dividend yields are lowest. When stock prices are low in a prolonged bear market, or when companies are under duress, yields are comparatively high.

A dividend yield is the closest an investor can get to a sure return on investment. Given the choice between a company with, say, a 13 percent growth rate and another company growing at an 8 percent rate and paying a 5 percent dividend yield, Neff ordinarily puts his money on the stock with a dividend.[4] "Graham and Dodd would tell you that the assured part, the yield, the dividend, is worth twice the weight assigned to the growth component," Neff observes.

"Earnings, even though they're reported, can be subject to all kinds of interpretations," says Neff, "but there's something about a dividend that is indisputable. It's calculable, it's real, it comes each quarter." It is also taxable, which can eat into returns. But at least tax bills are usually predictable. Growth rates can change instantaneously, Neff warns, at the moment institutional investors get a whiff that earnings might not meet expectations in the next quarter. "Whereas to have a dividend slashed or cut," Neff adds, "that would be a shortfall that's highly unusual." It is one of the last steps management takes, even in dire circumstances.

It's puzzling to Neff that investors seeking growth turn up their noses at dividends. He sees distinct advantages in, say, an 8 percent earnings growth and a 5 percent dividend yield, versus a 13 percent growth rate alone. Besides the obvious fact that shareholders can put dividends in their pockets, yields offer downside protection while one is waiting for a favorable upturn; at least there is something tangible to show when the stock price is marking time. But as long as dividends remain unfashionable, it's a plus for Neff, because the stock with the lower growth rate and the higher yield will normally fetch a lower PE than the stock with the higher growth rate.

"WE'RE TRYING TO PROVE SOMETHING"

Neff is a maverick with respect to diversification. He breaks the rules. When he retired, the $11-billion Windsor Fund owned about 70 stocks in a handful of market sectors, and a large portion of its funds concentrated in an even smaller group of stocks. The basic materials sector represented 23.4 percent of the portfolio when Neff retired—several times the relative weight for the sector in the S&P 500. Financial services were almost 20 percent, also a far larger representation than the S&P weighting. Banks, thrifts, and insurance companies, made up 37 percent of the Windsor fund when that sector was in the doghouse with investors in 1990–1991, even though financial services businesses comprise about 12 percent of the market. "We are trying to prove something," Neff says, "and there is some additional risk."

Barron's columnist and former editor Alan Abelson has observed a crucial difference in the way Neff and Fidelity money manager emeritus Peter Lynch diversify. Lynch, says Abelson, bought anything that promised to move in the right direction, even if it meant populating the Magellan portfolio with hundreds of stocks. Neff prefers an approach best described as putting eggs in fewer baskets and watching those baskets with extreme care: oils in the early 1980s after other investors bailed out; specialty retailers in 1982; Chrysler in 1990; financial services in 1989–1992.

While his counterparts tout the gospel of diversification, Neff warns that excessive diversification undermines the prospects of superior performance. Obsession with broad diversification is the sure road to mediocrity, Neff wrote in the 1994 *Money* magazine "Guide to Investing."[5] "Most people who own [more than two] mutual funds are overdiversified," Neff says.

What allows Neff to take big positions are his economic convictions. "I have a passion that any portfolio manager worth his salt has to be half an economist," Neff says. "For instance, after the 1987 cataclysm, the conventional wisdom was: the consumer was going to be spooked because the stock market had gone down 25 percent. And we said: Look, in Peoria and Oshkosh, they couldn't care less. They might even say it's about time those Wall Street guys got their comeuppance. As long as they're working and their neighbors are working, they're going to continue to spend. And it turned out in 1988, we did not have a recession."

On the strength of a bullish appraisal of the economy at the end of 1987, Neff poured $750 million into the stock market. *Barron's* took note: "A contrarian, Neff is buying into the bear market because of low prices and the opportunity to be selective."[6] *Barron's* had characterized Neff in similar fashion five years earlier, in July 1982: "A contrarian right down to his toes, John B. Neff . . . isn't bothered one bit to be buying stocks when most investors are heading for the hills."[7]

EMINENT CONTRARIAN

What does it mean to be a contrarian? "To go against the conventional wisdom," Neff says. That's easy enough to find. "It's in the paper every day and it's on the Street. It's what the majority of people think." Neff hastens to add that contrarian reactions do not guarantee prosperity. "You've got to also combine that with being right. In other words, the majority isn't always wrong. It's just that the odds aren't good on the majority's side. So you've got to make sure that you aren't doing this just to be difficult. It is useful only if it's in shareholders' interests. But the marketplace gives you very good odds because there is a great deal of groupthink out there." Thanks to the persistence of groupthink, or the herd mentality, "rather decent areas are routinely maligned, misunderstood, overlooked, and pummeled."

It's not an easy path to follow, as Neff warned in Windsor's 1990 annual report:

> It might be appropriate for shareholders to recall that our philosophy usually involves significant positions in overlooked, misunderstood, forgotten, woebegone companies and industries that are not in the mainstream of market popularity yet are fundamentally attractive in our view. Accordingly, this approach involves bucking the conventional wisdom and takes a strong stomach and a stiff backbone.

A strong stomach and a stiff backbone, to be sure, especially when the stock continues to slide. "It's like an anchor not grabbing on," says David Dreman of Dreman Value Management. "You buy a stock with all the fundamentals looking like they're in place but the stock keeps going down."

Investors who don't complain when investment managers buy a stock that goes up and up and up can get hot under the collar when a money manager buys on the way down, even though the drop lowers the average purchase price. Each day you look wrong versus the day before, says Neff. The response is, "You dummy, why did you buy that yesterday when you could have gotten it cheaper today?"

Being contrarian demands steadfast confidence. "When you have taken that tack, it's lonely," says Boanas. "It pits you against the rest of the investment community, which can make you look bloody wrong." Sure, Neff concedes, investors can pick out unpopular, low PE stocks with computer programs that are easy to find. It isn't enough. A contrarian strategy needs lots of intestinal fortitude, he says. And computers don't supply that.

Periodic reports to Windsor Fund directors spelled out Neff's steadfast contrarian approach to stock picking—before the results vindicated him. There are many examples, but one is classic. In 1973, he laid out the case for Tandy, an investment that eventually reaped a gigantic return. Although a lot of time has passed, the appraisal clearly evokes one of Neff's favorite axioms: Keep it simple.

Being a contrarian sometimes means going against your own conventional wisdom—in Tandy's case, a preference for dividend yields. When Neff recommended Tandy, it paid no dividend. However, it was genuinely woebegone and well off the PE ratio it had notched before the steep market slide of 1973–1974. For most investors, the company had lost its luster in 1973. Neff saw through the gloom:

> Another new purchase in the price-attractive, lesser-recognized growth segment is evidenced by Tandy Corp. Tandy is one of America's leading and most successful practitioners of the concept of specialty retailing. Management's strategy has been to seek out and then aggressively expand promising specialty formats with good growth potential and opportunities for leadership. This is dramatically illustrated in the case of Radio Shack (72 percent of fiscal 1973 profits), a failing regional chain when acquired ten years ago, now one of the largest national retailers of consumer audio goods. More recently, a group of chains appealing to hobbyists and do-it-yourselfers in home tiling, needlework and other handicrafts has been developed, and, together with the longer standing leather goods operation, represents an increasingly important profit center.
>
> Tandy's earnings have progressed every year in the last thirteen, compounding at 16 percent over the last four years. We would feel that 12–15 percent is a realistic appraisal of long-term prospects, and that fifteen times is a suitable reward multiple. Applied to our $2.15 estimate for fiscal 1974, this suggests a potential of $32.25, or 80 percent above our purchase price.[8]

What Windsor got, when it cashed in the last shares, was a price equal to 14 times the average cost.

At other times, whole sectors looked promising, as in February 1976, when Neff caught out-of-favor oils in the early stages of a prolonged market surge.

> A more important part of our strategy is to continue what we have always done fairly well, that is, recycle the proceeds from both realization and mistakes into "behind-the-market," undervalued, common stocks. This is particularly manifest in January in a very large purchase in the domestic oils. In a higher market we are conscious of the good yield and reasonable price–earnings ratios in this area that now has, thanks to the new energy bill, a virtually guaranteed upward path for pricing

over the next four years that will rebound to the benefit of the Company's bottom lines accordingly. The market has despaired somewhat over the politicizing of domestic crude oil and natural gas pricing, but in our judgment, they represent honest value and an excellent four-year track for earnings, not to mention the total oil prominence in the S&P 500 at some 15 percent of the total. If the market continues to enthuse, we will not be afraid to sell into it and perhaps acquire even more liquidity, but rest assured we will also continue to seek reinvestment opportunities that make sense.[9]

THE CITI SAGA

In 1987, Neff put his chips on the financial services sector—Citicorp, in particular. This is the investment he singles out as the most rewarding in his term at Windsor—and the most harrowing. Citicorp tested his deepest contrarian conviction to stick with an investment that flirted more than once with catastrophe and could have ended the career of a money manager with less staying power.

"It's a long and—at least at the start—a sad tale," Neff concedes. "It came onto our screen in 1987 when the stock price was maybe seven or eight times earnings." In the 1970s, Neff relates, Citi had belonged to the high-flying Nifty Fifty cadre, although its PE never made it to stratospheric levels. The PE ratio did reach the neighborhood of twenty-five, on the strength of hard-driving chairman Walter Wriston, who pulled out all the stops to transform a bank into a growth company. At 15 percent growth, Neff says, the bank was straining on all cylinders.

When the Nifty Fifty plummeted in 1974, Citi's growth rate settled down to below 12 percent, not enough to hold the imagination of investors still dreaming about 15 or even 20 percent a year. "But it had a good yield," Neff explains. Moreover, the 5 percent dividend yield plus the 12 percent growth rate meant a 17 percent growth rate available at less than eight times earnings. It was, in effect, an invitation addressed to Windsor from the biggest bank in the United States, sporting a bargain PE ratio. The price was in the low 30s, and Neff saw no better place to redeploy proceeds from the 1987 sale of an earlier value play, JP Morgan bank, which had tripled.

Citicorp had plenty of problems, in the form of nonperforming loans to governments of less developed countries. "Wriston said sovereign debt is always good, and it turned out in the underdeveloped countries that it was not good," Neff says bluntly. With greater exposure to these loans than other banks, which had similar problems, Citi's fortunes turned sour. The price continued its slide, and Neff bought more shares.

By taking a whopping $3 billion reserve against expected loan losses, Citi appeared to lance the foreign loan problem. In early 1988, securities analysts were projecting a good year. And they were right: 1988 produced robust profits. But before Citi reached Windsor's price target, bad news began to circulate. Having addressed bad loans in underdeveloped countries, Citi was facing a tidal wave of bad real estate loans right here in the United States, the legacy of lending practices gone amuck in a commercial real estate frenzy. By 1990, banks were lucky to collect 50 cents for every dollar they had loaned in their starry-eyed excess.

TAKEN BY SURPRISE

The proportions of the domestic lending crisis caught Windsor by surprise. "We were wary of it and we were asking questions. And we were thinking that not only Citicorp but the banking industry was overlending there. But we didn't visualize that it was going to be quite as catastrophic as it was." With Citi weakened by the reserve against loans to underdeveloped countries, real estate threatened to deliver a fatal blow. Vacancy rates went to the low 20s in desirable downtown office buildings all over the country.

To brace for expected losses, Citi wrote off nearly $4 billion in the first three quarters of 1991. A resulting $885 million loss in the year's third quarter was the second largest in Citicorp's history, after the dazzling $2.6 billion loss in 1987, stemming from the sovereign debt crisis. Meantime, Citi took a drastic step that really threw Windsor's yield-based calculations to the wind: it slashed and eventually eliminated the dividend. To balance an appetite for yield with the conviction that Citi would recover, Neff exchanged about 25 percent of the common stock for new shares of a preferred stock.

By late 1991, rumors of bankruptcy were circulating. Citicorp's ratio of reserves to delinquent loans was smaller than that of the nation's fifty largest banks, with the exception of the Continental Bank Corporation of Chicago, which had been rescued once before only with a federal bailout. House Banking Chairman John Dingle of Michigan stirred the pot with an assertion that Citi, because of tightened regulations, was "technically insolvent."[10] The stock slid still further. Windsor owned 23 million shares; the last ones had been bought for $15, a stake representing more than $500

million of investors' capital at risk. From Asia, word circulated of a run on
a Citibank branch in Hong Kong. "Citi's Nightmares Just Keep Getting
Worse," blared a *Business Week* headline on October 28.[11] In embarrassing
contrast with Citi's horrendous results, Chemical Banking Corporation,
its Park Avenue rival, earned $132 million in the third quarter of 1991.

How did Neff feel at that dicey juncture? "Not buoyant, obviously.
But we continued to analyze the situation as best we could." Despite a pro-
liferating supply of "see-through" office buildings (offices without tenants)
and resulting defaults, Neff and his team held on, convinced that the tide
would turn. They didn't have a lot of bullish company. Media reports examining the causes of Citi's perilous state heightened the sense of impend-
ing doom. In December 1991, *Institutional Investor* magazine published a
cover story about Citi that featured a prominent photo of a dead fish.[12]

Citi's new chairman John Reed was on shaky ground. "Rumors Fly
on Reed's Future," the *New York Times* reported on October 18, 1991.[13]
Loans to underdeveloped countries were his predecessor's legacy, but the
real estate loans were encouraged on his watch. "In Japan, he could not
have existed, because he was, in effect, not saving face," says Neff. "He
turned essentially 180 degrees around from being an aggressive lender to a
conservator. They actually got a letter from the Federal Reserve saying,
you know, you're on tenterhooks." A lot of people had Citi going bankrupt, including Ross Perot, who reportedly sold Citi stock short. "As bad
as Citibank's problems are," the *Times* reported, "many investors and Wall
Street analysts ask whether the full picture may be worse than portrayed in
the company's financial reports." By January 1992, circumstances left Citi
grasping for straws. "And these won't be good times," the *Wall Street Journal* reported, "given that Citicorp felt compelled Tuesday to announce that
it didn't flunk an exam by regulators."[14]

LOVE AMID THE RUINS

"There was a risk that the company was out of control," Reed admits,
"and that the regulators were very close in, and that our freedom to ma-
neuver, our freedom to operate, was severely constrained."

Still, Windsor stuck to its guns. "What was obvious was that commercial real estate was being dealt with," Neff says. "They weren't making any money, but that was because they were making untoward reserves
against commercial real estate, which meant that that part of the business
was losing four dollars a share. The rest of the business, which was pretty
much on track despite a difficult environment, was earning four dollars a

share." The credit card business in the United States and around the world proved sound. Losses increased, but high rates of interest supplied plenty of buffer. And Wriston's decision to establish footholds in underdeveloped countries eventually proved astute; in the late 1980s, their growth rate outpaced that of the industrialized countries.

"And we knew that at some point commercial real estate was going to break even. And the reason it was going to break even was because they weren't making any new loans, obviously, and at some point you're reserved up against the old ones." As it turned out, the reserves were more than enough. Eventually, Citi collected, if not a hundred cents on the dollar, at least sixty, seventy, or eighty cents on the dollar instead of forty or fifty cents. But the four dollars essentially grew to eight and a half dollars of current earnings; and, sure enough, commercial real estate broke even in 1996. Thus, when the stock was 8½ in late 1991, shares in the nation's largest bank were selling for the stunning bargain price of one times 1997 earnings.

Neff stresses that Citicorp was not a typical Windsor investment. "We obviously got in too early," he admits. "It lollygagged around for a while and then finally the fundamentals came together and then it had a sprint. But usually we suffer ennui rather than 55 percent depreciation."

Citi finally scraped bottom in December 1991. As the real estate panic receded, and Citi's strengths came into clearer focus, the stock price began to climb. For the average investor, Neff says, the Citi tale highlights three lessons: (1) look at the complete picture *and* its components; (2) don't be entirely persuaded by the media because there's a lot of panic out there; and (3) have a little patience.

"He really did get it exactly right," says Reed, who still seeks Neff's counsel. "He's exactly the kind of owner that a management likes to have. He is practical, at times he is critical, his advice is always sound."

At the end of 1992, Citi's price surpassed $22 a share. Windsor, which paid an average of $22 a share, was in the money at last. The news was good. Soon thereafter, the price began approaching the original price target of $29, and Windsor began to cash in shares that recorded a 30 percent gain. Not a huge gain, considering the length of time Windsor waited, but vindication became an easy claim to make when Citi's shares topped $100 in November 1996.

"WE'RE NOT THAT SMART"

Selling stock on the rise—standard operating procedure at Windsor—does not come naturally to most investors. "A lot of people can't bear to sell when a stock's price is going up," Neff told *Kiplinger's* magazine in February 1994. "They're convinced that they've made a mistake if they don't hold out for the last dollar. My attitude is, we're not that smart."[15]

Sell discipline centers on setting expectations at the outset. A target price is based not only on the earnings that Windsor projects, but also on subjective factors: quality of management, and competitive position within the industry, to name two. "All those things go into the price that we think the stock will eventually sell for," says Windsor analyst Jim Mordy. "And our sell discipline is tied to that target price, and we don't always wait to be at the target before we start selling. We're a big fund and have big positions, so we start selling as we approach the target price. And usually by the time the stock actually hits the target, we'll be gone."

Price targets are relative, because fundamentals can change and so can the market environment over the periods of time Windsor customarily holds a stock. If earnings prospects brighten over that time, Windsor adjusts the targets.

Neff would agree with Foster Friess that the best time to sell is when there's something left for the next investors, as opposed to waiting for the top. Instead of seeking 100 percent of that appreciation potential, Neff ordinarily starts selling when 70 percent of potential remains and often liquidates the last shares with as much as 40 percent of the upside left. This selling strategy ordinarily lets Windsor lock in its return and still capture a small portion of the frenzied overvaluations that often characterize the late stage of a rally.

Another time to sell is when the stock tanks—but not too hastily. Say there's adverse news. "Most of those things that happen you don't perceive uniquely," Mordy explains. "The company reports bad earnings, or something; the stock drops ten points, and usually by that time it's too late to sell the stock. Even though you've marked down your future earnings, the stock is now selling at the same multiple it was; it's just down ten points. In that case, we would hold on to it. There are other times where you've talked to the company and something they said wasn't quite consistent with your case for buying the stock. And in that case, we would be ahead of the game and that could be a reason to sell the stock."

Selling a stock didn't always sever a relationship permanently. "We bought Atlantic Richfield six times; we have five and a half round trips," Neff says. "The first time we sold it too early, subsequent ones we caught its relative performance in a twenty-year track, the times it was a relatively good performer." Freedom to revisit stocks bestows a significant advantage, in Neff's estimation. "We're ready to go on almost any decent company around because, one, we know it, or two, we not only know it, we've owned it."

Windsor also owned IBM more than once. On the last occasion, Neff pressed the company's new CEO, Louis Gerstner, not to slash the dividend as threatened. To no avail. So, after having bought IBM at $50 a share on the way down, Windsor sold IBM at $50 a share on the way up.

"But that happens," Neff says. "You do the best you can, and sometimes you don't entirely measure up individually. But I always slept nights because I gave it my best. You can't do much more than that."

A comparison to his tennis game is apt. "I didn't start playing until I was forty," he says. "And my strokes aren't great although my forehand and serve are not too bad. But basically, not totally unlike investing, I try to keep the ball in between the white lines. And play three times a week. Enjoy it, and kind of let the other guy make the mistakes."

3

Quantitative

THE AUTOMATED INVESTOR

F ew details, not even countless random ones, escape Barr Rosenberg. "We're looking for underlying patterns that disclose opportunities," Barr declares, concisely summarizing a computer-driven investment strategy that sifts through millions of bits of information every day and then decides which stocks to buy or sell.

It's tough to imagine anyone better suited to this daunting task than the brilliant Buddhist money manager known far and wide in the investment world as, simply, Barr. In the 1970s, he translated ivory-tower insights about risk into a lingua franca for investment professionals. Under the banner of his first investment firm, Barr Rosenberg & Associates, or BARRA, the one-time associate professor of economics ushered legions of professionals into the modern era, where risk can be measured and managed. Although he claims no authorship of the underlying ideas he elucidated, such was Barr's fame in 1978 that *Institutional Investor* magazine dubbed him the reigning guru of modern portfolio theory (MPT), and its very first celebrity.

BARRA and Barr's current firm, Rosenberg Institutional Equity Management (RIEM) rest squarely on concepts Barr popularized at a series of standing-room-only seminars that bordered on messianic.

Hearing Rosenberg address an audience of money managers these days, one has the distinct impression of listening to a sermon. You have been going about your job the wrong way, Rosenberg will say. You have all been using the wrong tools. You need new tools, new procedures, new ways of looking at the problem. As Rosenberg speaks, a hush typically falls over the audience. In the manner of sinners, heads are slightly bowed. Eyes are moist and a bit glassy. One can almost hear murmurs of "Amen, Brother" and "Praise the Lord."[1]

Barr exemplifies the legions of math- and computer-oriented portfolio managers called quantitative analysts, or "quants," a category that sounds awfully intimidating to average investors. "A quant is someone who uses publicly available data and systematic decision methods applied to that data," Barr explains. "A qualitative investor is someone who tries to glean a new understanding that's not yet available to the general public."

Until very recently, quantitative analysis and its cadres of practitioners were safely ignored by investors who lacked mainframe capabilities and a facility with numbers. But the world is changing, and the religion that swept institutional investors a generation ago is about to convert many ordinary investors via powerful personal computers, improved investment software, and online access to extensive market intelligence. Investors who still prefer to ignore quantitative analysis might consider another perspective: computers as the competition.

What's more, Barr's computer-driven strategies are not so remote as less-gifted math students fear. The truth is, they are firmly planted in the traditional, fundamental stock analysis that any thoughtful style of investing requires. Amid miles of computer code and complex mathematical formulas, three down-to-earth investment principles guide RIEM's quantitative strategy for beating the market:

1. Perform rigorous and prompt analysis of companies, markets, and investor sentiment.
2. Don't feel you have to know everything—just something other investors have not discovered.
3. Diversify.

As costs of computing and data gathering decline, professional quants are losing the technological edge they have enjoyed for decades. The quantitative arena is fast becoming more populated as investors armed with muscular PCs and Internet access enter the fray. "It's quite possible that the band is going to begin to narrow," Barr observes, "so that an amateur who is skilled in analysis won't be very much handicapped.

"The idea is to look at companies that are in similar businesses," Barr declares. "Compare them to one another and find the ones that are the most attractive. And that's really what we are trying to do, using the quantitative method." It's not rocket science, Barr insists, but a kind of rigorous analysis that reflects the way the smartest investors think—without the inconsistencies and biases that eventually trip humans up.

PATTERNS AND MEANING

"In a way, the computer gives us an edge in understanding our society, the economic aspects of our society," Barr explains. "We've studied the competitive pressures in economies, which influence future profitability by taking away company special advantages. Or investor behavior. We've studied people and how people participate in the market, and sometimes that gives us quite an interesting edge." He does not subscribe to the clamor for artificial intelligence to supplant human programmers. "We're not trying to make some kind of artificial life," Barr insists. "We're trying to understand regular patterns that underlie the society in which we live."

The patterns expose small opportunities, stocks that are likely to perform a little bit differently than Wall Street expects. "That's a lot easier than modeling all of life," Barr explains. "We just have to understand the regularities." Regularities are visible to everyone but are meaningful only to some. Newton discovered the law of gravitation, even though, for thousands of years, people knew that objects fall to the ground. By describing gravitation in precise terms, he opened the door to a wider understanding of the physical universe. "We're not doing anything big like that," Barr concedes. Instead, his interest lies in trying to describe a company's prospects more precisely than other investors. Will the company soar, or will it fall to earth? If his assessment doesn't coincide with the market's, that's a clue.

Toward this end, REIM's powerful mainframe computer replaces legions of living, breathing analysts vulnerable to physical exhaustion and the inevitable vagaries of human judgment. The operative distinction isn't methodology, it's a mix of quantity, speed, and, Barr hastens to add, accuracy. "Each day we get real-time prices on more than ten thousand stocks. That's literally millions of data items daily, overwhelmingly beyond the human capacity [to process]," says Barr. "The computer allows us to do the highest quality thinking we know how to do, systematically and tirelessly."

Some 200 phone lines connect news of more than 15,000 companies worldwide to RIEM, in Orinda, California. The lines import rivers of data, from fluctuating stock prices and trading volumes in dozens of global markets, to changes in companies' financial pictures and reactions by other institutional investors. Computer programs crunch these numbers and identify stocks to buy or sell. Trading is entrusted to humans, who can time the trades to conceal strategies. But unless flaws in the data are detected, no one, from Barr on down, can overrule the firm's electronic chief investment officer.

After selling his interest in BARRA, Barr started RIEM in 1985 on the conviction that a properly programmed computer can discern price inefficiencies even in a market that is largely efficient. The theory of efficient markets, a central tenet of modern portfolio theory, holds that stock prices reflect all meaningful information and, therefore, are correct. To do better than average requires information that is not already visible to other investors. Short of obtaining inside information, which is illegal, Barr uncovers fresh information by combing through innumerable details, a task best left to computers.

Does it work? "I think it's fair to say we beat the market," Barr claims. From its inception in July 1987 through November 1997, RIEM's U.S. Small Cap fund grew by 17.5 percent, before fees—well ahead of the 11.6 percent growth posted by the Russell 2000, a popular benchmark in the Small Cap stock category. RIEM's U.S. Core Equity strategy only beat its benchmark by a smaller edge from its launch in June 1985, posting 17.9 percent annual growth through November 1997 versus 16.8 for a composite benchmark based principally on the S&P 500, the Wilshire 5000, and the Russell 1000. After fees, however, the difference in core equity performance was almost a wash. RIEM has had extremely good performance in its "market neutral" strategy, which adds value by exploiting prices for undervalued stocks *and* overvalued stocks. Over the five-year period ended November 1997, the market neutral composite outperformed its benchmark by nearly 12 percent per year, before fees.

BRING ON THE EXPERT SYSTEMS

Quantitative investing can help boost the odds for ordinary investors, Barr says, even absent a multimillion-dollar investment in computers and communication technology. It's mainly a matter of choosing a manageable sample. Small stocks are promising, he remarks, because institutional investors just don't watch them as closely as they watch stocks that can bear multibillion-dollar investments without tilting the price level. "Beyond question," he says, "if you are looking at stocks where the capitalization is small, you have more opportunity and you are more likely to have a special insight about a part of the company's business that is big enough to make a difference."

With a big company, (but not a single-product company), even where there is evidence that one product will do very well or poorly, it may not be enough information to make money in the stock. But with the smaller companies, some instinct about one of their products might have a major impact on the stock price. Better yet, a few solid hits can boost an individual's portfolio and provide cocktail chatter for months. Barr, like other institutional investors, can't rest on occasional successes. If performance stalls, he loses customers.

To sustain long-term performance, RIEM relies on methods best compared to expert systems that govern such things as antilock braking in automobiles. "Expert systems are by their nature common sense," Barr explains. "They're doing something which a human knows needs to be done." Antilock brakes, for example, prevent skids when the road surface is slippery, by reacting faster than a person can. "The next generation [of drivers] will learn to drive cars that all have antilock brakes," Barr predicts, "and they won't realize that it used to be very dangerous to stop suddenly on a wet surface."

MASS, VELOCITY, AND STOCK PRICES

See a connection? Stopping a car begins with a qualitative human judgment about safety and ends with a quantitative challenge that can be expressed in terms of mass, velocity, and friction. Likewise, investing starts with something qualitative—human behavior—and ends with something quantitative—shares of stock and return on investment. Leaving emergencies aside, an expert system with updated information about traffic and road repair can plot the most efficient route from one place to another.

A whole world lies between qualitative and quantitative experience, says Barr, who is given to musing about metaphysical realms and investment. Yet people routinely translate qualitative experience into quantitative actions in many ways. "You can imagine the mixture of things going on. Some are unstructured human thought, full of ideas and insights and choices based upon factors that are difficult to quantify. Subjective factors.

Intuitive factors. Just what we do every day as we go about our daily lives—we're making decisions. Part of it was always going to be working out the consequences of what we know. So, for example, a spreadsheet to work out profitability five years into the future is usually a tool of the qualitative investor to work out in his own mind the implications of the ideas and possibilities he sees."

At RIEM, expert systems are built into three separate computer models that scour incoming information for pricing inefficiencies. An "optimization process" weighs the separate conclusions in terms of risks and rewards before recommendations are issued. Barr is touchy about revealing the guts of his proprietary black boxes, which essentially consist of hundreds of performance measurements and comparisons, from sales and net profits to complex market simulations using quadratic equations. "It isn't really a black box, in the sense that we open it up and every one of the elements makes common sense. But to the outside world we need to hide the secret workings. We don't want it to be reproduced."

An "appraisal model" has been in place since RIEM opened its doors in 1985. The original version has long since been replaced by subsequent iterations. "If you think about investment fundamentals, you want to know what the company's future earnings power is going to be, and the major determinant of that is the business already in place," Barr says. The business in place consists of the industries where it is established, how much capital is invested, the nature of the assets and liabilities that comprise capital structure, how much of future earnings must be earmarked to repay loans, and any delusions that face investors, based on these and other data.

SO MANY FACTORS, SO LITTLE TIME

The appraisal model slices U.S.-based companies into 166 groups of "similar businesses." A further cut, subject to the limitations of publicly reported information, isolates business segments and compares them with competitors and with market averages. Then the appraisal model reassembles the financial statements, adjusted to account for unique factors like taxes and pension funding. All told, 190 valuation factors characterize the income statement, the balance sheet, and the sales picture. The result is a single valuation for each of more than 5,000 companies in the United States and more than 7,000 non-U.S. companies.

The goal is to beat the market by exploiting differences between RIEM's valuations and current market prices. Expected rates of "extraordinary return" are calculated based on how fast the market has reacted to similar undervaluations or overvaluations in the past. Being quants, the folks at RIEM have a fancy name for these expected rates of extraordinary return: appraisal alphas. To investment connoisseurs, "alpha" suggests returns in excess of market returns.

After initial success, however, the appraisal model failed to deliver on Barr's objective: beating the market by four percentage points a year. The model, as constituted originally, failed to capture the changes that cause companies to increase earnings power. This deficiency became acute during the recession of 1990–1991. "When we underperformed, it was because the market was really concerned about future earnings," explains Marlis Fritz, marketing director and a principal of the firm. "They weren't looking at the fundamentals of the company at that point in time. And our strategy was a little vulnerable."

Barr and his colleagues attacked the glitch and produced an "earnings change model" designed to discern how a company's fortunes will play out in the subsequent twelve to eighteen months, based on unexpected changes in earnings. "We want to buy a stock before its earnings will do unexpectedly well," Barr explains. Positive earnings surprises enjoy a good reception on Wall Street. The price rises a little faster than the appraisal model would have predicted.

The earnings change model analyzes more than twenty variables with the aim of predicting individual company earnings over a one-year horizon. The variables fall into three categories: (1) measures of past profitability, (2) measures of company operations, and (3) consensus earnings forecasts. Using much of the same input, the earnings change model crunches away, completely independent of the appraisal model, until it produces a figure representing the projected earnings change. Multiplying this projected change by the market's historical response to changes of equal magnitude produces an expected rate of return, or the "earnings change alpha."

Earnings power can shrink as well as grow, of course, and the earnings change model is supposed to detect either trend. "We would sell the stock a little early if we're seeing that maybe its prospects in the next year are not so good," says Barr. The earnings change model would notice, for instance, if inventory is growing faster than sales. All other indications being equal, that's a sign of possible disappointment ahead.

The third model is subtler than the first two. Called the "investor sentiment" model, its purpose is to weigh factors that influence price but are ignored by the appraisal and earnings change models. It doesn't supplant stock-picking logarithms in the other two models so much as help RIEM's traders assess the trading climate—a value that should not be underestimated.

PEERING AT PEERS

The investor sentiment model, which studies past price patterns, senses market enthusiasm for particular stocks by scanning broker recommendations, analyst estimates, and other measures of market sentiment. "That's where we're looking at our peers. Other institutional investors. And in general we're looking at the stock market, the meeting within the market, the price changes, the turnover rate or the trading volume of the stock," Barr explains. "We're looking at all the different aspects of investor behavior or investor views about stocks, trying to judge what sentiment will be about a company in the near term. And this is often a very short-term horizon, going from a few hours out to, say, six weeks or two months. And this is strictly for the purpose of time and trades. In other words, if we're going to make a trade anyway, based on fundamentals, this would encourage us to buy sooner." If the sentiment looks positive, the goal is to trade ahead of the sentiment. If the sentiment looks negative, the strategy is to wait. On the sell side, the goal would be to sell sooner if the sentiment looks negative and to hold on for a while if the sentiment looks positive.

RIEM tracks, among others, the Brandywine Fund, run by Foster Friess, and the Windsor Fund, run by John Neff until December 1995. "The main point is that managers themselves sometimes exhibit a herd behavior," Barr observes. There are 1,200 managers in the United States today who manage more than $100 million. So, among the 1,200 managers, no matter how clever they are, there are some similarities, some common sentiments. One group RIEM watches closely is composed of momentum managers—professional investors who like to buy stocks fueled by favorable earnings momentum. "One of the challenges for us," Barr says, "is to try to determine whether a stock is going to be attractive to momentum managers in the future. That could clearly influence our decisions."

"Anyone who could predict these decisions by this group of managers would clearly be in a very good position to time investments." Now what we've done is to isolate one of the managers who turns out to be in that group of momentum managers, and that is the Brandywine Fund of Foster

Friess. You see that his strategy, in terms of prior performance, prior to the quarter in which he's buying, is roughly the same as the average. During the quarter in which these new purchases are made, the stocks are rising at an extraordinarily rapid rate. And thereafter again, we see that they're rising more rapidly than would be the average for that group."

A CLUE, NOT A CRYSTAL BALL

An effective, investor sentiment model also must sniff out downticks ahead of time, especially in the momentum category where prices ride a wave of nothing more palpable than enthusiasm. "Getting out quickly is desperately important," Barr warns, "because the only thing that's sustaining the high stock price is the price momentum. We see these precipitous declines in stock prices—10 percent, 20 percent in one day—when you scratch your head and ask: Is that news really that important to take away 20 percent of the worth of a company?" Reading investor sentiment provides a clue, not a crystal ball. Strategies can leverage these clues, within limits. "Not, perhaps, as the way one would dream of it—that you'd know the day before," Barr concedes.

Each model submits a list of companies where exceptional returns, or alphas, are predicted. An appraisal alpha is added to an earnings change alpha and an investor sentiment alpha. Stocks with the largest combined alpha scores become candidates for purchase. Stocks already owned go on the sell list if the combined alpha scores are only slightly positive, or are negative or zero.

The next step sounds like initiation rites for the local Optimists Club. The optimization process appraises all stock recommendations by investigating whether the expected returns warrant the risks inherent in each investment. The risks might not suit RIEM's overall portfolio risk profile, or they might exceed a customer's comfort level. Either way, the optimization process weeds out the stocks with risks not worth taking. Because every trade affects portfolio risk, everything gets fed back to the computer in order to assess the objective merits of subsequent trades. It's a continuous and exhaustive process far beyond the capacity of a team of humans toiling 24 hours a day.

Like drivers who may someday take for granted that brakes always work and all road surfaces are good, users of future generations of expert systems may find navigating the stock market much smoother. Meantime, it's not too soon to grow comfortable with quantitative investing. It is, after all, just a matter of extracting knowledge from scads of information—a skill that is increasingly crucial in all sorts of human activity.

Barr himself has enjoyed a rich mix of human activity. To represent his eclectic career as a pie chart, you'd need wedges for houseboat builder, teacher, iconoclast, economist, mathematician, medical researcher, philosopher, securities analyst, guru, and marketing whiz—not the most direct road to success in the relentless, single-minded investment business. But Barr was never single-minded. From an early age, his exceptional blend of high-voltage brainpower and uncanny attention to details propelled him in several directions at once. "He had a head for a lot of things," says his father, Marvin Rosenberg, a renowned Shakespeare scholar. "A head for literature. A head for philosophy. It was amazing to grow up with him. He waited for a while to talk, but when he began to talk, he talked very sensibly. He talked about phenomena. About relationships. He'd see one movement and compare it with another kind of movement."

From such a start, the eventual jump to his present metier isn't surprising. But finance was not Barr's first choice as a career. "When I got started in finance," he recalls, "it was not really because I was interested in finance at all, but because it was the most appropriate challenge for the set of skills I brought from my academic training and my interests."

Barr had focused initially on building mathematical models of social processes while pursuing a master's degree at the London School of Economics. He gobbled up books about models of political behavior and models of social interactions. His doctorate at Harvard explored risk models and decision making in the face of risk. "In 1966, when I was choosing a thesis topic, I wanted to study the decision-making process of individual investors or to draw inferences about it," Barr recalls. His biggest hurdle: "I just simply couldn't find enough data."

CALLING DR. ROSENBERG

Soon after joining the economics faculty at the University of California, Berkeley, in 1968, Barr applied similar models to solving medical problems—a task worthy of the latest methods available to a theoretical statistician. At the time, doctors were struggling with dosage levels for the drug lidocaine, which controls heart rhythm in cardiac patients.

"For most drugs, the recommended dosage is the amount that's required for the average person," Barr explains. "And of course people are not all average; they're unique—in the same way, as a matter of fact, that stocks are unique. So the question is how to arrive at the proper dosage for an individual. Typically, this would be done on a trial-and-error basis by the doctor. Try a dose; if it's too low, then you increase, and vice versa. But there are some drugs where the consequences of getting the wrong dose may be quite severe, and lidocaine is one of them." Short of injuring too many human guinea pigs, the answer is to devise mathematical models. Subject to variables such as weight and size, the models "absorb" lidocaine at different rates. Although Barr never saw a patient, doctors relied on him to help them carry out the first tenet of the Hippocratic Oath: Do no harm.

Although he welcomed the chance to help improve the quality of medical care, Barr yearned for the chance to mold larger quantities of data in productive ways. "I naturally ended up in finance," he recalls, "because it was the natural problem to work on, being rich in available data and a problem that society and business care a lot about." Moreover, lack of a medical training consigned Barr to medicine's periphery, and he prefers center stage. As he told Peter Bernstein, "My knowledge of medicine was limited. Capital markets were more congenial."[2] Had Barr been looking for a career ten years later, he speculates that he might have taken up gene mapping, where an even larger volume of data cries out for quantitative analysis.

"In finance, the challenge is to infer the character of opportunities offered by the capital markets," Barr says. "Each stock is unique, and the data we have about each company is limited. We need to infer the existence of an opportunity, and attempt to quantify its expected value, based upon patterns that we observe across all stocks. We do this in a situation where there is a great deal of individuality."

Companies are different, just as individual patients are different, but they also share common characteristics (industries, capital structure, and so on) just as individual patients share common characteristics (sex, age, weight, severity of illness, and so on). In both cases, the process is unpredictable and subject to risk. In both cases, the ability to accurately observe is limited by expense constraints (the cost of researching a company, and the cost of repeated tests of individual patients). "So," Barr says, "the individual company is a pretty close analogue to the individual patient."

By the middle 1970s, investors were hungering for ways to improve languishing investment performance. Answers were already available, but someone was needed to make them accessible. Barr rose to the occasion.

The gospel that Barr began to preach wasn't brand new, however. He freely admits that he repackaged the innovative work of others, including 1990 Nobel Prize laureates Harry Markowitz and William

Sharpe. Without their seminal insights into the nature and components of risk, Barr might still be teaching economics courses.

In 1952, Markowitz had published the academic paper that eventually vaulted portfolio management out of the dark ages. His insight dawned on him in reaction to prevailing wisdom expressed by John Burr Williams, author of *The Theory of Investment Value,* published by Harvard University Press in 1938. Williams had declared that the price of a security rests on the expected stream of future dividends, adjusted by the effect of inflation that makes one dollar received tomorrow worth less than a dollar already in an investor's pocket—the so-called "dividend discount" model. Markowitz shrewdly realized that this was only part of the equation in an uncertain world. By his lights, there had to be some accounting for the very real risk that expected dividends might not materialize, and a way to cope with that risk.

At first, the paper's profound implications were not apparent even to Markowitz. "It seemed like a reasonable solution to a problem," he says today, "and I was glad to have a dissertation topic." The dissertation centered on the merits of diversification as a way to achieve, depending on an investor's objective, the highest possible expected return for a given level of risk, or the lowest level of risk for an expected return. Thus was modern portfolio theory, or MPT, born. Not given to seeking publicity, Markowitz never pushed the idea beyond the academic realm.

The 1950s rolled past without drawing much attention to Markowitz; investors were just rediscovering equities in the third decade after the Great Crash had soured their appetite for stocks. Many institutions weren't even allowed to own stock, and large money managers saw little reason to expose clients to price fluctuations when treasury securities and bonds issued by big corporations supplied satisfactory returns. Owning even a few stocks was adventurous enough. Diversification was not a priority.

Meanwhile, Markowitz spent the decade refining his notions. In 1958, he hoped to publish a large sample of stocks to illustrate the merits of diversification, but computer time in those days was expensive and not easy to get. Eventually, he hijacked enough time to test the merits of diversification on a handful of stocks. This was, probably, the first instance of quantitative analysis, in the modern sense, applied to managing a stock portfolio.

A LITTLE BETA MUSIC

Then came Bill Sharpe, who approached Markowitz one day at RAND Corp., a think tank where both men were employed in the late 1950s.

Sharpe was keen to base his own PhD thesis on the ideas introduced by Markowitz. The upshot was a little concept called "beta." (For a fuller account of this historic meeting between two future Nobel Laureates, see Chapter 4, "If You Can't Beat 'Em . . .") Beta entered investors' lexicon only because that's the variable Sharpe used in the course of his computations—the same computations that also gave rise to alpha, or excess return, the other component of investment risk.

Rooted in what Markowitz had learned about diversifying risk, beta supplied, to investors who listened, a simple way to figure out whether a stock is more volatile or less volatile than the overall market, and by exactly how much. It highlighted the expected impact of a given move in the average price of many stocks on the price of a single stock. Better yet, selecting stocks with different betas could tailor the degree of investment risk in a portfolio. Beta, in other words, supplied a crucial key to effective diversification.

By 1970, this idea had begun to catch on, fueled by the proliferation of services that computed betas on the basis of a single stock's track record against the whole market. Rudimentary quantitative analysis became hot. Businesses sprouted up to supply legions of investors with betas for thousands of individual stocks, as well as for a handful of early mutual funds. Smart investors thought they had discovered a way to mint money: buy low-beta stocks to conserve value in bear markets; gather high-beta stocks primed for soaring increases in bull markets.

Barr saw a way to improve betas by adding a company's fundamental performance to the equation. Fundamentals consist of all the numbers that describe a company's performance, reported in financial statements and other public documents: sales, earnings, assets, liabilities, cash flow, debt, and the like. "The question became how do you predict [volatility], and one of the innovations that I contributed to in the early Seventies was to predict a stock's future beta. Using the most sophisticated methods we could conceive, it turned out that most of the prediction could be done based on fundamentals."

BARR'S BETTER BETAS

The upshot, "Barr's Better Betas" and, subsequently, "Barr's Bionic Betas," captured investors' attention and put Barr on the map. "There was a lot of originality," says Harry Markowitz, countering Barr's assertion that he merely applied existing principles of statistical decision theory.

In 1972, Barr formed the Fundamental Risk Measurement Service (FRMS) to provide customers with better betas, and a Conditional

Forecasting Service "designed to allow prediction of expected returns and variances for all determinants of investment risk." The fee: $10,500 a year.

The cash flow came in handy for a college professor who almost went broke trying to convert a tugboat into a floating home. His lucrative interest in financial consulting gave birth, in 1975, to Barr Rosenberg & Associates (BARRA). Besides supplying money managers with tools for keeping tabs on risks embedded in their portfolios, BARRA produced a pile of memorabilia. Such was the demand for Barr's services that his clients soon clamored for T-shirts emblazoned with the BARRA logo.

Beyond the hullabaloo, however, taking modern portfolio theory to the main stage was an ambitious goal. As late as 1977, a quarter century after Markowitz published his first paper outlining the notion of modern portfolio theory, skeptical money managers far outnumbered believers.

> The director of portfolio management at Crocker Bank in San Francisco, just down the street from Wells Fargo, confessed that modern portfolio theory "is something we look at, but I can't say we've been using much of it so far." Harold Arbit, vice president of American National Bank in Chicago, complained that "most of what I see is lip service. A lot of organizations simply keep some computer guru in the back office who they drag out for dog and pony shows and then put back again." The senior vice president for investment operations at IDS, one of the country's leading mutual fund management companies, regarded the new ideas as "pretty much in the realm of classroom debate and study." The most succinct comment was that of Barton Biggs, a widely respected market strategist: "I think it's just a lot of baloney."[3]

With no small sense of the importance of his undertaking, Barr began publishing a monthly newsletter in November 1977. Issue number one—a quaint relic of the days before desktop publishing—announced seminar dates for 1978, new subscribers, and news of the FRMS Users Group. "The letters will convey news, insight, and miscellany," Barr wrote. "Some will contain incidental essays, exercises, and problems. The papers may be valuable enough to warrant saving them for later reference, so we request that you keep these filed."

As "the papers" circulated, money managers began flocking to hear the word according to Barr for several days straight in Pebble Beach, California. Elliot Williams attended more than once on behalf of the money management arm of The Travelers Group, a large property and casualty insurance company. Williams recalls Barr's "profound ability to take incredibly complex notions and make you understand them, at least for the moment. Anybody who attended a Rosenberg seminar, while they were delightfully placed at Pebble Beach, they were very intensive sessions and yet you felt you followed it. I always was amazed that I could grasp some things. I'm not naturally quantitative and not a natural intellect but, boy, it made an awful lot of sense, and you became a believer."

TALES OF LAKE WOEBEGON

Money managers who paid richly for the privilege of attending BARRA seminars were not accustomed to browbeatings from anyone except their clients, but Barr hammered away with unequivocal fervor. Speaking on modern portfolio theory at the 10th Institutional Investor conference in 1978, Barr announced to all concerned—several hundred money managers—that their heroic attempts to beat the market were largely doomed to failure. "Inescapably, a properly constructed index fund should outperform the average performance you provide," he told the stunned audience. Needless to say, according to one eyewitness, there were no requests for an encore. Like the children in Lake Woebegon, all money managers are supposed to be above-average.

"I tried to be diplomatic," says Barr, "and I don't think I rubbed many people the wrong way. I think they resisted hearing what I was talking about because it did imply a vulnerability that they would have wished wasn't there." Much as money managers hated the taste of Barr's elixir, they had to swallow it.

Hung over following a manic succession of feasts and famines—from the flaky "Tronics" boom in 1960–1961 to the sexy Go-Go era in the late 1960s, and then the rise and subsequent collapse (in 1974) of fifty blue-chip stocks that were supposed to keep rising forever—money managers grasped for a better handle on risk. If they had to take it with a dose of humility, so be it. By the late 1970s, they were overseeing immense investment portfolios, and excessive risk was something they could ill afford if they wanted to retain customers.

Supplying money managers with tools to cope with these risks flourished as a business, but it didn't satisfy Barr's ambition to beat the market himself. "I got into this business of active management because I felt that there was a role to be played by my own personal skills, in the sense of building models that would come up with fair valuations and be good guides for buying and selling stocks." Because managing money while supplying risk management tools to competitors presented an obvious conflict, Barr cut his financial ties to BARRA and launched Rosenberg Institutional Equity Management (RIEM) in the summer of 1985, with a simple if elusive goal: "We're trying to find stocks that will outperform the market that we can buy, and stocks that will underperform the market that we can sell short," Barr declares. "That is the essence of our business."

BARRA VS. RIEM

Although the beta and the efficient markets concepts underlie both firms that Barr has launched, BARRA and RIEM are different in at least one profound way. At BARRA, says Barr, various versions of beta became part of the industry's common sense. Competitors copied them and used them in precisely the same fashion; they became the accepted description of the way to invest. "Those ideas were confirmed and strengthened by others using them," says Barr. Not so at RIEM. "Active investment management, where you are trying to outperform, is by nature the opposite. *Any systematic idea that anyone can reproduce to make money will destroy itself, because as people try to use it they will destroy the same opportunities that it exploits.*" The money-making idea, when shared with others, loses value.

According to Barr, such a fate doomed more than one lucrative venture, so he keeps a tight lid on the innards of his black box. One overexposed strategy: neglected stocks. "There was a concept that neglected stocks would give a higher total return because no one was looking at them," Barr says. "So if you bought a portfolio of these neglected stocks, you would outperform the market. Well, at least for the last 15 years or so, that certainly has not worked. And why? Because people who have a lot of diversification said, 'All right, I'm diversified relative to the small risk that one or two of these companies will do badly. Even though I don't really know what they're like, I'll just buy a portfolio of them and I'll ride the crest of the wave, so to speak, as the average one outperforms.' And then, as people catch on to neglected stocks, they're not neglected any more."

WHERE'S ALPHA?

What's an active manager to do in an environment where successful strategies are perishable? RIEM's solution: Hunt for alpha.

"We would like to be an alpha factory," Barr declares. The goal is to spot opportunities, or market inefficiencies, first by examining the fundamental strength of companies, and then by diversifying so that being right on average delivers satisfactory results, notwithstanding inevitable mistakes.

Chasing alpha, outside the trappings of modern portfolio theory, is in fact what all investors do. Much like Molière's *Bourgeois Gentilhomme,* who was impressed to learn that, unbeknownst to him, he had been speaking prose all his life (prose sounded so esoteric), ordinary investors routinely speak the language of alpha and beta but seldom think of it in such elevated terms.

Owners of houses understand that painting and decorating and refinishing the basement add to the market value of a home, but, ultimately, the market value is driven by demand for the neighborhood. Putting a jacuzzi and a modern kitchen into a two-bedroom apartment won't increase the value twofold over the identical apartments on the floors above and below; it will probably only increase the value roughly by the cost of the jacuzzi and the new kitchen. Nearly all of the market value rests on the value for two-bedroom apartments in that building and in that neighborhood, not on the amenities installed in the apartment itself. In market terms, beta describes the underlying risk, or systematic risk, of owning a house in that neighborhood or a two-bedrooom apartment in that building. It's the risk an owner cannot eliminate with paint and polish. "Location, location, location" is just a way of saying that beta matters to homeowners.

Alpha represents the value that exceeds the expected value for a house, renovations included. A diligent investor might determine that the white elephant at the end of the street, with the stream running through it, was a throwaway design by Frank Lloyd Wright. When that information becomes available, then the house with the water in the basement might sell for eight times its next-door neighbor. That's alpha, the component of risk that pays off above and beyond expectation.[4]

Want to sell a used 1992 BMW? A rational buyer won't pay significantly more, or less, than the average price for all similar 1992 BMWs, unless you can prove that Jerry Garcia once took it for a spin. In that case, Jerry would bestow alpha.

THE EFFICIENT USED-CAR-LOT THEORY

Using a used-car lot as an example helps Barr describe the way alpha and beta work. Imagine that all the cars are of the same make and model.

They've all logged 18,000 miles and the price tag on every windshield is the average price.

Besides the element of personal taste, however, simple reason suggests that some cars are worth more or less than the average price because of the way they were driven, serviced, or manufactured in the first place. It behooves a buyer to look at each car carefully, with a mechanic on hand if possible. A superior car will run better, use less gas, and require less maintenance than an average car. "There is an opportunity for analysis, to find a car that will perform better than the others," says Barr. This is an inefficient car market, where alphas abound.

Where markets are efficient, alphas disappear. In a used-car lot identical to the one described above, suppose that 100 professional mechanics have bid on every car, and the price on the windshield is the average of all the bids for that particular car. In this lot, it would be awfully hard for a car buyer to find a used car selling at a bargain price because 100 mechanics all examined it. It's probably safe to assume, in other words, that the market is efficient. That means, says Barr, there would be no alpha. "All you would have to do would be to go in and apply your personal taste, realizing that every one of the prices is fair."

The stock market lies somewhere between the two used-car lots. It is very efficient, but far from perfectly efficient. Alpha exists—if not in abundance, at least in sufficient quantity for a small number of money managers to beat the market.

Barr aims for lots of modest alphas, not home runs. The secret lies in spotting overreactions and riding the pendulum as it swings back to where it belongs. "We do not make judgments about the absolute value of a company," Barr told the *San Francisco Chronicle*. "Rather, we exploit the errors which other companies make."[5]

It's somewhat like investing in a new restaurant in, say, San Francisco. "The reason you were hot to invest is, you thought for sure it was going to succeed because you were the brother of the chef," explains RIEM partner Marlis Fritz. "It's a family thing and you've known them forever and there is no way this restaurant is going to fail. It's your story and you have insider information that others don't have. But you're not properly weighting the fact that 95 percent of all new restaurants fail within the first year. This is a very important statistic that should be part of your decision to go into this investment. But it is ignored, or improperly weighted, because the investor thinks he has so much information that he is overly enthusiastic. At Rosenberg, that doesn't happen to us. We don't know the story. We don't get caught up in the story. We are much more involved in what the facts are. What are the data telling us about the prospects for this restaurant going forward?"

On average, the stocks that RIEM purchases are 10 to 12 percent cheaper than similar stocks. That's not a lot; it means a $45 stock ought to be trading at $50, according to the expert systems. These stocks don't ordinarily ignite much interest. "We'll never be able to find a stock that's going to go up 100 percent or 50 percent," Fritz admits. "But that doesn't mean our strategy isn't successful. It succeeds because what we know about all of these stocks is sufficient and because we have this very high batting average. With two or three hundred stocks in a portfolio, and 56 percent of the time we're right—that kind of strategy can and does succeed."

IS BARR FOR REAL?

Inherent merits of his investment strategy aside, Barr has succeeded beyond the dreams of ordinary college professors in no small measure because of superb salesmanship. Nevertheless, he retains a wide-eyed, curious nature—or fakes it exceptionally well. "Barr is so bright he could use it in a way that was deceptive and it would be hard for you to know," says a friend and former Berkeley colleague.

Does Barr believe his own messages about thorough analysis and diversification? In fact, what he claims as his best personal investment—other than BARRA—was a flyer that broke all the rules of diversification. "A friend told me that he knew a stock was going to rise in price, and I believed him. I put all of my Keogh funds into it, just for a few months between investing them in one place and investing them in another, which was a crazy thing to do," Barr admits. "He told me what his price target was, and I waited till the stock price got there and I sold it." By waiting for the stock to reach its target, Barr outdid his source, who bailed out at a lower price. "So I think that was pure luck, but I credit it as a good investment." His worst investment, a walnut farm in the Sacramento Valley, fared poorly. "I should have invested in stocks," he says, "because in stocks I'm able to really generate some superior performance. I would have had much more money if I'd put that money in stocks."

Taken at his word, Barr's philosophical tone still reflects his former residence in the ivory tower. "This is work that perhaps I'm good at," Barr says of his investing career. "There is some intellectual satisfaction, but I really enjoy the understanding. I'm a bit of a scientist by nature, so I really would like to know more about how things work. And we have tools that really do open up some extraordinary insights that I wouldn't have expected."

One prominent example: the degree to which free enterprise is a natural human impulse across cultures. "It has been fascinating to me to see how much the competitive process is really alike in different places," says Barr. The only real barrier to robust capitalism in China, in his view, is the lingering image that capitalism is completely amoral, or worse. "Russia has that image too, but I think Russia really likes entrepreneurs."

The world is catching up with us, but Americans still embrace risk to an extent not seen anywhere else. "We're certainly a country of rapid change," Barr says, "and change always brings uncertainty and risk. If you look at our databases for the U.S., perhaps 300 companies a year will disappear. They will be very successful and someone else will buy them, or they will merge, or they'll fail."

In Japan, by contrast, it was rare until recently for more than two companies a year to drop out. "The Japanese keep their companies as if they're a valuable part of the society," says Barr, "whereas we seem to keep something—an organizational flavor, if you will—that transcends any individual organization." These days, as Japan awakens to the effects of intense global competition, it's becoming more commonplace for Japan's business landscape to suffer attrition.

"All of the successful, mature economies envy us our dynamic quality," Barr declares. A descendant of European Jews on his father's side and Scottish missionaries on his mother's, Barr sounds deeply enamored of a culture that easily mixes traditions. "We're not a disciplined country where everyone does the same thing," he says. "We're always running around, disputing with one another and yet it seems that despite that, we succeed very well. We don't have a 'buy American' discipline. Other countries have the 'buy Japanese' or the 'buy French' disciplines. We just buy from anywhere. We don't have that loyalty to one another and yet there is something else about our cooperation in the society which is really very meaningful, and makes this a strong and powerful country in terms of business of all kinds."

Add to this list the world's most advanced and liquid capital markets. "What the stock market does," Barr says, "is allow individual investors to participate in this tremendous ferment with the safety that diversification allows."

Barr embraces this noisy backdrop of fresh data constantly reshaping the world's financial markets. "What's interesting," he observes with religious overtones, "is that it must have a pattern. The pattern is generated by society. In most cases, we instinctively understand what the pattern is, but we may not have been able to observe it. And we may never think to look for it unless we had the computer and the resources to look at the data intensively."

YOU CAN'T WIN 'EM ALL

The most adroit expert systems cannot reduce every situation to quantitative terms and meaningful conclusions. Given a wealth of statistics on baseball—batting averages, fielding percentages, pitching performance, for example—it is tempting to wonder about picking the winner of the World Series before a season starts. "When I was a student I did a little bit of work on that," says Barr, true to his restless curiosity. "The basic answer is, it's very difficult because no team is that much better than the others. A season is not long enough to average out all the uncertainties. So the answer is, you can use quantitative analysis to pick odds which will give you some reasonable odds, as for a race course, and of course people do that. I'm sure there are lots of people out there handicapping baseball, football, all different sports based on statistics. It's got human beings in there, so you can try. But there's the element of randomness, and one season is not nearly long enough for things to average out, unless you have a dominant team—like the Atlanta Braves lately, or the Yankees in the time of Babe Ruth."

"What cannot be quantified is both what's knowable now but you don't understand it," says Barr, "and then also what's intrinsically unpredictable." What we don't understand is random for us but would not be random for someone who perfectly understood, say, what makes athletes tick or stock prices fluctuate. As for what is intrinsically unpredictable, we cannot know it because it hasn't been determined yet, because human beings are not very predictable. "Bless their hearts," says Barr.

Despite his ardent faith in computers, Barr seems to admire still more the unpredictability that is distinctly human. It is both endearing and a wellspring of opportunity. "Profitability of a company is part of the functioning of human society," he observes. "Human society is human. It has all of these completely unpredictable aspects. And we like surprise. We make a culture which is continually giving us a new view of the world. A computer is designed to work with a predictable or regular pattern. Human beings can be relied upon to make that pattern irregular. The first assessment of that pattern needs to be done always by another human being who perceives what is happening."

Always introspective, Barr was about twenty-five years old when he began to embrace Buddhism. "My father is from a Jewish background and my mother a Presbyterian missionary background. And so I was brought up with some kind of openness in terms of religion, and Buddhist philosophy was very interesting to me." He sounds ambivalent about how Buddhism affects his investment style. "What a question," he says. "I'm not sure that's really the way it works. There are countries which are Buddhist and people have the same range of professions that we have here. So I don't suppose that there is any direct connection that way—that is, that Buddhism would make me a different sort of investor. Perhaps a little bit, but I think that the same orientation that led me toward Buddhism, which is perhaps the same kind of intellectual curiosity, may have been what took me also into investment management in the long run. I've always wanted to go deeply into things."

WHERE WORLDS COLLIDE

These days, Barr's home spans two worlds: one is a room full of computers, crunching millions of numbers; the other, surrounding his Mediterranean-style villa, is a lush garden replete with Buddhist statuary. One of them, a stupa, symbolizes, to Barr, enlightenment, transcendence of knowledge over ignorance, and some sense of understanding what is fundamentally important. The earliest versions contained relics of great masters, from the Buddha on down. The garden is very tranquil, a resting place for owls, ducks, and an occasional heron.[6] "A garden to me," says Barr, "represents a living force and natural beauty, which really transcend what humans can accomplish."

The link between Barr's religion and his investment career seems to be a penchant for reflection. "Buddhism certainly encourages a reflective attitude toward life," Barr explains. "And, in a way, building an expert system has that quality. Because you're trying to emulate your own decisions, based on a lifetime of training and the like. And so there is an element of self-analysis. How do I make this decision? What are the factors that I really take into account? Once you've abstracted from the day-to-day details of making a decision to some understanding of underlying structure, then you can build an expert system that will make that same decision and, perhaps, make it better. I certainly find that I learn about myself and I learn about flaws in my thinking when I try to translate my thinking into a computer process."

As for flaws in the data arriving from some thirty suppliers, a battery of checks and balances is on guard. A primary protection is a cross-check across the suppliers that highlights discrepancies. This system flagged a difference of 25 percent between two figures for the number of shares outstanding for Barclays PLC, a British banking concern. It turned out that one figure was for Barclays Bank, a wholly owned subsidiary of Barclays PLC. As it happens, the most common errors are figures for shares outstanding. Other means of error detection feature internal consistency checks (examples: the sum of all assets equals total assets) and reasonableness checks that monitor key financial ratios for obvious anomalies.

"When things go wrong for us, it is generally that we didn't know enough," Barr says. "Our models were not incisive enough or the data didn't inform us fully of the opportunity that was present. In a situation like that, the frustrating thing is that we can't solve the problem until it is understood fully. So you have to look deeply in the hope that the models can then be improved. And in many cases, we can make a better model, a more refined description of the way the world works."

4

Index Funds

"If You Can't Beat 'Em . . ."

I f anyone deserves the credit for dislodging the investment profession
from age-old complacency about the elusive risk–reward ratio, financial economist William F. Sharpe, the affable winner of a 1990 Nobel
prize in economics, tops the short list of brilliant candidates. By advancing
established notions of risk and reward and then adding fresh dimensions of
his own, Sharpe challenged professional money managers to surpass market performance—a mathematical hurdle that few can clear without taking above-market investment risks—and paved the way for index funds.

Sharpe's choice of car for traveling to and from his beloved Stanford
University football games helps illustrate his far-reaching contribution to
the field of finance. The peppy little *Deux Chevaux* (French for *two horses*)
gets him around town mighty close to the average time clocked by much
swankier automobiles, which are subject to the same delays, detours,
breakdowns, and fender-benders. It's not fancy, but it takes Sharpe where
he wants to go.

Similar traits are found in a no frills investment strategy grounded in
a financial model that Sharpe unveiled in 1964. That strategy, called *indexing,* outperforms most professional money managers most of the time.
Index funds are designed to match or closely replicate the overall market's
performance.

81

Because cost rules out owning shares of every available stock, index funds frequently rely on a proxy created many years ago by Standard & Poor's Corp., now a division of McGraw-Hill Cos. The so-called S&P 500 consists of 500 companies chosen to reflect the relative contributions of the industries that comprise the U.S. economy. The list changes over time as companies merge or fail, and replacements are added as needed. Each of the companies in the S&P 500 is included in proportion to the aggregate value of all the shares that constitute the full index.

If stock issued by a company that makes cars equals two percent of the value of all the stocks in the S&P 500, then the car maker's stock would account for two percent of the indexed portfolio. The investment would always be matched to the market and little trading would be needed to periodically balance the fund, which is why index funds are often called passive investments. The S&P 500 is by far the most popular benchmark for index funds, but an index can be linked just as easily nowadays to almost any benchmark or combination of benchmarks consisting of stocks or bonds issued in the United States or anywhere else. Sharpe's personal wealth is invested almost entirely in a global collection of index funds, each sized to match the portion of the assets that different regions of the world represent.

Although index funds still constitute a small fraction of total world's investment assets, it is difficult nevertheless, to overstate the significance of an investment strategy that has zoomed to prominence in recent years. The first indexed mutual fund was launched in 1976, and no one followed suit for almost a decade. But during the twelve years from 1985 through 1997, the number of stock index mutual funds in the United States rose from just two funds to 138. Meanwhile, assets held in these index funds soared to more than $132 billion, a 19,357 percent increase. Bond funds caught on later, but their growth is also dramatic. From two funds in 1985, the number had grown to 18 funds by the end of 1997, with $8.4 billion under management, according to Morningstar Incorporated. Institutional investors, who embraced index funds several years before the first indexed mutual fund, now routinely allocate pension assets to index funds.

In the return-on-investment sweepstakes, index funds enjoy two key advantages: (1) certainty of keeping up with the market's return and (2) low taxes and operating costs. Active, stock-picking money managers must pay for research by legions of securities analysts who ferret out companies to buy or sell, triggering burdensome transaction costs at both ends. Passive money managers can run index funds with modest mainframes that track changes in stock prices. There is no cumbersome stock picking. Except when one company replaces another that has fallen out of the S&P 500 universe or has disappeared in a corporate merger, index funds change only in price, not in composition. That means few transaction costs and lower tax payments for investors who must report capital gains every time they buy or sell a stock. Because they are designed to match overall market performance, index funds will never produce eye-popping returns that exceed the market. But, for investors content to match the market each year, while incurring minimal expenses, it's tough to find a surer method.

Students who flock to Sharpe's standing-room-only lectures hear a rather surprising admission from this super-achieving Nobel Prize winner: Market performance is just fine. He concedes that indexing appears to lack the excitement of the hunt for winners even though it provides above average returns over time, thanks to low expenses. "It's a very boring way to get rich," he admits. But ten years from now, Sharpe would expect his best and brightest students to report that they had matched market performance by investing in index funds. "If they listened to what I said," Sharpe says, "they probably all would have invested in index funds, and they would all have the same amount of money."

THE ARITHMETIC OF ACTIVE MANAGEMENT

An investment strategy geared to performance sounds downright un-American—especially to money managers who claim they can beat the market. Given facts collected over four decades, however, a cultural obsession with superior performance is at odds with powerful evidence in support of index funds.

To underscore the point, Sharpe invented a game he calls "The Arithmetic of Active Management." He starts by splitting one-third of an audience from the rest. Members of the smaller group are to manage index funds; members of the larger group are to be active managers who get to choose the securities they think will beat the market. "We pick a universe—the French stock market, the British bond market; it doesn't matter," Sharpe says. However many securities there are in the universe, they are owned collectively by all the participants in the game, just as in a real market.

The game's passive managers simply buy each security in exact proportion to its market-weighted share of the whole universe. If a stock constitutes one percent of the market, it will also constitute one percent of the indexed portfolio. "Then we go to the active managers," Sharpe says.

"They're doing their research and visiting companies and studying macro events." One of the active managers buys Company A-B-C and another buys Company D-E-F. Other active managers buy companies with little regard for their proportionate share of the universe. "Then I usually ham it up," Sharpe admits. "God forbid you should get stuck at a cocktail party with one of the passive managers. They're so damned dull, they don't know anything. Active managers are fascinating. They're brilliant." (Knocking passive managers is pure jest, of course. With Sharpe himself supplying exhibit A, early advocates of index funds were some of the most fascinating and influential investors in the burgeoning investment field.)

Once all the securities in Sharpe's game have been divided among passive and active managers, they pick a time period. Whether it is a week, a month, or a year, the outcome won't vary. "Let's say the return in this market was 10.3 percent," Sharpe says. Next question: "What is the return of all the active managers?" Answer: 10.3 percent. That is the only possible answer, because market performance represents the sum of the returns each manager chalks up, divided by the number of managers, active and passive. If active managers had done even better, rules of arithmetic dictate that the market would have been up also.

OK, so some active managers outperform the average and some underperform it, but the average performance by all active managers is identical to the average that passive managers produce. That being the case, it stands to reason that active managers as a group must *exceed* average performance just to do as well as passive managers, whose expenses are lower. End of story, says Sharpe. "So any time you read that active managers beat passive managers or active managers beat the index funds, it just means there's a mistake somewhere. You haven't compared a broad enough set of managers, you've got the wrong index fund, or something else is going on, because the arithmetic is indisputable."

The proliferation of index funds has spawned new, hybrid benchmarks embracing almost limitless combinations of underlying assets. Sharpe sees no harm in these benchmarks, provided managers don't change them midstream. If a manager claims to have beaten the market he was not competing against at the start, that's a red flag. Sharpe warns also against the claim that an "average actively managed dollar" has outpaced the market. Because small stocks tend to outperform the market as a whole, investors should insist that managers of small-stock portfolios measure their performance against small-stock benchmarks.

Sharpe is not saying that shrewd investors cannot beat the market. The same math that condemns average active managers to underperformance also requires that some of them will outperform the average every year, though seldom the same ones. "We know that in any given period there will be a minority of people who will beat the market," Sharpe admits. "I mean, that's definitely the case. And we know that over fairly extensive periods there are people who beat the market. And there is some reason to believe that maybe, if you're in the minority that can figure out the minority [of fund managers] that are going to beat [the market] next time, you should put some serious money with those people. But I would ask them either to limit their bets, or if they are making big bets, I would limit the amount of money I put with them." All the evidence at hand shows, moreover, that managers who outperform the market one year are no more likely than any other manager to outperform it the following year, much less two, three, or more years hence.

Besides the out-of-pocket expenses that active management requires, Sharpe warns that active funds ignore the most reliable bulwark against catastrophe: optimal diversification. "Do I think that you should *not* have some money actively managed with people who are doing research and making bets? No. I think it is perfectly acceptable, even if you don't find it entertaining. But it's a matter of gradation: how far you want to go in losing diversification."

An investor has only to study the track records of John Neff and Foster Friess for evidence that the market is beatable, over significant stretches of time, by investors who shun broad diversification.[1] For ordinary part-time investors, who lack resources or access to the vast quantities of information that cause securities prices to fluctuate, any attempt to beat the market in the long term pits them against the money managers described in this book and the hundreds of other professionals who comb the market daily for underpriced securities. The part-timers' information search is likely to be fruitless, if not disastrous. "It always helps to be smart and it always helps to work hard," says Sharpe, "but the stock market is a very difficult place in which to do significantly better than [other] people who are reasonably smart and work reasonably hard."

Anyone who has waited in a checkout line at a supermarket or has crossed a toll bridge understands why it is so tough for investors to sneak ahead of the pack. "You go to the bridge and you see all the toll booths," says Sharpe. "And it's sort of amazing that the lines seem to be the same in each lane. Go to the grocery store. It's amazing that the lines seem to be the same. And if you see a shorter line, you go over there and, sure enough, it's because somebody's got a basket piled with goods. People are searching for a good deal and the very process of searching means there aren't that many good deals." For much the same reason, on a jammed highway, one lane is seldom moving faster than the others—except perhaps the shoulder, and that can get dicey.

The stock market has thousands of checkout counters, and tens of thousands of shoppers in as many lanes, all looking to buy or sell stock for its optimal price. Every trade ascribes new public information to the stock price, and any change in the stock price implicitly communicates that new information to other investors. It is, say experts, an efficient process. Being experts, they have coined a lofty term: the efficient market theory, or the efficient market hypothesis.

The efficient market theory comes in different nuances and shadings, Sharpe explains, but the basic notion is that financial markets in general, and the stock market in particular, are very competitive, and no stock can be purchased other than for a price determined by the sum of other investors' evaluations. "If somebody is going to sell it to you for ten dollars, that person thinks that it is worth somewhat less than ten," Sharpe says. "Prices of financial securities get determined in a very competitive environment, and the efficient market theory says, simply put, those prices are probably pretty good estimates of an uncertain future. Who knows what is going to happen in most companies? But it is unlikely you're going to pick up the paper and find a stock that is woefully underpriced and, hopefully, you won't find one that is woefully overpriced. And so the price is a very important piece of information because it is determined by the push and pull of demand and supply."

Stocks follow a random walk, moreover. Previous price changes tell investors nothing about future prices—a further obstacle to investors who try to outwit the market. But the historical price information says a lot about price volatility. By putting that information to work, investors can construct diversified portfolios in which risk factors offset one another. In an efficient market, Sharpe believes, it's the only sensible way to invest. Otherwise, the investor is rolling loaded dice.

According to Sharpe, efficient markets prevailed even in horse-and-buggy days. Although investment research has improved dramatically since then, it has a higher wall to scale. "The markets are much, much bigger now," Sharpe observes. "Financial markets are much more extensive. We have securities for things that we never thought of having securities for twenty-five years ago. So, while there are many more people studying the markets, and communications are infinitely better, there is also more to study."

SHARPE'S ROOTS

Sharpe's mother, Evelyn Moloy, an elementary-school principal with a graduate degree in education from the University of California at Pomona, would not have predicted her oldest son's influential role in the seismic events that have shaped securities markets in recent decades. "It never entered my head that math would be his forte," says Moloy—a caveat for modern parents plotting a path for their offspring to the Nobel Prize. Growing up in a southern California household more steeped in humanities than in science or mathematics, Sharpe, who was born in Boston, studied violin and piano and, not surprisingly, always did well in school without having to be pushed.

When Sharpe entered the University of a California at Berkeley in 1951, his plan was to study science and, eventually, medicine. That didn't last long. In his sophomore year, he transferred to the University of California at Los Angeles (UCLA) where his interests turned to economics, a switch that left scarce time for the humanities. "Once I got going on economics," he says, "unfortunately my education was stunted. I mean, I'm one of those people who read [F. Scott] Fitzgerald in his forties, so I've had to fill in a bit. I wish I'd had a better, more extensive liberal education."

The humanities did not elude him altogether. During a summer break from college one year, he ran a parts room in a garage that housed cars and trucks belonging to the county. "The guy who ran it was always claiming to be overworked, but I was able to get his work done in about a half-hour every day. Then I had to sit there to be available in case people needed parts." Besides using the idle time for a correspondence course in Far Eastern political science, Sharpe read the complete works of George Bernard Shaw—not just his plays, but lengthy prologues and epilogues—plus music criticism that Sharpe, an opera buff and jazz aficionado, recommends.

Economics suited Sharpe's analytical bent, but the first required course he took toward a business degree left him cold. "I didn't hate it, I just thought it was kind of vacuous. It was really what we would now call an old-fashioned investment course: how to read financial statements, project earnings, and find hot stocks and all the rest of that. It just lacked any sense of intellectual rigor. There were so many questions brought up and I was very disappointed with it." Accounting was no great shakes either, by his lights. He takes no credit, however, for spotting the need at that juncture for the more elevated debate he stirred up ten years later.

He was sufficiently encouraged, nonetheless, to become the first UCLA student with a dual major in economics and finance. That path eventually led him to a post as a graduate research assistant to Professor J. Fred Weston, a serendipitous matchup for the field of financial economics. "[Weston] was teaching a course in which he was very interested in Harry Markowitz's work. I didn't teach the course, but he was very busy and he asked me to do a lot of the preparation. With this, that, and the other thing, I got involved in what Harry was doing and I thought, 'Now this is really interesting stuff.' That's what got me into investments as a subject matter—being very excited by the structure that Harry was putting onto it. The rest is history."

Not quite, actually. Markowitz himself fills in some pertinent details before and after Sharpe arrived at his door at the RAND Corporation, an early post-World War II think tank. Its name was derived from the phrase "research and development," and, not surprisingly, many high-powered intellects found their way to RAND in the 1950s and 1960s.[2]

"I had published an article in 1952 called 'Portfolio Selection,'" says Markowitz. It was a groundbreaking article that stemmed from Markowitz's PhD dissertation at the University of Chicago, in which he suggested a way for risk measurement to guide the investment process. Until then, investing had been largely a game of shooting for the highest possible returns, and risk be damned. Ten years passed, however, before Sharpe came along to make sense of a powerful theory that had not resonated outside of academic circles. "Maybe I wasn't mathematical enough for the mathematicians and simple enough for the nonmathematicians," says Markowitz. "But by the time Bill came in, all that changed."

Sharpe brought an unusual combination of talents to the task, says Robert Litzenberger, a former Stanford professor and Sharpe colleague with his own long list of publishing credentials. Most finance professors at that point fell into two schools of thought. The new school concentrated on economic theory and largely ignored the practical implications, while the old school directed attention to markets and investment with little attention to economic theory. "With Sharpe, there was a difference. He was very good in theory and yet very practical, and the world adapted to the theories. That's the amazing thing about finance," says Litzenberger, a managing director at Goldman Sachs, a Wall Street investment banking firm. "It's not a matter of financial economists adapting to the world, but financial markets adapting to the new theory."

BIRTH OF BETA

At Weston's suggestion, Sharpe visited Markowitz at RAND, where Sharpe was also working, to discuss the seminal 1952 paper as a springboard for Sharpe's PhD dissertation. At their first meeting, the two men explored their common interest in portfolio theory and in finding ways to overcome the hurdles posed by the conclusions Markowitz had reached. To put those conclusions to work was not feasible. An investor would have had to examine tens of thousands of relationships, or covariances, among thousands of stocks—a formidable challenge now, to say nothing of its difficulty in an era or room-size computers that had a fraction of the power of a single desktop computer today. Markowitz recalls: "We talked about needing a model of covariance, and, in my book, I had suggested a possible first thing to look at was what is called the one-factor model. It says that everything is related to everything else because they are all related to the market or some other underlying single factor."

Single factor models have intuitive appeal in other walks of life. We conclude that a car is a lemon or a honey based on our expectations for cars in general. It's not necessary first to measure its flaws or its virtues against those of every other vehicle on the road. Likewise, Markowitz and Sharpe sought a means to decide if a stock was more risky or less risky than the market without measuring it against the riskiness of every other stock, one-by-one.

On the basis of their discussions, Sharpe decided to test a one-factor model as the basis for a doctoral dissertation exploring the measurement of market risk. "He did this one-factor model but he didn't just publish it," Markowitz points out. "He also made available a Fortran program (an early computer language) whereby people could use this one-factor model. And a lot of people did dissertations after that, using the one-factor model [and] Bill's code, and testing how well one would do if one used portfolio selection in this or that manner." Sharpe published important findings from the dissertation in 1963, in *Management Science*. The single-factor model has long since been eclipsed by multifactor models, a claim to fame for Barr Rosenberg, among others. But it was Sharpe who let the genie out of the bottle. Investing has not been the same since.

Useful as the single-factor model was, Sharpe was just warming up for an even more significant contribution to finance. "Capital Asset Prices: A Theory of Market Equilibrium Under Conditions of Risk" was published in the September 1964 issue of *The Journal of Finance*—two years after it had been rejected. Once published, it filled a gaping hole in the investment process.

In their preface to an excerpt from Sharpe's paper, in *Classics: An Investor's Anthology,* editors Charles Ellis and James Vertin summed up the enormous significance of the CAPM model:

> In this landmark paper, appearing some 12 years after Harry Markowitz's *Portfolio Selection* article first introduced the outline of a systematic framework for the process of investment management, Bill Sharpe provided the crucial missing element of what was shortly to become a Modern Portfolio Theory: namely, a compelling explanation of security pricing under the conditions of uncertainty faced by all investment managers. Before this paper, there was no positive descriptive answer to the question, "What *is* the relationship between present value and future prospects, taking risk into account?" After it, there was a Capital Asset Pricing Model (CAPM)—an insight which has significantly changed both the academic and practitioner investment worlds.[3]

To economists, a state of equilibrium exists when all the sellers and buyers are satisfied with the status quo. Looking at portfolio selection under conditions of equilibrium sounds humdrum, but it was an exceptional insight that resonated immediately and sparked the creation of CAPM. Sharpe downplays it, however. "Economists are trained to say, 'Well, let's assume everybody is engaging in violently optimal behavior and figure out what the equilibrium implications are.' That's just sort of what microeconomists do. I thought that was kind of the obvious thing." Markowitz had supplied the prescription for selecting stocks. Sharpe closed the loop by explaining why it worked.

Some high-level jockeying had preceded publication of "Capital Asset Prices. . . . " Papers on similar themes were exchanged among their authors, including John Lintner, a full professor at Harvard, and Jack Treynor, a Harvard-trained management consultant employed by Arthur D. Little & Co. "There was a certain tension between John Lintner and myself when John read my paper," Sharpe says. "John was distressed. I remember I was at an economics meeting in New York and he flew down from Harvard and talked me into writing a little note for the [*Financial Analysts*] *Journal* saying that something was wrong when in fact it wasn't. He was swaggering a bit. I was then a young untenured assistant professor at the University of Washington, and he was a full professor at Harvard, so that was a little bit awkward. But that didn't last."

Events turned out to favor Sharpe, who published first, following an initial rejection, an appeal, a two-year delay, and finally a salutary change of editors at *The Journal of Finance*. The new editor was Jack Treynor. But Sharpe downplays his achievement by describing it as an idea whose time had come. "I don't have enough hubris to think that, had I not done what I've done, the world would be significantly different," he says. "But I did it sooner and in some ways did it a little better than it might have been done otherwise. Who knows?"

COME AND GO-GO

As a practical matter, CAPM should have put an end to the freewheeling assertions of stock pickers that one investment is superior to another, without taking risk into account. But as fate would dictate, CAPM came along just as the stock market was becoming enamored of so-called "story stocks," in the mid-1960s. Those stocks were traded largely on the strength of the rosy earnings that investors hoped would materialize. "It is ironic that Sharpe was arguing that the optimal investment strategy was simply to buy and hold as widely a diversified basket of stocks as possible, just as the performance cult was taking hold," Peter L. Bernstein observed in *Capital Ideas*.[4]

The market's fixation on extremely risky stocks was a peculiar counterpoint to a model designed to warn investors that risk was getting out of hand. But hot specialty retailers, cowboy-boot makers, student marketing schemes, and other such investments were all the rage in those days. Investors' enthusiasm pushed the Dow Jones Industrial Average over the 1,000 mark for the first time during intraday trading in January 1966.[5]

At the "go-go" era's height, a handful of hot-shot money-managers dominated the horizon. Too many were named Fred, declared David L. Babson, a highly respected manager who made his mark recommending growth stocks like Dow Chemical, Eastman Kodak, and IBM in the early 1950s. Babson's comment was aimed at Fred Alger, Fred Mates, and Fred Carr, three money managers who enjoyed rock-star status until high-flying go-go stocks suffered a crashing end in 1968. "In the mid-1960s," Peter L. Bernstein noted in *Capital Ideas*, "the investing public's faith in the capabilities of professional investment managers was leading to a degree of hero worship comparable to the general public's adulation of the Beatles and the Jets' quarterback Joe Namath. John Hartwell, one of the towering figures in the world of professional investing at that time, declared: 'It is a basic fact that we should look upon performance as something that is at-tained with a great deal of consistency if one organizes to do it.' "[6]

While the go-go climate prevailed, flouting Sharpe's powerful evi-dence that risk is meaningful and measurable, Sharpe waited in obscurity so far as Wall Street was concerned. No fanfare greeted his capital asset pricing model. "I sat up there in the outskirts of the nation—in Seattle, which was pretty much out of it at that time—waiting for the phone to ring and [for] people to beat a path to my door. And absolutely nothing happened. Nothing. Zero. Nada," he says.

"What I didn't realize was that people read journals maybe a year or two after they get them, and then they think about it a while. The time period was long then. It's not as long now with people running around giving talks on the university circuit. Ideas spread much more quickly and are tested much more quickly. So for a couple of years I thought, 'Damn, it's the best thing I'm ever going to do and nobody cares.' So I was disap-pointed. Then, little by little, slowly, people began to think there might be something there. And then people started picking up on and critiquing it and expanding it and testing it."

Sharpe welcomed the mounting criticism. "You know something has really made its mark when people start attacking it," he says. "You know when you go to a seminar and somebody starts talking about 'traditional' investment theory and you know they're using it in a derogatory sense and you know it's yours they're talking about. So you know it has impact."

As the smoke cleared following the collapse of the go-go era, investors woke up to the practical aspects of CAPM, principally "beta," a means for measuring risk in a stock apart from risk in the market, and the "reward-to-variability" ratio, a means of measuring incremental risk per unit of in-cremental return—a test most go-go stocks would have flunked. Before long, however, "reward-to-variability" became known by another name that has stuck: the Sharpe Ratio.

YOU BETA BELIEVE

"Beta," which Sharpe used in his early computations, provides a measure of how much a share of stock or a portfolio of stocks is likely to move in response to a move by the market as a whole. It's not too far removed from common sense. If you are walking on a busy street, you might walk slightly faster or slightly slower than most pedestrians, depending on how long your legs are and what shape you are in. But, in a crowd, your pace is largely governed by the crowd's pace. It's hard to sprint when everyone else is ambling along taking in the sights. On the other hand, it's hard to amble along a block away from a train station at rush hour without getting jostled.

How you walk might have a high beta, in CAPM terms. If your gait has a low beta, you are not likely to speed up or slow down quite as much when the crowd speeds up or slows down. But if your gait has a high beta, you are likely to overreact, taking off like a shot when the crowd speeds up, and slowing to a crawl when it slows down.[7]

Particular circumstances may influence a certain stock, but the degree to which that stock moves up or down in response to the circumstances is largely determined by the traffic around it in the stock market. Using beta separates stocks that travel more or less at the same speed as the market from skittish stocks that fluctuate widely. Low-beta stocks are "defensive," says Sharpe, meaning they are relatively less sensitive to the market's gyrations. "They're the utilities, for example. They don't move a lot when things go bad. High-beta stocks are things like airline stocks. They tend to be very sensitive to economic conditions and tend to move a lot when the economic forecasts change."

The market as a whole has a beta equal to one; it goes up and down in step with itself. Each stock has its own individual beta. Taken together, all the individual betas comprise the beta of a portfolio. "If the beta is .8 for a utility stock or a utility fund, that means that when the market falls 10 percent, you generally can expect the price to fall about 8 percent," says Sharpe, the father of beta. "When the market rises 10 percent, you can generally expect the stock to rise about 8 percent. Not always, but sort of on average. And so beta is a measure, not of total risk but of sort of a move-with-the-market kind of risk."

TWO RISKS IN ONE

The stock of any company exhibits two kinds of risk: (1) move-with-the-market kind of risk, and (2) risk peculiar to the company and the business it's in. By diversifying, investors can reduce or eliminate the portion of risk peculiar to the company. To avoid the risk that an investment in one particular drug company will lag the performance of other drug companies, an investor can buy shares of several drug companies with confidence that their risks offset each other. Own all the drug companies, and market performance in the drug sector is a sure bet. But move-with-the-market risk cannot be mitigated. It's the risk that any investor embraces when investing assets in the stock market. CAPM identifies the portion of the risk that cannot be diversified, because that is the risk an investor should expect to be compensated for ultimately.

By sifting skittish, high-beta stocks from more stable, low-beta stocks, CAPM supplies investors with the means to build portfolios that avoid unacceptable risk levels or that offset risk with diversification. Among published sources, Value Line supplies betas for individual stocks and Morningstar Inc. supplies betas for mutual funds. Bear in mind that one beta is not inherently better than another, provided the aggregate risk lets an investor sleep nights.

The Sharpe Ratio supplies additional assistance in managing risk in a portfolio. "It's a measure that takes into account not only how you did but how much risk you took," says Sharpe. "Here are two funds. This one earned, let's say, 18 percent and it was just like clockwork. Every single month it just went up, up, up, smooth as silk. The other one—one month it earned a lot, the next month it lost a lot. It was all over the map. It happened to end *up* 18 percent. Now which would you like to put your money in for next year? Clockwork sounds good, because there is more chance that there is something real there rather than just dumb luck." A low Sharpe Ratio signals low return per unit of risk, either for a stock or for a portfolio. A high Sharpe ratio signals the opposite—a high return per unit of risk. In a choice of actively managed funds, says Sharpe, the one with the higher predicted Sharpe Ratio is normally more desirable.

In 1969, Sharpe left his teaching post at the University of Washington to help set up an experimental School of Social Science at the University of California at Irvine. The experiment was short-lived, so Sharpe then accepted an invitation to join the faculty of Stanford University. By pure coincidence, Stanford was not far from an energetic team that was literally taking Sharpe's ideas to the bank—the Wells Fargo Bank. Wells Fargo in those days was trying to win a spot on the lucrative money-management map. Unlike competitors with large actively managed portfolios already under management, Wells Fargo harped on the failure of active managers to achieve average returns.

Wells Fargo did, however, have some funds under management, and, to avoid conflict in that area, it had launched a clandestine operation in 1963 under the aegis of a Management Sciences Department headed by a maverick banker named John A. "Mack" McQuown. "We spent Wells Fargo's money pursuing ideas with great enthusiasm," says Wayne Wagner, an early member of the Management Sciences team and an IBM veteran with a Stanford diploma. McQuown invited a succession of luminaries to Wells Fargo to share their ideas. They included many of the most illustrious names in financial economics: Fisher Black, Eugene Fama, Michael Jensen, and Robert Litzenberger to name a partial list. The group also included two future Nobel laureates, Myron Scholes and Robert Merton, who were to share the 1997 prize for economics. Members of this group were instrumental in testing the conceptual merits of an index fund and in designing the novel technology needed to make it work.

Much of the time and money was spent in search of "a method of managing money that was consistent with Bill Sharpe's ideas," Wagner says. The connection between Sharpe's ideas and indexing required only a short step, according to Robert Litzenberger. "If you believed in the capital asset pricing model you have to implicitly believe in indexing," says Litzenberger. "People who try to outperform the market are playing a zero sum game. If you have no comparative advantage relative to the typical market professional who picks individual securities, you're just incurring transaction costs. This concept tied in with Bill's work showing that actively managed mutual funds do not do better on average than passively managed portfolios. Once we recognize the impact of transaction costs, indexing follows as a natural conclusion."

A HATED IDEA

Notwithstanding such logic, a hard-fought battle remained: to overcome the deep-seated antagonism of active managers. They took to calling the very idea of an index fund unpatriotic. Though they themselves seldom turned in above-average results, they referred to average performance pejoratively. Who, they asked, wants to be operated on by an average surgeon? Or advised by an average lawyer?

"It was anathema. It wasn't just passive resistance; this was a highly charged, emotionally charged issue because it was an indictment of the traditionalists, and they saw it as that," says William Fouse, who arrived at Wells Fargo in late 1970 with a mandate to spread the CAPM gospel to the bank's traditional money-management arm. Mocking the active managers' animosity, the Leuthold Group, a management consulting firm to the financial services industry, created a poster that portrayed Uncle Sam declaring: "Help stamp out index funds. Index funds are un-American!"

"With the blessings of the board and the president of Wells Fargo, I was inserted like a germ into this traditional management group," says Fouse, who had left his position at Mellon Bank because it had refused to launch an index fund. (He returned to the Mellon fold several years later, as founder and chairman of the bank's Mellon Capital Management subsidiary.) At Wells Fargo, the audience was more receptive to Fouse from the very start, and the first index fund was already in the works—under the direction of McQuown's Management Sciences group.

Sharpe's calculations were pivotal in documenting the case for indexing, but many factors contributed to the emergence of index funds. "Indexing is one of the mechanical outgrowths of a body of academic insights about markets and managers," says Dean LeBaron, a founder and former chairman of Batterymarch Financial Management Corporation, which began to advocate indexing about the same time as Wells Fargo.

The process required a spark, however. It came from a recent graduate of the University of Chicago's Graduate School of business, a hothouse of revolutionary ideas about finance, and a home to a bevy of Nobel laureates in economics, including Paul Samuelson (1970), Merton Miller (1990, with Sharpe and Markowitz), and Ronald Coase (1991). Imbued with new ideas about investment risks, Keith Schwayder collected a diploma in 1970 and went home to join the family business, a luggage manufacturer called Samsonite Corporation. One look at the company's pension fund, which was being handled by a mix of active managers, convinced Schwayder that something had to be done. He got in touch with McQuown's group at Wells Fargo and, by July 1971, Samsonite had invested $6 million in the very first index fund.

MA BELL SIGNS ON

The Samsonite fund was up and running, but indexing had yet to prove itself to a wider audience. The second investor, the Illinois Bell Telephone Company, had more clout. Its action had come as an indirect consequence of an earlier revelation at Illinois Bell's parent, AT&T. "The Bell system played a pivotal role in indexing because they had data from all the managers working for all of the operating companies," Fouse says. The data showed AT&T that the dozens of high-priced active money managers it employed produced, in the aggregate, average results. To remedy the situation, AT&T sponsored a series of seminars around the country to introduce its pension managers to passive investing. Two other firms eager to enter the indexing business also ran seminars: Batterymarch Financial Corporation, in Boston, and American National Bank, in Chicago.

Illinois Bell signed on with Wells Fargo. But a new strategy was required. Instead of attempting to match, as Samsonite did, the performance of 1,500 stocks listed on the New York Stock Exchange, the Bell companies became the first to base performance on the S&P 500, which eventually became the standard benchmark for index funds. For a major corporation to adopt an unconventional investment strategy took more than an ordinary degree of faith. LeBaron credits a former telephone executive, Tom Owens, with putting indexing on the map where other institutional investors could no longer ignore it.

Before committing $5 million, however, Illinois Bell exacted a condition: a like contribution from Wells Fargo's own pension fund. It was agreed, but even $10 million fell short of the $25 million needed, in those days, to purchase 1,000 shares of each company in the S&P 500, so Wells Fargo devised a sampling strategy. The fund bought enough shares in a given industry to produce average results, give or take some tracking error. Once the fund reached $25 million in size, Wells Fargo abandoned the sampling approach in favor of owning proportionate stakes in all 500 stocks.

The call to indexing began to grow louder. "The investment management business is built upon a simple and basic belief: Professional managers can beat the market. That premise appears to be false," wrote Charles D. Ellis, president of Greenwich Associates, a firm that tracks the performance of investment managers.[8] In the same month, July 1975, *Fortune* Magazine published an article by associate editor A. F. Ehrbar, "Some Kinds of Mutual Funds Make Sense." The article took aim at the chronic inability of active funds to compensate investors for the hefty fees they charged.[9]

One reader who opened that issue of *Fortune* was John C. Bogle, the combative founder and chairman of The Vanguard Group, who was seeking a niche for his fledgling company. Bogle's philosophy at the time was low transaction costs investing for individual investors. But separation from his former employer barred him from conventional investment management or distribution. "We were all wondering what the hell we were going to do," Bogle says. "I had done a lot of reading about index funds and I said, 'Why don't we start an index fund?' It turned out to be right on the mark in terms of what the future looked like, because it was what the past looked like." An index fund would certainly satisfy his determination to become a low-cost supplier. A typical money manager collected fees approaching 2 percent of assets in those days; Bogle told his board of directors that Vanguard could operate profitably charging only a half of one percentage point.

Lots of ideas in the investment business have a time in the sun and then fade away, but Bogle persuaded his directors that indexing would last. "The theory is correct; everybody after costs can't beat a market before costs."

The board was skeptical. One reason was their doubt that nonmanaged funds could beat managed funds. Another was their fear that Bogle was plotting to circumvent his agreement to stay away from fund management. Together with James S. Riepe and Jan M. Twardowski, Bogle finally won the board's approval. Vanguard filed the Declaration of Trust for First Index Investment Trust on December 31, 1975. Declares Bogle: "This was the first significant decision that we made, other than declaring dividends, at Vanguard, this new little company. It was opportunity writ large."

Unexpectedly, however, the index fund fell far short of enthusiastic expectations. "For the first three or four years, the index surprised me by totally underperforming," Bogle concedes. The worst year was 1977, when Vanguard outperformed only 15 percent of actively managed stock mutual funds—all the other funds, in effect. Bogle kept faith, however, partly on the evidence supplied by *Fortune* writer A. F. Ehrbar in a July 1976 article titled, "Index Funds—An Idea Whose Time Is Coming." It was a self-confident assault on the fortress of active money management: "Index funds have thus far captured only a small fraction of professionally managed investments, and they will not put conventional money managers out of business soon. On the other hand, the logic of the funds is compelling, and it is hard not to believe that at some point the logic will transform the money management industry."[10]

Performance by the index bobbed up in 1980, to outperform slightly more than half of the equity fund population. But high hopes suffered more setbacks in 1981 and 1982 at the outset of the great bull market, when it failed to surpass performance by more than 38 percent of active managers. Although it is tempting to conclude that index funds have only proven themselves in a bull market, much of the early academic work that gave rise to index funds was gathered during the 1950s and 1960s, when the stock market experienced swings in both directions.

All of this movement, Bogle rationalizes, was merely the pendulum swinging back toward the center. "A typical regression to the mean is always part of this business," he says. "And the same thing may be true now—only it doesn't appear that it is going to be, after this tremendous performance of the last two or three years." But with the costs of active management at record levels, active funds carry hefty jockeys in the race against index funds.

If nothing else, the slow start discouraged competition. No other funds challenged Vanguard for nearly a decade. But even though the number of index funds has ballooned since, many investors still cling to the conviction that active managers deliver superior returns. In mid-1997, index funds still represented less than 7 percent of all assets managed in equity mutual funds. But that portion of managed assets was double the level in 1991, and Vanguard's flagship Index Trust, twenty-one years after its introduction, was the second largest mutual fund in the United States, behind Fidelity's actively managed Magellan Fund—but catching up.

SLINGS AND ARROWS

The growing success of index funds has not silenced critics of efficient market theory or of Sharpe's capital asset pricing model. How can markets be efficient, they ask, when there is evidence that small stocks often outperform large stocks; stocks bought in January do better than statistics predict; and value stocks with low price–earnings ratios have historically produced abnormally high returns. Or consider the market frenzies that have taken place since the Middle Ages. All are signs that prices are not inherently right at any given instant, a situation that opens up opportunities for the most astute investors.

"The efficient market is in its death throes," investment adviser David Dreman proclaimed in *Forbes* Magazine in 1994, in commenting on a theory he considers bankrupt in light of voluminous evidence of market inefficiencies.[11] "I think the markets are not efficient nor do I think they ever will be efficient," Dreman declared. "One of the problems that I have with efficient market theory is: the theorists equate enormous amounts of data with the ability to analyze the data, and that's very, very different. An analogy might be that there are millions of us who can play chess but there is only one [Gary] Kasperov, and maybe one or two [Anatoly] Karpovs. Very few of us can reach the same level of efficiency with the information [that is available]."

Dreman is not the only skeptic. "Efficient market hypothesis is taught as gospel but [is] patently wrong," says Harvard psychiatrist John Schott, who has made a study of psychological barriers that impede rational investing. How can the markets be rational if investors aren't? In the Winter 1993 issue of *The Journal of Investing,* George M. Frankfurter, the Lloyd F. Collette Professor of Financial Services at Louisiana State University in Baton Rouge, blasted CAPM in an article titled "The End of Modern Finance?" In surprisingly harsh terms for an academic publication, Frankfurter pronounced CAPM dead on arrival and suggested it is to blame for the intellectual demise of the finance field.

The very fact that many studies show the existence of the Monday, end-of-the-month, end-of-the-year, small-firm, etc., effects—effects that put the first dents in the armor of the CAPM in academe—is proof positive that the market does not behave according to the logic of the CAPM. If it did, none of these effects would show up.[12]

Sharpe replies that critics have not kept up with CAPM. "It's easy to attack the first version of the capital expectations model, which was the simplest possible model," says Sharpe. "We've gone much beyond that. We now include much more of reality in the models. But the basic insight stands despite [critics] who claim empirically that they can't find as much evidence as one might wish in certain markets." CAPM is not supposed to rule out anomalies. The basic idea, according to Sharpe, is that the risk that ought to be rewarded is the risk of doing badly when the whole market does badly. An investor can take other risks, and some will pay off for periods of time, but ultimately the excessive risks will curtail the rewards. "If economies don't work that way," Sharpe says, "then it is hard to understand why anybody gets a premium for bearing risk of any kind. That fundamental notion, which we now see as a much more general proposition than when I wrote the first paper, is still bedrock theory."

Others have no axes to grind. They have never been converted to indexing for the simple reason that they *do* beat the market. "It doesn't sound like a very intellectual approach," says Foster Friess, manager of the highly successful Brandywine Fund (see Chapter 1). "It sounds intellectually bankrupt to be in a stock and you don't have any idea why."

Peter Lynch, who piloted Fidelity's Magellan growth fund to the number-one position in the equity fund universe, was never swayed by the argument that markets are efficient. Early in his career, signs of inefficiency were impossible to ignore. "I also found it difficult to integrate the efficient market hypothesis (that everything in the stock market is 'known' and prices are always 'rational') with the random-walk hypothesis (that the ups and downs of the market are irrational and entirely unpredictable)," he wrote in his 1989 memoir, *One Up On Wall Street*. "Already I'd seen enough odd fluctuations to doubt the rational part, and the success of the great Fidelity fund managers was hardly unpredictable."[13]

According to probability, such exceptions to the rule are inevitable, says Sharpe. There ought always to be active managers who outperform. The other side of the argument, in favor of index funds, makes use of the expected distribution of performance results. "I'm certainly not going to say for a moment that those are not brilliant people," says Sharpe. "But I will tell you the following: If you have a group of fifty people and you ask them to flip coins, and I were to ask you, 'What's the chance that after flipping the coins thirteen times you will come up heads eleven times?' you'd say, 'That's minuscule, it couldn't happen. It's a very small chance.' And that's true. But if you have a group of fifty people flipping coins thirteen times, you are going to find that one of them comes up heads ten times, nine times, maybe eleven times."

Admittedly, investing includes an element of skill. But skilled investors who beat the market one year usually lag behind it in other years, so it is very hard to tell how much of performance is guided by luck. "Somebody will do it even if they have no skill whatsoever, relative to others. They're all skillful."

Recent criticism of indexing has centered on the charge that a handful of big blue-chip stocks, namely General Electric and Coca-Cola, have grown so large that index funds mainly reflect their performance rather than that of a diversified portfolio. Sharpe dismisses the charge. "If you divided them into six parts, then you might feel better because it's now being driven by twelve stocks instead of two, but the point is, it is driven by the economy and if the stock represents a large part of the economy, it should have a big influence on the value of the market."

With the dust still flying, it seems to Peter L. Bernstein that Sharpe's contribution, subject to adjustments, has staying power: " . . . CAPM combines so many strands of theoretical innovation that it remains the keystone in investment theory, theories of market behavior, and the allocation of capital in both private and public enterprises. Moreover, its theoretical significance is equaled if not surpassed by its widespread use in business and finance."[14]

As the STANCO Professor of Finance at Stanford University's graduate business school, Sharpe takes the slings and arrows as an occupational hazard. He remains a prodigious generator of new ideas, says his Stanford colleague James Van Horne, the school's Gianinni Professor of Finance. "Bill has an extremely lively mind. He just jumps from one thing to the next," Van Horne says. "He basically is water on a hot skillet. He just is continually going."

On Sharpe's Website,[15] where a casual surfer can find his key papers, current and past syllabi for the courses he teaches, and a very long work in progress (a text on investment), Sharpe also fields questions from anyone seeking investment advice from a Nobel laureate. "I encourage people to send me mail, and they do, from literally all over the world." From Australia, a writer with $1,000 wants to know whether to invest in stocks, gold, or oil. "I don't offer investment advice on the Web, but I'll send a reply to him suggesting that perhaps he wants to put his thousand dollars in something like a diversified equity mutual fund, rather than oil or gas. I'm not able to answer all the e-mail I receive, but I try to answer as much as I can. It's an incredibly efficient way to communicate. It's also wonderful to hear from people all over the world who are reading some of my material."

A Cautionary Note

If his correspondents take Sharpe's advice, they will heed his first three rules of investing: Diversify. Diversify. Diversify. In the mistakes category, he says, "Putting their chips on too few horses is right up there." Second on his list of mistakes individual investors make: spending far too much money on commissions and transaction costs generated by brokers, money managers, and financial planners. "That's not to say you shouldn't spend money; but the point is, it is easy to spend too much. And that eats into you nest egg remarkably quickly."

Third on Sharpe's mistakes list: too little risk. It's one thing to be cautious, another to be so cautious that the future is jeopardized. Risk tolerance is a matter for investors to decide for themselves, however. Sharpe's advice is to begin the investment process by spending time on asset allocation: how much to invest in stock, in bonds, in value stocks or growth stocks, in non-U.S. stocks. "That's the big decision," he says. When selecting a mutual fund, don't jump at the first sign of great returns. "First look to see what they do," Sharpe cautions. "Are they a growth manager or a European stock manager or a bond manager? Second, I look at the expense ratio. The third [parameter] is historic performance data."

Once the investment parameters are set, says Sharpe, relax and get on to other things. "Pick the right amount of risk and return for your situation, your willingness to bear risk. And then leave it alone. Leave it alone. Don't jump just because there is a headline in the paper, don't call your broker or your mutual fund manager and sell something and buy something; you're just going to incur cost, and you'll just as likely get it wrong as get it right. Leave it alone."

Sharpe and his wife, Kathy, an accomplished painter, manage his wide-ranging consulting business. In the biography he wrote for the Nobel Foundation in 1990, he gave a succinct account of their extracurricular activities. "We enjoy sailing, opera, and Stanford football and basketball games, especially when the weather is good, the music well performed and the opponents vanquished."

5

Emerging Markets

BRAVING THE FRONTIER

The economic news from Asia sounded dire in August 1997. Thailand's fledgling stock market was reeling, and its currency was in free fall. Even a $17 billion rescue plan by the International Monetary Fund would probably not be enough to bail out Thailand's overleveraged banking system. The top central banker, Chaiyawat Wibulswasdi, voiced a grim assessment. "These are not days for economic policy," he moaned, "but for surviving until tomorrow."[1]

Such scenarios send most investors scampering for cover. J. Mark Mobius, president of the $13 billion Templeton Emerging Markets Fund, cuts a bolder swath. "We're here because the market is down substantially," Mobius declares. "We like it when markets are bearish. It's an interesting psychological phenomenon that when markets are bullish, I feel very uncomfortable and not too happy, because it's more difficult for us to find bargains. When markets are down, I'm a much happier person." Tumult is good. "When we hear about recessions, disasters, revolutions," Mobius says, "we know there will be an opportunity."

Welcome to Russia, China, India, Thailand, Trinidad, Ecuador, Malaysia, Brazil, Botswana, Nigeria, and several dozen other nations whose economic output seldom rivals that of Illinois. These are the world's emerging capital markets. Despite lofty management fees, volatile performance, and

103

liquidity risks that can impose severe penalties or delays on recovery of capital, they are lucrative stomping grounds for a fast growing cadre of investors who have trailed Mobius in search of superior investment returns.

"Mark Mobius was one of the first American fund managers to invest in these countries, fighting his way through their byzantine bureaucracies and laying the groundwork for other managers to follow. And make no mistake: They do follow." So declared *Smart Money,* in September 1997, when naming Mobius to the eighth spot on its list of the world's thirty most influential money managers.[2] According to Tricia Rothschild, Morningstar's international editor, other fund managers routinely call Morningstar to find out what Mobius is up to.

KICKING TIRES

What he's usually up to, most days a year, is what he's famous for: kicking tires. "By seeing companies firsthand," Mobius says, "you gain confidence. If you only read the press, you get swamped by negative information. Traveling helps you stay with an investment in a firm—despite all the negatives you may hear." On a typical outing in August 1997, Mobius visited 36 Russian companies in three different time zones, from an energy supplier in central Russia to diamond-mining projects as far north as Archangel and to oil and gas projects in Siberia's distant reaches.

Critics carp that Mobius is more marketer than money manager, which sounds a little like complaining that P.T. Barnum was more capitalist than circus impresario. When results are impressive, what's not to like? Mobius, who was a marketing consultant before he started managing money, appears to have succeeded on both counts. "The Templeton Emerging Markets Fund truly can claim to be No. 1," the *Los Angeles Times* reported in May 1997.[3] The fund recently celebrated its tenth birthday with the best total return, over the past decade, of any mutual fund tracked by Morningstar Inc. Along the path, Mobius has earned a rich share of kudos. "His name has become synonymous with new global markets," *Fortune* magazine observed in October 1994.[4]

With a shaved pate and Eurasian features, Mobius is a near ringer for the late actor Yul Brynner, whose celebrated portrayal of the King of Siam in the Rodgers and Hammerstein musical *The King and I* seems strangely pertinent. Mobius is not shy about the connection. In fact, when a retrospective series ran Yul Brynner films back-to-back in Hong Kong a few years ago, Templeton snapped up the ad time to plug Mobius and the emerging markets funds. It's worth noting that, in China, tradition associates bald heads with wealth.

Bald or not, canny investors can suffer severe haircuts in emerging markets. Or they can obtain superior long-term investment performance—provided they investigate before they invest. The challenge is to understand particular risks and then make informed investment decisions based on attention to details, a bargain-hunting mindset, and no small measure of fortitude.

IF IT'S 10 P.M., THIS MUST BE BOTSWANA

Other money managers voice the same bold investment philosophy, but few go to the same lengths to ensure its success. Mobius logs nearly 100,000 air miles a year in search of promising companies located in countries prone to social, political, and economic upheaval. He admits to almost no personal life and rarely takes a vacation. "In this business, we have to be so lonely, so independent," he admits. "You're going against the grain anyway. When other people buy, you sell. When others sell, you buy. It's almost antisocial."[5]

Most nights, a hotel provides his home, and his itinerary is so packed he needs a watch showing several time zones to tell him *where* he is. Mobius often works seven days a week, and after jogging for an hour and eating a light breakfast, office hours—wherever he happens to be—begin about 8:30 A.M. and frequently end after midnight. His primary means of communication is a cell phone connected through Singapore, the home office, where Mobius seldom spends more than one month a year.

Investing in far-flung emerging markets means keeping tabs on investments that make the volatility of U.S. stocks seem very tame by comparison. Emerging markets returns soared in the early 1990s, prompting the British newspaper, *The Sunday Telegraph,* to name Mobius Fund Manager of the Year in 1992.[6] "The award results from Mobius's achievement in turning the Emerging Markets trust into a £131 million fund within three years while generating returns of 100 percent plus for shareholders," the newspaper gushed. The Templeton Emerging Markets Fund doubled its net assets, moreover, when the average mutual fund gained 18 percent and when Templeton's nearest competitor, in New Zealand, rose by 68 percent based on three-year performance. In the United States, Morningstar named Mobius Closed-End Fund Manager of the Year in 1993.

After taking flight, however, emerging markets fell sharply in 1994. One enthusiast who had jumped in at the peak was the wife of Mark's brother, Hans. By the following November, she was in no mood to entertain her globe-trotting brother-in-law. "I was invited by my brother for dinner, and my sister-in-law was not too happy to see me," recalls Mobius. His suggestion for recouping her investment did not win instant acceptance, to say the least. "I said the best thing to do is to buy more. Well, that really surprised her."

HOPE SPRINGS ETERNAL

Mobius is nothing if not an optimist. It's a crucial prerequisite in his line of work.

> In emerging markets investment, it is necessary to be optimistic since the world belongs to optimists; the pessimists are only spectators. The fact remains that there have always been problems and there will continue to be so in the coming years throughout the world. But we are entering an era which is perhaps unparalleled in the history of mankind. With better communications, improved travel, more international commerce and generally better relations between nations, the opportunities for emerging markets investors are better than they have ever been before.[7]

Serious investors, Mobius contends, cannot afford to ignore markets that constitute around 80 percent of the world's habitable land area and more than two-thirds of the world's population—but only about one-fifth of the world's wealth. The entire African continent, excluding South Africa, trails tiny Belgium in terms of gross domestic product. New stock markets are surfacing around the world, but they still comprise less than one-tenth of global market capitalization.

The gap between rich and poor nations is shrinking, however. "That's the reason why we're in emerging markets," says Mobius, "because the current growth rate is double that of the developed nations. In Thailand, it has more than doubled. They've been having high single-digit and sometimes double-digit growth. This growth is going to make them catch up with other countries. We want to be here because the growth is here."

So does General Motors, the largest automobile manufacturer in the United States. To ensure that the "expected explosive growth of developing markets"[8] doesn't pass it by, the giant automaker is building factories in Argentina, Thailand, Poland, China, and Brazil, at a cost upward of $2.5 billion a year.

Although dramatic growth by an emerging market hardly matches absolute economic output from a smaller gain by the U.S. economy, faster growth rates turbocharge investment performance in several ways. "Two things are happening," Mobius observes. "One, the economies themselves are growing at double the rate. But the capital markets are growing too, at far greater rates." Thus, emerging markets are poised to capture far more than their share of the world's growth:

World Growth Rate	GDP Growth Rate (%)
1. China	9.3
2. Vietnam	8.5
3. Malaysia	8.0
4. Albania	8.0
5. Indonesia	7.4
6. South Korea	7.3
7. Thailand	7.1
8. Singapore	6.8
9. Georgia	6.0
10. Armenia	6.0
11. Serbia	6.0
12. Uganda	6.0
13. Côte d'Ivoire	6.0
14. Botswana	6.0
15. Bangladesh	5.8
16. Philippines	5.8
17. Taiwan	5.7
18. Angola	5.7
19. Zimbabwe	5.5
Japan	2.1
USA	2.1
Germany	2.2

Source: © Country Reports, EIU World Outlook 1997.
Reproduced by permission of the Economist Intelligence Unit.

And as companies increase their earnings power, their asset values increase, yielding additional returns for early investors. "You put together the growth and the valuation and it becomes rather attractive," Mobius suggests.

Although growth rates in several emerging markets lag behind U.S. rates, Mobius predicts that population trends must ultimately shift the world's wealth to emerging markets. "America will rue the day it taught

Russia to be capitalist," he says. Emerging markets have youth in their favor, as a "population pyramid" illustrates. Bars representing age groups in emerging markets tend to form a proper pyramid, with the bars growing smaller as the size of the age group's population declines. In developed markets, however, population pyramids exhibit midriff bulges, signifying that a larger portion of the population is in the higher age groups.

Never mind the fact that in the United States the bulge reflects healthier and better-cared-for older citizens. To Mobius, population pyramids reveal that older populations must compete increasingly with younger populations in a world driven by rapid technological and social change—a climate in which youth enjoys distinct advantages.

"You'll see the same pattern in India, same thing in China. Some exceptions, but generally that's the pattern." When Mobius first visited Singapore, in 1960, the government was trying to limit the number of children born, for fear that the population would grow too large for the small island to support. But it has since reversed that policy, realizing that a larger population is needed to sustain rapid growth in production and consumption. Meantime, emerging economies bestow benefits ranging from improved food and health care to better education, higher literacy rates, and longer life spans.

"This process is just beginning in these countries," Mobius observes. "If you are interested in consumer goods, cars, tools, or any product whatever, you would want to be in a country like this because this is where the future market is. The growth is there and the population; the number of potential customers is there. You must be close to these markets otherwise you will lose out."

Visiting an emerging market takes a traveler forward *and* backward in time. Economies that have never had reliable telephone systems are better poised than developed economies to embrace the newest telephone technology. "Mexico City has digital telephones while Frankfurt is still in the electromechanical age," Mobius told the *Evening Standard,* noting also that China has 100 million TV sets—even more than the United States.[9] "The upshot of all these developments—economic, political, sociological, and demographic—is that productivity is skyrocketing in these countries," Mobius said. "It took the first industrial country, Britain, 58 years to double output per person. It took the U.S. 47 years. Japan did it in 34 years but Turkey took only 20, Brazil 18, Korea 11, and China is doing it in 10."

It's a matter of technology leapfrogging itself. "You don't need to build a whole telephone system of wires underground if you do it [with] cellular [technology]," Mobius says. "You don't have to have a room full of cross-bar electrical mechanical equipment for a switching system when you can do it with a small box of digital microelectronics." And, to keep up the pace, overnight couriers can deliver parts needed from the United States or Europe in 24 hours.

Meantime, the denizens of emerging markets can observe for themselves the trappings of an affluent society. They clamor for television's portrayal of the well-heeled and idle, including such fare as *Dallas, Dynasty, Melrose Place,* and, leading the pack, *Baywatch*—the world's most popular TV program. "They see people with emotions, with feelings, with weaknesses, and they say, 'Why can't I be like that?'" says Mobius, taking this voracious appetite for American culture as a sure sign that emerging markets are headed for prosperity.[10]

THE PEOPLE'S CAPITALISM

Few signs of change in emerging markets are more telling than the recent curriculum change at the People's University of China, where young communists once trained for world revolution. According to Mobius, lack of interest in courses devoted to Marxist dogma moved the university to supplement them with courses in business studies.[11]

For investors with stamina, the confluence of free markets, technology, a youthful population, and a demand for goods of all kinds promotes an environment full of investment bargains—especially when there's turmoil. "That's the nice thing about it," Mobius says. "Very often you don't have to pay for the growth that makes these stock markets very attractive." A company operating in an emerging market will normally fetch a fraction of the market multiple accorded a company with similar growth prospects in a developed economy.

Braving upheaval in Argentina resulted in exceptional payoff. Shares of Compania Naviera Perez Companc, an oil company with sales of around $700 million, gained 340 percent in two years. Its shares are traded on the Buenos Aires Stock Exchange, one of the largest in Latin America, but on on par with the Philadelphia Stock Exchange in the United States.

"Argentina was suffering from very, very high inflation at the time," Mobius remembers. People were losing confidence in the economy. Political upheaval added to uncertainty, as disciples of the late dictator Juan Peron fought for control of the government under the banner of rejuvenated nationalism. When Carlos Menem, a Peronist, won the presidential election, pundits predicted disaster.

BAD NEWS BULL

"We knew from what we were observing and hearing that there was no way Argentina could continue on that way, with the inflation the way it was going and with the way the economy was working. It just could not go on," says Mobius, who snapped up shares to a point where 16 percent of the funds he managed were invested in Argentine companies. "And of course you know what happened. [Menem] just turned things around and the economy took off." Fueled by privatization (the sale of government-operated businesses to private investors), the country's stock market rose.

Mobius claims no credit for discovering the principles that make emerging markets attractive. Emerging markets are far from new, although the term is of recent vintage, predated by "Third World" and "Lesser Developed Countries." A century ago, wealthy Scots formed the Edinburgh Investment Trust and put much of their money to work building railroads across North America. But as a vehicle for the modern investor, emerging markets funds date back only to 1987 and the advent of the Templeton Emerging Markets Fund, with Mobius at its helm.

It was a post to which Mobius was ideally suited, but not one he envisioned when he began attending Boston University. "I was more interested in psychology," he told Bill Griffith, author of *The Mutual Fund Masters*.[12] "I wanted to become a psychologist, and I eventually gravitated to social psychology and then to mass communications. I got interested in survey research work." One of his first jobs after finishing college led to his conducting surveys related to economics, which in turn led to his enrollment at the Massachusetts Institute of Technology, where he earned a doctorate in economics and political science.

PIANO MAN

Hans Mobius, the middle member of the three Mobius brothers, never dreamed that his younger brother would end up managing money, much less $12 billion in markets from Amman to Zagreb. "I figured he was going to be a pianist," says Hans, who recalls how Mark supplemented scholarships to college and graduate school by playing piano and singing in nightclubs—which helps explain his fondness for Marlene Dietrich. The three sons of Paul Erich Mobius and his wife, Maria Louisa Colon, were all musically inclined. In the 1950s, they formed a classical trio with Hans on cello, Mark on piano, and older brother Paul on violin.

After Mark was born, the family moved from the Bronx, in New York City, to North Bellmore, on Long Island. With a father from Germany and a mother from Puerto Rico, Sunday dinners nurtured a multicultural atmosphere. "We would have all our Puerto Rican Spanish-speaking family over, and sometimes we'd have German-speaking relatives over," Mobius remembers. "It definitely gave me a global view of things. There's no question about that." (That his father was not yet a U.S. citizen when Mark was born entitled Mark to obtain German citizenship later in life. He travels nowadays on a German passport.)

The boys' father, a master baker who had emigrated from the German province of Saxony before the Second World War, died while the boys were teenagers, leaving their care and support to a single working mother and any income they themselves could provide. "If anybody passed on business sense, it was my mother," says Hans, who owns his own business in upstate New York. "Mark got it from her." Thanks to Maria Louisa's hard work and astute management of scarce financial resources, the family managed to live comfortably. But modest comfort was small recompense for the lamented loss of a valuable tract of land in her native Baranquitas, a tract that had been given to her great, great grandfather by the King of Spain in gratitude for establishing vast agricultural projects then gradually sold off by descendants.

Mark's workaholic traits were in evidence even in childhood. "It was my older brother, Paul, and myself who were always in trouble," Hans recalls. "Mark was working. He always had projects. Once he got on a project, he stayed on it until he solved it. If it got a little tough, he'd stick to it. We'd go bicycle riding and he'd stay home working."

Mobius was graduated from college with credits in psychology and the fine arts. Both, he says, are useful today. The fine arts foster a sensitivity to different peoples and cultures, and psychology helps him cut through the fog that often clouds an investment scenario.

On a visit to a shipping company in Murmansk, Russia, for example, Mobius recalls meeting the company's director in an enormous office in an old colonial-style building. The director greeted Mobius with a mix of curiosity, defensiveness, and arrogance, culminating in a tirade against America, against Europe, and against capitalists trying to take advantage of his country.

"I could see, thanks to my background in psychology, that this guy had an inferiority complex," Mobius recollects. "He started talking about how great his company was and I started admiring his office, once I got a word in edgewise." Mobius complimented him on the office's décor, with predictable results. "He started to warm up. You could see a different person coming out." After an hour, the director offered to show Mobius the plant—including a tour of the perks he was most proud of, a basement sauna and swimming pool. "With a little training, a little education, you can get to understand." Add to that a sense of humility and a sense of humor. "You've got to have a sense of humor in this business," Mobius suggests.

"I laugh a lot in Russia, you know. These guys are very serious but I laugh. Recently, one of our analysts went into a trading company and as he started his presentation the managing director said, 'Stop. I don't want to hear any more. I want to know if the destruction of the Russian economy by you capitalists is on schedule.' If I was there," Mobius says, "I would have laughed."

Long before Mobius could locate Kazakhstan on a map, a semester in Japan during his junior year of college had hooked him on the Orient. He had earned a PhD in economics and political science from MIT, however, before a second opportunity to journey east presented itself. On behalf of Hong Kong-based Monsanto Overseas Enterprises Company, Mobius went abroad to test the waters for a soybean-based soft drink that ultimately fizzled—but not in the way that was intended. Monsanto's Midwestern technicians didn't want the drink to smell like soybeans. But the sweetened drink they cooked up made people ill, and ultimately was rejected.

After completing the soybean study, Mobius weighed the merits of staying in Hong Kong versus joining Monsanto at its headquarters in St. Louis. It was not a difficult choice for him. He hung up a shingle as a marketing consultant. One of his first efforts at self-promotion was a 1972 booklet, *Investing in China,* meant to guide Westerners seeking to invest in China. Its subject: "Accurate, Up to the Minute Information on the Conditions, Requirements, Policies, and Trading Practices of the People's Republic of China—for all businessmen interested in starting or expanding their China trade."

FROM SOAP TO TRACTORS

"I did studies on every industry from soap to tractors," he told *Business-Week*. "It was wonderful training."[13] Another time, he gave marketing advice to leather producers in Madras, India, on behalf of the United Nations Development Agency. Mobius would seize almost any opportunity to expand his knowledge of the region. At one time, according to his brother Paul, Mobius worked knee-deep in water, helping to harvest rice.

Under the banner of his own marketing consulting firm, Mobius conducted a study in the 1960s on fats and oils, with an eye to selling soap in Moslem Indonesia. He surveyed the Indonesian population from Sumatra to Bali, only to conclude that the plan wouldn't wash, so to speak. Soap at the time, much of which came from China, often included a mixture of animal fats plus palm oils and other oils. The National Renderers Association in the United States (a bloodless way of describing the trade organization for operators of slaughterhouses), which paid for the survey, couldn't guarantee that the animal fats did not come from pigs. That was an unacceptable drawback for Moslems, who consider pigs unclean—and doubtless a drawback for many non-Moslems as well.

Eventually, one of his clients asked for a study of Asian stock markets. "That hooked me," Mobius says. In the late 1960s, he began investing his own money in Asian stock markets. Although conditions have improved greatly since then, the stakes, along with the risks, have increased commensurately.

Reading Gerald Loeb's *The Battle for Investment Survival* reinforced Mobius's confidence that fundamental, long-term, commonsense investing surpasses any other investment methodology. Buddhism, a pervasive force in the region he has called home for three decades, instills patience and tolerance. "Unless you're tolerant," he says, "you can't have an open mind. If you don't have an open mind, you can't be a good investor. You've got to let everything in and be willing to digest it."

OUT OF THIS WORLD

Then there was the influence of his first investment: shares of Communications Satellite Corporation (COMSAT), the quasi-governmental agency launched under the spell of President John F. Kennedy's call for exploration of outer space. COMSAT was far from his most lucrative investment, but Mobius insists that it was his best. "It was the best to me in the sense that it was the first one. Of course I've made investments that are much, much better in percentage increase terms, you know. But the most memorable to me is the very first one, an insight into stock market investing when I knew nothing about the stock market."

Ironically, when Mobius made that first investment, outer space was more accessible than emerging markets were. A quarter century later, when the Templeton Fund broached the idea of an emerging markets fund to the Securities and Exchange Commission (SEC), the concept still lacked a working definition. A process of elimination helped. "It's very much a judgmental thing, and the criteria cannot be hard and fast," Mobius told the *Wall Street Transcript* in April 1992.[14] "We know the United States is not [an emerging market]. We know Canada is not. We know most of the Western European countries are not. We know Japan is not. So that knocks out by far the bulk of the world's stock market capitalization, and we're dealing with relatively small market capitalization numbers at this stage of the game, but they are increasing."

SO, WHAT'S AN EMERGING MARKET?

Without a preexisting category, Templeton's proposal for an emerging markets fund drew puzzled scrutiny from the SEC regulators. Eventually, to their satisfaction, the fund defined emerging markets as the low- and middle-income countries so identified by the World Bank. "And it fit our intuitive definition of what we thought emerging markets should be," Mobius says. "That was all of Latin America, all of Africa, all of Asia except Japan, Australia, and New Zealand. In those days, of course, Russia was not even a twinkle in our eye. But now that's changed and [former communist countries] meet the criteria. Now what happens when a country gets rich: Is it still an emerging market? No, but we haven't gotten to that point yet."

Mobius has also offered a somewhat more candid definition. "The recent term 'emerging markets' may be a euphemism," he confessed to *Global Investment Management,* a British publication. "But it is also a declaration of hope and faith on the part of us specialising in the study of emerging stock markets. We believe that although some of the stock markets of developing nations may sometimes seem to be 'submerged,' they are generally emerging into bigger and better things."[15]

In mid-1997, according to the World Bank, an emerging market was a country with a gross domestic product (GDP) below US $8,956 per capita. That includes countries where water is still drawn by hand from wells and carried by oxen, and where there is no telephone system to speak of, much less fax machines or computers. The minimum wage in Thailand, in 1997, was $6.50 a week—a six-day workweek. Medical insurance is unheard of, to say nothing of modern medical facilities. The only fringe benefit many workers enjoy might be bowl of rice at lunch.

Mobius retains flexibility to operate in countries where the economic infrastructure is not all that might be desired. The fund has started investing in Vietnam, for example, although that country has yet to create a stock exchange. "It is important not to define emerging markets too narrowly," Mobius warned in the fund's March 1997 report to investors. The danger: Too few markets exhibit enough trading activity, or liquidity, to allow the fund to move in and out of investments in a timely fashion.

This is no venue for perfectionists or for investors inclined to second-guess themselves. "We don't always pick winners," Mobius admits. "In fact, I would say that if we are right 60 percent of the time we are doing well." Poor investments go with the territory. "Hopefully," says Mobius, "we've learned from them. But the problem in this business is you don't have the chance to correct mistakes very often because they're beyond your control."

FLIPSIDE OF VENTURE CAPITAL

Because emerging markets commonly lack infrastructure, the risks associated with them resemble the flip side of the risks that venture capital investors encounter in developed markets. Venture capital usually bankrolls unproven products in unproven markets, backed by a body of commercial law, court systems to back up claims, and stable governments and banking systems. Investors who brave emerging markets look instead for companies with existing markets for goods or services, that operate in countries *lacking* stable political regimes, sound banks, regulatory infrastructures, commercial law, and court systems to enforce what law there is. Absent this infrastructure, minor problems can balloon into financial catastrophe, and sorting out claims becomes a nightmare.

As events in Southeast Asia underscored in autumn 1997, sudden upheaval can rock fragile stock prices, and thinly traded markets can make timely exits near to impossible. Because of such conditions, Mobius proposes a warning label for prospectuses: "Don't expect to get out during a downswing. Don't take money out of a fund when markets are going down. If you want some cash, take it when the markets are good. Think like we think. Give us money when markets are bad. Don't trade these funds. Invest with a five-year time horizon. Five years, five years, five years."[16]

Mobius groups emerging markets' risks into five categories:

1. Political risks.
2. Financial risks.
3. Investment risks.
4. Systemic risks.
5. Transactional risks.

These categories sound daunting, but they can be identified, analyzed, and managed, insists Templeton's emerging markets analyst, Jim Root. "And if you do it right," he says, "you can get a better risk-adjusted return than in the regular markets."

POLITICAL RISKS

Governments can change policies, and countries can change governments. When either event happens, investors with assets at stake may find themselves in deep trouble.

"If you're the kind of investor who can't sleep at night when the country is going through a revolution, emerging markets might not be for you," money manager Edward Games warned when he was heading the Brazil Fund for Scudder, Stevens & Clark. "The most important thing for the individual investor to understand, and understand fully, is that he can lose his shirt, socks, and pants very quickly due to volatility, and [anyone] not prepared for this possibility . . . should not buy into these markets."[17]

If political risks kept Mobius awake, he'd seldom get the six hours of sleep a night that he requires. Something is always afoot in one country or another. His take on investing in Brazil: It's risky; that's why it's cheap.

The Indiana Jones of Emerging Markets

Because of his reputation for embracing tumult, fans call Mobius the "Indiana Jones" of emerging markets, a reference to the fictional archeologist of Hollywood fame, who searched the sites of the ancient world for the Ark of the Covenant. The moniker fits to the extent that Mobius will go anywhere at any time, enduring occupational hazards fearlessly—a trait that has given rise to legend in Templeton circles. "What I like are the riskiest and most dangerous places," Mobius told an interviewer in April 1997, confessing to a special fondness for risks and dangers in Russia and Hong Kong.[18]

Insofar as the Indiana Jones tag might suggest adventuresome, devil-may-care investments beset by excessive risk, Root claims it is misleading. Caution and homework are paramount. "Mobius would not find himself in as risky situations as Indiana Jones would have," says Root, "because Mobius would have been more prudent in the first place about seeking them out." That is, after all, why he travels so much.

"People may have the image of emerging markets investing as running off to the four corners of the world to invest. It's actually a lot more cautious than many people imagine. It's not just a question of traveling to some far-flung place and improvising. You start with an awareness of the risk—what could go wrong, in a nutshell." But Root concedes that when the time comes to buy or sell shares of stock, you might not know everything you would like to know. If you wait to gather all the information you think you need, it's going to be too late.

Occupational Hazards

Caution notwithstanding, Mobius has encountered some pretty dicey situations, including a crash landing in a Chilean cornfield, a white-knuckle flight in Reykjavik, Iceland, amid gale-force winds, and a driver outside São Paulo, Brazil, who stopped midroute to demand more money. More harrowing than these, though, was a helicopter ride between two São Paulo skyscrapers. "It was a pretty frightening experience when you see this little pin that you're descending onto. And it's one pilot, not two pilots. So if something happens to him, you've had it."

Investing in emerging markets has threatened life and limb in other ways. "We would obviously not go into a market if there was a full-scale war—but we have come pretty close,"[19] Mobius says. Ask him about his visit to the Philippines in December 1989. Then-President Corazon Aquino was under attack by members of the army, who were attempting to overthrow the country's first elected government. "We were in the Mandarin Hotel and the coup started soon after we arrived. And they started shooting all around that area. We couldn't get out of the hotel. It wasn't even safe to go to the windows, because they were shooting at windows as well."

Trapped in a Manila hotel in the midst of a military coup, with people being shot in the streets, what did Mobius do? What he was there to do. "Well, we were investing. We were still investing because it was a great time to invest," Mobius recalls. "I remember we were buying [stocks] at a fraction of the prices today. So of course we had to make an assessment of the outcome if the rebels won. And what would be the outcome if they didn't? And we concluded that regardless of what happened, the country would continue on the path it was going. And the economic situation was certainly getting better at the time. So we felt that it was a good risk–reward equation." Indeed. "Over the next three years," says Mobius, "we doubled our money."

When mobs hit the streets in tiny Albania in 1996, angered by a gigantic Ponzi scheme that collapsed after their savings had been exchanged for shares of bogus mutual funds, Mobius was again sanguine. "The first thing on my mind," he says, "was what opportunities there might be." There's a stock market in Iran these days, he notes, and even Iraq is moving toward a stock market of it's own.

Faith in the manifest destiny of free markets has limits, however. Islamabad, the capital of Pakistan, was not on his investment itinerary in late 1997. "Islamabad is too chaotic right now," he explains. "The government is changing. It's a possibility of war or revolution. Who know what's going on? I prefer not to visit Islamabad at this stage of the game."

Nothing to Fear but Expropriation

Until emerging markets sincerely embrace free-market principles, wise investors will keep their eyes trained on the political climate for the one political risk that stops Mobius cold: expropriation of assets.

That risk continues to exist for a time, even after privatization sweeps a country. "It could happen," Mobius concedes. "These things go in cycles. The people forget what happened to state-owned enterprises and how they decimated these countries. There's a saying, you know, that those who forget the past are doomed to repeat it and I think it's a very important point. I mean nothing is forever. Nothing is forever."

Not that Mobius fears any significant movement toward restoring government ownership. "I can't think of any country that is moving in that direction," he says. "Even Cuba is moving away from [state-owned industries] slowly, but surely. I think the concept of privatization is well embedded in government leaders almost everywhere. It's just a matter of what degree and how fast they're moving in that direction, because the results speak for themselves." China, too, is rapidly expanding free-trade zones where capitalism flourishes.

FINANCIAL RISKS

After promising repeatedly to support the peso, Mexican government reversed itself in late 1995 and let its currency float freely against the U.S. dollar and other world currencies. Financial catastrophe followed, necessitating a controversial bailout by the U.S. government to retrieve Mexico's beleaguered banking system from the brink of collapse. Stocks listed on Mexico's stock exchanges plummeted in value, and—adding insult to injury—skittish investors who bailed out faced the sad fact that the pesos they salvaged bought far fewer U.S. dollars than they had just a month earlier—despite pledges by the Mexican government that it would not devalue its currency. Similar predicaments in Thailand and Malaysia required international bailouts in 1997.

Financial risks like those that tripped up investors in Mexico and Southeast Asia are part of the landscape in emerging markets. Even in the absence of wholesale devaluation, runaway inflation can frustrate efforts to create value in a stock market. Funds under Templeton's control were investing in Brazil and Argentina when inflation was 3,000 percent a year, according to Mobius.

Just keeping up with hyperinflation requires nimble calculations that quarterly financial statements fail to convey. In Brazil, says Mobius, there was no way to predict a company's earnings for the year without adjusting daily earnings by the rate of inflation that day. It required a different means of analyzing prospective investments." So we had to shift our valuation methods to looking at net asset value. That was the best indication of value at the time."

Fortunately for investors in emerging markets, investing in stock can offset routine fluctuations in currency—provided the investors don't panic and pull the plug. "We are not concerned about currency, because an investment in an equity is a hedge on the currency," Mobius told the *Wall Street Transcript*.[20] "If you examine some of these very high-inflation countries which are subject to devaluations, you will find that the stock market adjusts to inflation."

Because local stock prices constantly adjust to inflation, currency fluctuations are not a problem. "We learned this in Argentina," Mobius declares. "We were investing in Argentina in late 1987 and early 1988, and of course a lot of people said, 'Aren't you worried about the currency?' We said no, because by buying assets we're protecting ourselves—just like the local investors are protecting themselves." Moreover, Mobius has yet to find someone who can accurately and consistently predict currency movements. "That's the most difficult thing in the world, and we haven't found any experts who have been able to guide us on this and be consistently successful."

INVESTMENT RISKS

Investors face certain fundamental risks in every company, wherever it's located. The questions they must ask are the same, whether the company is in India or in Indiana. What are the company's markets? What is its market share? How solid are its profits and profit margins? Can the company set prices? Can it charge a premium, or is it compelled to follow suit when its competitors lower prices? What are its prospects for expansion? How stiff is the competition—and what do its most successful competitors think of it? "If a competitor speaks highly, that's a good sign," Mobius says.

"The key problem for the investor is not a scarcity of opportunities. There are many good companies, and many people who can turn loss-making enterprises into profit-generating empires," Mobius says. "The problem is finding true information."[21]

Rude surprises often await U.S. investors who are accustomed to information generated by routine investment analysis. The companies they are interested in may not disclose crucial details about the cost of goods sold, depreciation allowances, or directors' salaries. Extraordinary gains or losses may not appear in financial statements, masking tax impact. The valuations companies put on their machinery may reflect its purchase price, its possible sale price, a cost-to-repurchase price, or some other figure that disguises the effects of depreciation.[22]

Such risks make travel imperative. Telephones and fax machines supplement but do not substitute for time spent face-to-face with company managers in emerging markets—which is why Mobius visits upward of 600 companies a year, picking up, en route, by his own estimate, every cold germ that flourishes in an airplane cabin. "Mobius is the ultimate road warrior, circling the globe three or four times a year in a Gulfstream jet that once belong to RJR Nabisco," USA Today reported in November 1995.[23]

"I can't just sit before a computer screen and bring up all the alternatives and hope I'll be able to get good information," he says. "There is no way we can do that, that's why we have to get out. That is also, by the way, why we are constantly opening up new markets, because we realize that tremendous risks have to be evened out by diversification. As much as possible, we have to try to diversify so we're protected against the tremendous risks."

The sheer geography of emerging markets imposes a heavy burden on money managers. "The amount of time you've got to spend is way out of proportion very often to what you get back," Mobius says. "You have to visit maybe twenty to thirty companies before you can find something you'd feel willing to buy. So I'd say you've got to spend a lot more of yourself personally on Saturdays, Sundays, Mondays, with time zone differences. In the Middle East, people work on Saturdays. So there's a lot more involved with emerging markets than you normally would have."

Numbers Are Not Everything

Analysts who work for Mobius typically spend about half their time poring over numbers in the office, and the rest on the road. Analyses begin with audited financial statements. "Numbers are absolutely necessary to you," Root says. "You want to see at the end of the day what everybody is looking for: the profit margin. But the numbers are just a consequence of management's actions and programs. You have to meet with them. It's both the factual information they give and also a question of judgment. Are they aware of certain issues? Are they caught unawares by certain questions? How do they interact with employees? What is the quality and efficiency of contact with employees?" Root asks.

"You are generally speaking with the top manager or the top finance executive, but it takes more than one person to make a company. Is he being a leader? Is the work flow organized optimally?" Root continues. "You look for any signs of sloppiness that may creep in, signs that maybe an especially successful company may be starting to rest on its laurels. You may need to pursue a line of questioning you hadn't anticipated. There's a certain amount of adjusting to the answers that you get."

Mobius began to hone his ability to assess investment risk long before the phrase "emerging markets" entered the investment lexicon. But skillful questions, straight answers, and a knack for reading body language never guarantee success by themselves. "You hear the horror stories, the cheating, the lying, but at the end of the day," Mobius observes, "by and large most people are honest. The thing you've got to be more careful about is what they actually know."

Five years after Mobius snapped up 12 percent of Asia Fiber Company, Ltd., the leading manufacturer of nylon cord and fabric in Thailand with $65 million in sales, the stock was languishing amid news of crashing Asian currencies and stock markets. Listed on the Stock Exchange of Thailand, shares of Asia Fiber changed hands in September 1997 for roughly the price Mobius had paid five years before. "It's had problems because the industry itself has had problems," Mobius explains, blaming a currency exchange rate that puts Asia Fiber and other Thai companies at a competitive disadvantage. But it was still a good company, and Mobius elected to stick with it a while longer. He knew the company and trusted its management, and the currency devaluation that rocked Thailand in the late summer of 1997 could put Asia Fiber in a better export position.

Companies anywhere in the world may go belly-up despite the best efforts of management, or they may fail because of fraud. The fate of a Thai company called Alphatec illustrates the pervasive investment risks that lie in wait for investors in emerging markets.

> Once lionized as Thailand's best hope for leapfrogging into the upper ranks of the world's technology producers, Alphatec now stands as an object lesson in the dangers of doing business in a country where management accountability is spotty at best. The stark absence of corporate controls at Alphatec—the mingling of funds among listed and closely held companies run by the same family, the use of multiple sets of accounting books and misleading accounting methods, the highly paid, rubber stamp board—mirrors the problems at other Thai companies that have brought this country's economy to the brink of collapse.
>
> During Thailand's go-go decade after 1985, such deficiencies could be papered over with easy credit and soaring stock prices. But now the reckoning has begun. Parisbas Asia Equity, a regional securities brokerage firm, has reconstructed income statements of 20 listed Thai companies using stricter accounting standards. The result: about $1.6 billion of reported profits from the past five years turned into cumulative losses of more than $700 million.[24]

Aggrieved investors in emerging markets often lack the means of recourse that are commonly available in developed countries. "There is lawlessness, to put it mildly," Mobius observes, "and you can't depend on protection from the law or from the authorities."

Despite many reasons for suspicion, Mobius resists jumping to conclusions. "People do lie to you," he says. "More often than not, people are telling you the truth, but their version of the truth." Rule number one, in that case: Avoid asking leading questions. Don't ask, for example, if the economy is getting better. "We ask, 'What do you think of the economy?' And then we observe people." Very often the nonverbal communication can be as revealing as the verbal. "That's where experience plays a role," says Mobius. "I lived in Thailand for a year and got some understanding of the culture, and it's amazing how scrutable people actually are. You can tell a lot by their body language."

One Bangkok executive couldn't hide the real condition of his bank's loan portfolio. "When we started asking him more penetrating questions, he said, 'I can't give you any details. I'll call my assistant in.'" The assistant was called in, and she didn't have any more details than her boss. "We realized he was trying to evade the question. The clue came when he started shifting and looking a little uncomfortable." Postscript: Mobius elected not to invest in that bank.

SYSTEMIC RISKS

Opening up an emerging market entails more than putting out a welcome mat. To lure investors, an emerging-market country needs stock markets, settlement agreements, tax treaties, regulations with teeth, and custodial institutions to hold the physical shares of stock and to process dividends. If the market framework is deficient or discriminates against outsiders, investors face serious systemic risk.

"I never go into a country unless I can see my way out. In other words, I will not go into a country unless they have laws and regulations which allow foreigners to take their profits and their capital out again when they want to get them out." An adequate market framework is characterized by four traits represented by the acronym FELT, which stands for Fair, Efficient, Liquid, and Transparent. "If you have FELT, that's fantastic," Mobius says.[25]

- In a market that is *fair,* all investors, large and small, insiders and outsiders, compete on a level playing field.
- An *efficient* system reduces paperwork and conducts operations in the simplest and most direct way, keeping costs as low as possible. In addition, it facilitates settlement so that trading contracts don't get hung up by cumbersome procedures.
- When there is *liquidity,* shares of many companies are always available and there is always a market for them, with enough daily trading volume to keep investors from easily driving prices up or down.

- The markets should be *transparent* in two ways: (1) with respect to the operations of traded companies and (2) with respect to trading activity. When markets are transparent, they foster fairness, efficiency, and liquidity.

Absent FELT, emerging markets cannot achieve their potential. They invite scandals like the one that closed the Bombay Stock Exchange when a handful of traders conspired to push stock prices to record levels until regulators discovered that $1.2 billion had vanished. Mobius escaped unscathed; he was out of the market before the news hit.

Rapid strides to eliminate systemic risk are visible in some countries. Progress is slow in others, and occasional backsliding is evident in a few. "Unfortunately, the history of these countries is that it has been a little club of the elite running the stock markets for their own sake and not for the general good of the nation," Mobius says.[26] Although pundits might level the same charge at major U.S. exchanges, Mobius notes, it's not really a close contest. Despite the progress, emerging markets still lack size, depth, regulators, enforcement, audit standards, and intermediaries called custodians that hold stock certificates and make sure dividends are paid. Efficient means of communication and transportation, as well as consistent accounting standards, may also be wanting. These are not risks to be taken lightly.

Unfortunately, free-market concepts are not accepted automatically everywhere, not even in Eastern Europe, with its extensive cultural, ethnic, and commercial ties to Western countries. A dinner with the minister of finance of Czechoslovakia highlighted for Mobius the hurdles that emerging markets must overcome. "It was interesting to hear him talk. He said: 'Look, I know about all these capitalist ideas. I've read all the books.' But you could tell he knew nothing—he hadn't lived it. I began to realize that there is a process of osmosis in capitalist societies. Youngsters absorb the ideas by living [surrounded by them]. Eastern Europe has to go through a total mentality change. It has to start thinking in terms of profits, of eliminating waste. All that is not easy. There are tremendous forces that do not want to be eliminated."[27]

A Brief World Tour

Thailand launched the Securities Exchange of Thailand (SET) in 1975. Until the late 1980s, however, international investors other than Mobius pretty much ignored it.[28] Then the Composite Index shot upward. It peaked in December 1993, then promptly lost almost 20 percent of its value in 1994—the year Mobius's sister-in-law nearly barred him from her house. It had yet to regain lost ground in late 1997.

Hungary set up a bond market in 1982, when it was a member of the communist bloc. The bonds enabled municipal and national governments to tap the global capital pool. The Budapest Stock Exchange, which enjoyed a brief life prior to communist rule, reopened in June 1990 with eight publicly traded companies. In 1996, the index of 25 stocks showed record volume and prices.

On the African continent, stock markets were still miniscule in late 1995, with the exception of South Africa. But Nigeria's stock exchange had six branches, and even tiny Botswana listed 12 stocks worth around $326 million, according to the *Economist* Intelligence Unit:

Sub-Saharan Stock Markets

South Africa	$280.5
Zimbabwe	2.0
Nigeria	2.0
Kenya	1.9
Ghana	1.7
Mauritius	1.4
Côte d'Ivoire	0.9

Source: International Finance Corp., © EIU Country Profile, Kenya, 1996–1997. Reproduced by permission of the Economist Intelligence Unit.

The Kingdom of Jordan launched the Amman Financial Market in the late 1970s. With 115 stocks in 1997, and a $5 billion market capitalization, Amman was the second most active exchange in the Arab world after Egypt, which had 700 listings. Morocco and Tunisia, whose governments have pushed reforms to attract increased investment, listed 55 and 23 companies, respectively, in 1995.

TRANSACTIONAL RISKS

Transactional risks have to do with the physical processing of an investment, from the verbal commitment to buy shares to the delivery of the share certificates. In developed markets, investors take much of this process for granted. In emerging markets, it's wise to be alert to irregularities.

When Mobius visits an emerging market, he goes straight to the stock exchange and examines the quality of the printing on the share certificates. That's a precaution against the sort of counterfeit shares that plagued a Turkish electric company in the early 1990s. What started as a rumor turned out to be true. To determine whether the shares owned by Templeton were real or fake, Mobius approached the local branch of Chase Manhattan, which was acting as custodian for the shares. Appointing such a custodian is a routine procedure in emerging markets. Where there is none, Mobius stays away. Indeed, some counterfeit shares turned up in the vault. According to Mobius, Chase said that it had a contractual obligation to do its best to determine whether certificates were real, but that it was not obliged to guarantee their authenticity. It advised Mobius to see the broker. The broker, in turn, blamed the stock exchange, which was in the early stages of setting up a central clearing facility.

Mobius was unsuccessful in his efforts to win compensation until he accepted an invitation to give a speech about emerging markets. His audience included the chairman of the Istanbul Stock Exchange and members of his official entourage. Mobius seized the opportunity. "I stood up and said, 'Gentlemen, you owe me money.'"

That the Turkish government covered the losses that Templeton had incurred on the counterfeit notes underscores the importance of having good connections in emerging markets, instead of relying exclusively on the frail legal framework. At times, Mobius observes bluntly, "The effective way of doing business is by gifts and by benefiting the players involved who can bend the law for you. Your benefit will come not from following the law but from bending the law, because that's the way it's done and you'd be at a big disadvantage [if you didn't follow local practices]."[29]

Never assume that stockbrokers in emerging markets are your friends. There's always a likelihood that they stand to gain far more from the stock they're pushing than the investor will. Even when a broker is on the level, by the time most investors receive a glossy brochure, the bargains have vanished.

Transactions that seem innocent at first can cost dearly in the end if investors are not exceedingly careful. Mobius relates how one company printed its share certificates in two denominations, 500 shares to local investors and 20,000 shares to foreigners. When the business climate turned sour, the owners of the larger denominations were unable to find buyers for their shares.

Trading scandals go with the territory: from elaborate Ponzi schemes to petty theft. In his long career, Mobius has seen just about everything.[30]

- In 1992, officials misplaced 75,000 certificates representing 75 million shares of stock traded on the Kuala Lumpur Exchange.

- The principal stock exchange in Greece suspended trading of a leading blue-chip company, Titan Cement, after it came to light in 1991 that thousands of stock certificates had been forged.
- In April 1992, the State Bank of India came up short millions of dollars owing to falsified records of government securities transactions.
- In March 1993, counterfeit shares of stock turned up in four Indonesian brokerage firms, forcing the state's regulatory arm, Bapepam, to suspend trading in the five stocks affected.

Transaction risks also encompass exorbitant fees charged by unscrupulous brokers, and, as everywhere, the potential for computer crime. The speed with which emerging markets have embraced high technology leaves them vulnerable to high-tech criminals who need not fear thorough backup systems. Moreover, investors need to be wary of the time it takes to settle transactions. In some countries, red tape can tie up assets for enormous periods of time, preventing investors from moving quickly when speed is essential.

Routine transactions sometimes entail bid–ask spreads wide enough for a tractor to drive through—a far cry from the $\frac{1}{16}$ of a dollar spreads on the New York Stock Exchange. "We compare offers from various brokers and try, of course, to get the narrowest [bid–ask] spreads possible," says Mobius. "At the beginning it was difficult because we had very, very wide spreads for a lot of these stocks, and that makes it particularly difficult when you're running an open-end fund. You have to price the securities in the midrange between the bid and the offer, and if the range is wide, you have real problems because you immediately lose money when you start pricing [the assets] on paper." It's not uncommon to find a 20 to 30 percent gap between buyers and sellers. On a recent visit to Russia, Mobius elected not to invest in a small rural company trading on the St. Petersburg Exchange, where bidders were offering $5 and sellers were asking $15.

THE GOOD NEWS ABOUT EMERGING-MARKETS RISKS

The litany of risks associated with emerging markets might suggest that investors would be wise to stay clear of them. But there are two powerful offsetting factors: diversification and covariance.

Operating in upward of 40 economies in four regions of the world, an investor enjoys more ways to diversify than are available in a single market, even one as large as the United States. "In our view, it lowers the risk because you've got different things happening in different times all over the world," Mobius observes. "For example, right now we have a disastrous investment in Brazil, but we have a very successful one in Argentina. We have a disastrous investment in Hungary, we have a fantastically successful one in Hong Kong." Far from canceling each other out, the winners outweigh the losers. "The good news is that, on average, we do better, there are more successes than disasters, and the successes tend to be very good successes. They tend to, in percentage terms, move up more than the disasters move down."

Meantime, emerging markets seldom fluctuate in lockstep with developed markets or even with one another. In the parlance of experts, they tend to exhibit low covariance. Far from scaring off risk-averse investors, out-of-step fluctuations offer a chance to reduce a portfolio's overall volatility and increase the likelihood of a satisfactory return.

Wary investors do not mistake low covariance for a guarantee that some stocks always rise in price while others go down. Events in October 1997 demonstrated otherwise. When U.S. markets opened on the morning of Tuesday, October 28, after plunging 7.18 percent on Monday, they faced a backdrop of one-day market declines in 41 stock markets worldwide. The declines ranged, however, from less than 1 percent in the United Kingdom and India to declines exceeding 14 percent in Russia and Hungary. Canada and Slovakia supplied the best news awaiting U.S. traders on Tuesday morning: they recorded no losses and no gains. Moreover, widely used measures of covariance rely on historical data that may ignore the recent flow of funds into emerging markets. Critics warn that too much faith in outdated statistics can lead to unpleasant consequences, especially in thinly traded markets dominated by a handful of institutions.

Whatever degrees of covariance actually prevail, it is clear that all markets do not behave alike. This being the case, Mobius contends that growth-seeking investors must look beyond their own shores for superior returns. "The U.S. market can never be the best performing market year after year," he says. "In fact, the studies that we've done show that no market in the world has been, in two consecutive years, the best performing. And in a twenty-year period, only a few markets were the best performing in two years of those twenty. So the simple fact tells you that if you want to have the best performance, you don't want to stay in one market. And this, by the way, is true not only of the United States, but of any of the European countries, any emerging markets. In fact, I was talking recently to a group in Hong Kong and of course they were very hot on the Hong Kong market. And I said, this is not the place to have all your money. You must diversify. You must get out."

Average investors who stick to two or even three developed markets fail to appreciate the value that a wider choice of markets bestows. "That's the advantage we have now," Mobius says. "You may have a bull market in emerging markets generally, but there's always a country that is going down, or has gone down and is presenting a bargain."

Mobius does not belong to the camp of professional investment managers who start by choosing markets and selecting the degree of exposure desirable, based on each market's historical performance. One of the foremost practitioners of asset allocation is Gary Brinson, the subject of Chapter 7. Brinson sets "policy weights" for different markets, a top-down framework that supersedes individual asset selection.

STRICTLY BOTTOM-UP

Mobius follows a strictly bottom-up approach. "Even though in our reports you'll see a breakdown by industry, it's not relevant to our investment thinking. When we pick stocks, we don't pick industries," he told the *Wall Street Transcript.* "We look for the bargains, put them on a bargain list and then begin buying. We find that we end up with a highly diversified portfolio, but that's not by design; it's just chance, really. I don't mind being heavy in a particular industry if I find the bargains are in that industry."[31]

When Mobius concludes that the stock of a company in the portfolio is very expensive, meaning that it is no longer a bargain with good growth prospects, he will find a stock that is 50 percent cheaper, and, if fundamental value exists, he buys it—no matter where he finds it.

> The bottom up makes eminent sense to the emerging market for one very simple reason. Information about the macroeconomic political environment in these emerging market countries is very, very difficult to get. And whatever you do get is often inaccurate and late, so by focusing on a bottom up approach we learn more about what's happening in the country than by trying to look at the macro statistics.[32]

"If you make a big decision on a country, you're more likely to make the wrong decision," Mobius insists. There are so many companies in each country, some doing well and some doing poorly, that even in a bull market or a bear market he can find bargains. "That alone is sufficient reason for emphasizing a bottom-up rather than a top-down approach in emerging markets. But it's not all.

"If you're taking the countrywide decision, your view of the country will be influenced by the headlines, by what other people are talking about, which can be misleading," Mobius finds. "Very often, the headlines will not give you a micro picture, which is more important from an investor's point of view. If I go talk to one of the banks in Thailand or a textile company and ask them how the economy's affecting them, I will get a much more accurate picture than if I talk to an economist who's looking at a macro picture."

The resulting decisions may at times resemble a top-down approach, however. "Now the conclusion may be that I will sell many, many stocks in a country that, from a macro point of view, does not look interesting. But I'm less likely to make the big macro mistake." (He was largely out of Asia in 1997.)

A decidedly contrarian outlook helps guard against the big mistakes that inevitably befall investors crowding into hot markets. Mobius is a contrarian in the tradition of Templeton Fund's founder Sir John Templeton, who bought Japanese stocks in the 1960s, when Hitachi, Sony, and Mitsubishi were bargains. "People are always asking me where is the outlook good, but that's the wrong question." Sir John told *Forbes* in 1995. "The right question is: Where is the outlook most miserable?"

> In almost every activity of normal life people try to go where the outlook is best. You look for a job in an industry with a good future, or build a factory where the prospects are best. But my contention is, if you're selecting publicly traded investments, you have to do the opposite. You're trying to buy a share at the lowest possible price in relation to what the corporation is worth. And there's only one reason a share goes to a bargain price: because people are selling. There is no other reason.[33]

"We are value investors," Mobius declares. "Value is in what other people are not buying. What other people are selling. Because, otherwise, it wouldn't be cheap."

Toward this end in Asia, Latin America, Africa, and Eastern Europe, Mobius and his team of stock analysts scan all the companies in particular markets for good bargains, using a database culled from annual reports and audited statements going back as far as ten years. Companies that have relatively low debt, sound financials, and good earnings potential, but that are out of favor with investors for one reason or another, earn further consideration based on brokerage reports, credit analyses, and, ultimately, company visits.

"We will weight risk, there's no question about that," says Mobius. "But that's after we've looked at the structure. Very often, we will omit companies that obviously have weak financial structures. Some that are on the borderline, we will look at. Then we look at earnings. What do they look like? What have they been in the past? What can we expect in the future? Of course, nobody can predict the future, but you can get some idea because the past is prologue, you know. You can see what the company has been doing and whether there has been a big variation in earnings per share after all kinds of adjustments."

The reason for scrutinizing all the components of performance, including cash flow, is to figure out what earnings will look like in five years. The rule of thumb is to find companies that are currently trading for less than what five times earnings are projected to be five years in the future. A stock that is changing hands for ten or even twenty times earnings can still represent a bargain to Mobius—if the five-year outlook is favorable enough.

This investment strategy underscores the contrarian preference for unpopular stocks. "If you start out at a very, very high price relative to current earnings," Mobius says, "it's difficult to justify growth of, let's say, 50 percent a year." Much like John Neff, but on a global scale, Mobius wants stocks that make other investors uncomfortable. "In order to get that kind of stock," says Mobius, "you need to go to companies which are not well liked by the market at this stage. It also means you are buying stocks that are going down in price and will probably continue to go down for some time."[34]

PATIENCE IS A VIRTUE

Sticking to a contrarian strategy imposes tough discipline even for practitioners of the Templeton approach. "You've got to have a very strong stomach. You've got to have a lot of willpower," Mobius observes. "And, most of all, you've got to have clients who are patient and will agree with this philosophy."

Once Mobius okays a stock, it's likely to remain in the portfolio for five years, the fund's average holding period. This reflects commitment, of course, but it also reflects the fact that trading volume in emerging markets is much less robust than in the United States, Europe, or Japan, and large positions can't easily be liquidated, especially in a bear market. In any event, Mobius says, "You can't sell anything unless you have something that's 15 percent cheaper to buy."

Timing markets is a game that Mobius avoids. "Even with all our analysts researching the market constantly, we are not clever enough to 'call' the bottom of the market," says Stewart Aldcroft, a Templeton fund manager. "It may not occur for another three to six months, or maybe longer. It may be now. We won't know until after it has occurred, and then it may be too late to buy 'at the bottom.'"

At 61, daily exercise keeps Mobius fit and vigorous and at a pace that exhausts younger analysts. Retirement seems out of the question so long as his motivation remains strong. He still relishes the challenge of building assets. "You want to see if you can do better than you did the year before," he declares. "And you know, you're only as good as your last performance. I may have won a prize for being the best manager in 1995, but it's now 1997 and we have to keep on moving, doing it again. So there's the challenge."

Mobius's drive also reflects the value of experience and his admiration for his 83-year-old mentor, Sir John Templeton. "That's a great thing about our business," says Mobius, "we get better." When you've gone through a few crashes and booms around the world, you don't get so upset anymore, and moreover, you learn to take advantage of upheaval. "It's kind of a pity to throw that all away and retire," says Mobius. "It doesn't make sense."

6

Fixed Income

BETTING ON BONDS

On a typical workday, Bill Gross faces a decidedly modern challenge: putting hundreds of millions of dollars to work in the bond market.

With close to $110 billion under management, Pacific Investment Management Company, better known as PIMCO, commands a sum nearly equal to 1 percent of the $11 trillion U.S. bond market, where daily trading activity approaches $300 million. One-day fluctuations in PIMCO's portfolio may approach the annual sales of many large public companies. "If the market is strong, our assets could be half a billion dollars more than when I woke up this morning," says Gross. "That's a very sobering thought as you approach the trading desk."

Gross has been approaching a trading desk since 1971, when trading bonds was a novel idea. Preparation for the job included a stint clipping coupons for Pacific Mutual Insurance Company, his first employer after graduate school at the University of Southern California. Except in rare situations, bondholders bought, for example, a ten-year bond to match a ten-year liability and collected the interest until the loan came due. When Gross arrived, every bond had coupons attached. Investors clipped the coupons, usually every six months, mailed them back to the paying agent, and received an interest check a few weeks later.

Unlike his contemporaries, who were hot to get in on a burgeoning stock market, Gross liked bonds and volunteered to help launch and run Pacific Mutual's fledgling bond trading operation. He didn't have much competition—in fact, he had no competition at all after the company's only other bond trader requested a different assignment. Getting rich certainly wasn't Gross's primary motive—not in the bond market at that time. Bonds just suited the personality of a low-key guy with an infectious laugh, a cowlick that wouldn't stay down, and an appetite for trying something new, recalls Howard Raykoff, a fellow bond market pioneer. "Billy was the one who accepted the responsibility for trying to trade these things. And everyone else said, 'Fine, I'd rather do something else,'" Raykoff says. "I'm telling you, it was very avant garde for an insurance company to set up a pilot portfolio to trade bonds."

Thanks to visionaries who hauled bond trading into the twentieth century, bonds have emerged from basement vaults. Virtually all transactions these days occur instantaneously in cyberspace. At PIMCO, fourteen professional bond managers keep tabs on the marketplace from a fashionable post in Newport Beach, California. The trading floor, replete with dozens of blinking computer screens, overlooks the Pacific Ocean. The view is a distraction, Gross admits, but not one that interrupts exceptional performance.

BASIC PRINCIPLES

The multifaceted bond market in which Gross and other bond traders operate is intimidating. But while it looks exceedingly complex to casual observers, its appealing logic and internal consistency are within the grasp of investors who understand three basic principles:

1. A bond represents a borrower's agreement to pay lenders a fixed rate of interest, and, ultimately, to repay the loan when it is due.
2. What matters ultimately is the borrower's ability to pay interest on time and repay the loan when due.
3. Bond prices and bond yields move in opposite directions in response to inflation.

Investing in bonds requires attention to more than one event at a time. Driving a car requires a foot on the gas, hands on the wheel, and eyes on the road. Navigating the bond market requires a foot on interest rates, a handle on the prospects for being repaid, and an eye on inflation.

GENTLEMEN NO MORE

It is hard to envision more sweeping changes than those that transformed the bond landscape in one generation. Andrew Mellon's wry observation that gentlemen prefer bonds is now as quaint and irrelevant as it sounds. It's a rough and tumble world these days.

Bonds, in one form or another, have been around for centuries. Italian merchants and bankers exchanged *prestiti* in the sixteenth century. These, like bonds that followed, represented contractual obligations by borrowers to repay lenders loan amounts plus interest. The first bonds in the modern sense appeared in Holland 300 years ago. They were called "Dutch Perpetuals"—bonds that never mature. Once bonds began to proliferate, few were traded, even during much of the twentieth century. Although bond markets existed in the United States for decades, they were largely static. When Gross appeared on the scene, most of the trading, such as it was, involved bonds issued by utilities, transportation companies, and government agencies. There were no long-term Treasury bonds, much less junk bonds, mortgage bonds, or derivatives. AT&T bonds, not U.S. Treasury securities, supplied the pricing benchmarks.

Gross's timing was serendipitous, if not brilliant. He had hardly established a bond-trading operation when a bear market in stocks drove investors to bonds, and a manager who could squeeze returns had something very attractive to sell. Returns of 8 to 9 percent from bonds looked mighty good in 1973, when the S&P 500 declined by 15 percent, and in 1974, when investors suffered an even worse drubbing as the stock market lost a quarter of its value.

Meantime, buy-and-hold days were disappearing for even more compelling reasons. Gaping government budget deficits and soaring oil prices in the 1970s put a rude end to the bond market's sleepy ways. The related inflation drove prevailing interest rates to double digits. Rising interest rates clobbered bondholders who were counting on fixed rates of return as market yields rose and market values declined. Investors who were holding bonds scheduled to mature in five years or more endured severe beatings. Short-term investors, luckily, suffered less violent price swings. Still, all bondholders felt the unsettling effects of inflation.

Far from protecting wealth, investors soon learned, bonds that fail to keep up with inflation eat into savings. When investors are caught with these bonds, selling them poses a still more vexing problem: How to collect the face amount of a bond with a below-market interest rate. It's a salvage operation that always incurs a loss. Because bonds pay fixed amounts of interest, the only way to boost return on, say, a bond paying $50 a year in interest was to buy it for less than face value. By 1979, this process resembled a fire sale. Instead of collecting 100 cents on the dollar of initial investment, beleaguered sellers, in order to lure buyers, had to take less. When rates peaked, some bonds fetched half their face value. All of a sudden, with prices tumbling as never before, bonds did not look so safe.

CERTIFICATES OF CONFISCATION

Aging bonds in the late 1970s became known as "certificates of confiscation." Inflation confiscated capital from beleaguered investors who sold bonds at fire sale prices. The alternative? Remain captive to an investment as capital slips away with every passing interest payment. Who could say which was worse? When interest rates hit 15 percent, some bonds issued a few years earlier by the U.S. Treasury, paying less than eight percent, changed hands for 50 cents on the dollar, or even less. Not because they were defaulting or going under, but simply because inflation was propelling interest rates on new bonds to stratospheric heights.

When interest rates started to recede, most investors missed the boat again. Panic dulled judgment, in Gross's opinion. Fearful of move losses, they jettisoned the bonds from their portfolios—exactly the wrong move it turned out. High yields and low prices had run their course. It was time to move in and capture attractive long-term rates. As for the risk that rates might go higher still, as has happened in tumultuous economic times, Gross kept faith that the interest rate pendulum could swing only so far.

While investors fumbled, the era of active bond management dawned. The goal for the new breed of active bond managers was to restore a measure of order and safety to bonds by trading them in response to expected changes in inflation. The bulk of trading at PIMCO consists of selling and then reinvesting nearly one-third of the bonds in the portfolio every year, with an eye to protecting principal while maximizing interest payments, or yield. Such volume means that PIMCO is on one side or the other of transactions totaling $60 billion a year—or $240 million on an average day.

GHOULS OF THE INVESTMENT WORLD

"Trying to decipher what inflation is going to be is what we're all about," Gross says. Short of trying to predict the future, Gross advises wary investors to track the strength of economic activity and productivity in the United States and, to some extent, the global forces shaping the world's economy. The fact that capitalism appears to have triumphed over communism, for instance, allows for competition that fosters lower wages and, as a result, lower prices. "That's a dramatic element for a bond investor," says Gross. "You mention low inflation and all of a sudden a light bulb goes on."

When inflation is low, bond prices and yields fluctuate in a modest range that creates opportunities for nimble investors without posing a heavy risk of catastrophic loss. Bond traders profit by exploiting the ups and downs exhibited by bond prices and yields in response to inflation.

LIKE A TEETER-TOTTER

Although a higher yield sounds good for bond holders, at first blush, the opposite is true. When yields go up for newly issued bonds, prices for existing bonds go down—and vice versa. Gross likens this seesaw movement to that of a teeter-totter. Yield sits on one side and price on the other.

This inverse relationship is difficult to grasp, not least because it's hard for average investors to interpret news that affects bonds. A bull market means that bond yields are down and prices are up. Is that good news? Existing bondholders might enjoy the rising prices, but cashing in those gains means reinvesting at lower rates of return. Investors whose bonds mature, get none of the price boost and must also settle for lower interest rates. In a bear market, yields on new bonds rise but prices on existing bonds fall.

In general, bondholders applaud lower yields and higher prices, which usually signify economic weakness. Because bond investors welcome these unsettling signs, Gross calls them "the ghouls of the investment world." News that weakens yields and lifts bond prices is well received in the bond market. "We depend upon sour economic news, slow economic growth, and slow inflation," Gross says. "We basically want an economy that doesn't improve dramatically." Lower interest rates are good news also for borrowers, including anyone seeking to finance or refinance a home mortgage.

Besides an uncanny knack for reading the bond market's signals, PIMCO's founder attributes the firm's success to a laundry list of winning factors: discipline, hard work, common sense, good luck, prudent risks, and consistent application of a sound investment strategy.

In addition to these traits, Gross displayed an entrepreneurial bent during California's housing boom in the early 1970s. He literally stood on line for a day and a half to secure the right to buy a house in a trendy housing development—and then sold his right to the highest bidder. Another time, he was stubborn enough to carry a placard in front of a gas station in a one-man protest against lousy service.

When bond trading really took off and it became painfully apparent that Gross and his team were reaping huge profits for Pacific Mutual but taking none of it home, Gross confronted his employer and put his job on the line. "I remember Billy saying 'I'm going over there, I'm either out of a job or a new firm,'" Raykoff recalls. "So I waited until he called me and said 'We're a new firm.'"

MR. NOT-SO-NICE GUY

Gross admits to a tough side, at least in his earlier days. He tended to pit bond dealers against one another, to drive the best prices for PIMCO. It's a technique that many bond traders use, but PIMCO, by dint of size, played a little harder than most. "He was always a tough trader, bidding us back, always tenacious with levels," says Raykoff, one of Gross's first customers. If the going price was at one level, Gross would press for a lower price in order to boost the yield. Dealers would have to decide whether it was worthwhile to earn less on each trade but trade more often with PIMCO.

But Gross could push and cajole with style—with ruinous results for competitors who tried to imitate his trading tactics. "They didn't do it with the finesse Billy had," says Raykoff. "He had a special feel for how far to push. Others were just mean and nasty. They felt it was in their power to push around Wall Street. They figured they could just get the Street to do anything." The upshot: Gross often snapped up the most attractive deals before clumsier rivals had a chance to see them.

(During Gross's early days at Pacific Mutual, one shameless ploy failed to pan out. To attract the attention of top management, he arranged for vanity license plates: "BONDS1." He always parked his car as near as possible to the car belonging to the company's chairman, figuring that one day the license plates would come up in conversation. Frustrating months passed, however, and no one said anything, until one day a woman in a supermarket approached him for help in securing a bail bond for her son.)

Trading bonds is not the only activity that spurs in Gross a single-minded determination to win. Like Sky Masterson, Damon Runyon's fictional gambler who bet on which raindrop would win the race to the bottom of a window pane, he wants to be best or first or fastest. "I just see it all the time," says Bill Thompson, PIMCO's CEO since April 1993. After meetings at a country club, says Thompson, "we might walk out [to the practice greens] with a putter in our hands and a golf ball and I'm telling you, if he doesn't get it closest to the hole he's mad as hell. For five dollars or just a handshake, it doesn't matter." Adds Gross's wife, Sue, "If you say, let's race to the highway, he's there."

Exceptional insight into people gives Gross a competitive edge in the bond market, Thompson says. "The *people* component adds in two ways. One, the people we have to deal with every day—basically, the Street and the world of investors—it's very important to understand how they function, where they take their ideas, what motivates them, their biases, and how selective their memories and reasoning are. Number two, in a broad sense, understanding people and their reactions is very helpful in assessing market psychology. Bill is very good at being able to see all the things that are going on out there, from the Fed to momentum investors and you name it. He can cut through all that and has a pretty good understanding of what is really important—in other words, put aside the emotion and the herd instinct that drives a crowd. I find him uniquely able to do the type of thinking that is not so widely done by a lot of other people. He understands where everybody is, but he looks in a different direction. I think there is a lot of people instinct in that."

CRAWDADS AND SALAMANDERS

Confidence, clarity of purpose, a capacity for seeing through the tumult—they all took root near Butler Creek, a stream that ran through Middletown, Ohio, where Gross spent much of his childhood. In those days, Gross wrote later on, Butler Creek represented "crawdads and salamanders and all sorts of fun things that little boys dream pleasant dreams of."

It's a long way from Middletown to a roiling bond market, but some simple lessons that Gross learned along Butler Creek still figure prominently at PIMCO. "Common sense is the number-one criterion in this business," Gross insists. "Intelligence is fine and hard work is fine, but if you don't have common sense, you're going to lose your shirt." Common sense, together with intelligence and hard work, bestows the critical ability to diagnose change, and that ability "produces the return we are looking for."

In the bond market, a commonsense philosophy exploits the "noise" created by short-term investors looking for quick gains, especially in hedge funds. "We've known for several years now that it pays to 'just say no' to fallacious volatility that intimidates other money managers with little willpower and below-average market performance." Proof lies in the results. Interest rates in 1994 didn't behave as Gross predicted they would, for example, but he never lost his composure. Instead, his patient strategies, together with excellent international and high-yield investments, more than compensated for any shortfalls.

To sharpen his insights into people and markets, Gross reads widely, from economic history like Paul Johnson's *Birth of the Modern* to sociology, book reviews, and novels by John Updike. "Books of this sort tend to give you depth and a bug for investing," he says. "You need to know about history, you need to know about people."

This is all part of the investment process. To Gross, investing calls for a much wider scope than predicting upticks and downticks. "I've always managed money from a conceptual standpoint," says Gross, who trained for the bond business in Las Vegas, where he once played blackjack for five straight months. "Investing for me takes into consideration human character and psychology. That's what tends to produce bull markets and bear markets. And when you intertwine that with analysis of economic history and concepts like the fall of the Berlin Wall, the flow of capital around the world, and your own sense of yourself, that produces positive results over time."

Although luck alone cannot chalk up long-running investment success, Gross confesses to a few superstitious traits. "A lucky penny will always attract my eye," he admits. Mornings, in the trading room in his basement, he'll hit the buttons in the same order each day for fear of disrupting the markets. He keeps a pair of dice on his office wall with a seven or eleven exposed. When he rolls them from time to time, he won't stop until he hits a seven or an eleven. If the dice get jostled by a cleaning woman and the market goes down, he suspects a link. "Even though we're employing our wits and intelligence on an ongoing basis," he says, "you need a lot of luck in this business or any business. And this pair of dice helps to promote that."

ANCHORS TO WINDWARD

Properly managed, bonds should provide a haven from luck's ill winds. In an uncertain world, where risks are great, they should act as anchors to windward that help keep the ship safe and asset values secure. Gross says, "That's what the charge of the bond market is: to provide stable fixed income over a period of time." Stocks may tend to produce average total returns in excess of 12 percent, taking dividends and capital gains into consideration. Total returns from bonds seldom exceed 8 percent over the long run. But Gross warns investors not to become too greedy or fearful. Regression to the mean—a fancy way to say the pendulum always swings back to the middle—is inevitable for a stock market that has nearly doubled in 1996 and 1997, and now perches on heights that many investors consider perilous.

Gross believes that at least some bonds belong in every investment portfolio. Through the years, bonds can provide a fixed flow of income to retirees and to anyone meeting specific objectives: college education, retirement plans, a second home. "If you're saving for a goal and you want to make sure that it is within reach," Gross counsels, "then bonds have a place because they provide that fixed-income cash flow."

An old rule of thumb advises investors to subtract their age from 100, treat the result as a percent, and let that determine how much of a portfolio should be invested in stock. This "decent" rule, says Gross, is best applied to investors between age 40 and retirement age. The rule "loses validity at the tails," he says. People in their mid-twenties, he reckons, should put 90 percent of their assets in stocks unless they depend on current income. Anyone over 70 with a need for current income should have upward of 90 percent of an investment portfolio in bonds. For older investors more concerned with estate taxes than income however, a larger component of stocks can help reduce heirs' tax bill.

A NEW RISK SPECTRUM

As cadres of professional bond managers developed an appetite for beating inflation, Wall Street's investment bankers cooked up more and more confections. New types of bonds featured myriad complexities and all degrees of risk. The new risk spectrum expanded beyond government securities with no risk of bankruptcy and bonds issued by powerful corporations where the risk of bankruptcy was remote.

Floating-rate bonds arose, as any homeowner knows who purchased a mortgage that readjusts with changes in prevailing interest rates. Companies also began issuing bonds with floating rates that float, or fluctuate, in tandem with a fixed benchmark, often a U.S. Treasury security with an equivalent maturity. Another popular benchmark in the corporate bond arena is the London Interbank Offered Rate (LIBOR). Because corporate bonds are riskier than bonds carrying government guarantees, borrowers must pay something extra to attract lenders. The extra amount, usually a fraction of a percentage point, is called the *risk premium*.

Junk bonds began to appear, largely on the strength of Michael Milken's insight that fledgling companies could pay interest rates out of proportion to increases in bankruptcy risk. Until Milken demonstrated that bankruptcy risk for companies beneath the investment grade radar was overrated, few bond investors paid much attention to them.

As subordinated lenders, junk-bond investors were low on the totem pole in the event of bankruptcy, when senior lenders recoup their cash first. (Subordinated lenders are next in line, followed by stockholders.) But handsome yields and lower-than-expected rates of bankruptcy prompted investors to change their outlook. From obscurity in 1980, the junk-bond market had bloomed into a flourishing industry by 1997 thanks to lower interest rates and corporate takeovers.

"[Milken] developed a new niche that developed into a very vibrant part of the capital markets," says Gross, who attribute's Milken's ensuing downfall to a mix of factors, not least some fear and loathing on Wall Street where junk bonds were greeted at first with suspicion and envy. "But junk bonds as a category certainly have been proven over the years to be appropriate vehicles for companies that issue them to raise capital and for investors who buy them in the appropriate quantity at the appropriate rate."

Early purveyors of junk bonds liked to tout the promise of improvements in credit quality. If improvements materialized, it would mean that investors eventually would collect yields superior to the yields for equivalent risks. Higher yields were supposed to command higher prices. Often times the credit improvements followed, but there was a hitch that few investors recognized: call provisions. These provisions permitted successful companies to call, or redeem, junk bonds before investors could cash in. But on the downside, risks were not mitigated. Junk bonds could sink in value to zero if companies defaulted. That capped the upside and left lots of downside for an investor—reasons enough for Gross to largely steer clear of junk bonds. Moreover, Gross didn't trust a market in which one player was so dominant as Milken's firm, Drexel Burnham Lambert, and he remains circumspect.

"We didn't invest in junk bonds at the time," he says, "and still don't to a substantial degree." When fixed-income investors were clamoring for yields in excess of 13 and 14 percent, Gross placated them with forays into the burgeoning mortgage market, where PIMCO was an enthusiastic participant. Each mortgage bond repackaged thousands of ordinary home mortgage payments, and sold them to investors seeking the income, chiefly under the auspices of the Government National Mortgage Association (Ginnie Mae), a quasi-governmental agency at the time, and the Federal National Mortgage Association (Fannie Mae). Issuers fashioned bonds featuring a wide array of risks and returns when interest rates were still very high. Confident that risks were less than feared, and that receding interest rates would boost bond prices, Gross bought these securities in huge quantity and made out extremely well.

ALPHABET SOUP

Spawned in part by the junk bond revolution and mortgage-backed bonds, the bond business became an alphabet soup, as Wall Street invented new names for new ways to sell a bond's interest payments to one investor and the principal repayment to another. Derivatives, or fixed-income investments derived from underlying U.S. Treasury securities, credit card receivables, or other streams of income, took off as a way for issuers to hedge interest rate risks and for investors to boost interest income. Practically unheard of in 1985, a decade later derivatives ballooned into an enormous market driven by investors' hunger for income improvement and cash flows with special characteristics.

U.S. Treasury bonds that paid no interest or principal payments (until maturity) became popular. These bonds eventually paid patient investors relatively high rates of interest and earned a moniker that stuck: zero coupons. Huge demand for these bonds fostered a brisk secondary market where zero coupons are bought and sold every day. Encouraged by the voracious appetite of investors for bonds of all kinds, cash-strapped companies in the late 1980s started issuing "payment-in-kind" bonds (PIKs); investors received interest in the form of additional bonds. Still other bonds bore unfathomable acronyms. New species of bonds were often convertible, redeemable, exchangeable, and subordinated. New names like LYONS (liquid yield option notes), STRYPES (structured yield product exchangeable for stock), PRIDES (preferred redeemable increased dividend equity), and FE-LINEs (flexible equity linked exchangeables) emerged.

When Wall Street cooked up a way to sell bonds based on prices at a future date, Gross embraced the new futures market with zest. PIMCO even distributed T-shirts that read "Buy Futures." Competitors faltered during the bond market's vicissitudes, but not Gross. He thrived. His philosophy: Always trade. According to observers, he always wanted something from the bond store. He was always shopping and always enthusiastic.

Despite the wild profusion of bonds, Gross insists that the domestic fixed-income market "really isn't that mysterious." For tax paying investors within the United States, the market boils down to three main components, and bonds from borrowers in other countries comprise a fourth category:

1. *Government bonds.* Every time a government or federal agency finances a multi-billion shortfall, companies like PIMCO compete to buy the bonds. The much-publicized federal deficit supplies most of the bonds that PIMCO buys.

2. *Corporate bonds.* When corporations decide to borrow money to build a new factory or buy another company, they issue corporate bonds. Unlike the U.S. Government, which can print money to pay its bills, corporations are not exempt from bankruptcy risk.

3. *Home mortgages.* In effect, these are bonds issued by homeowners. A single home mortgage cannot attract much attention, but bundled together, a few thousand mortgages add up to serious investments. Thanks to the government agencies that figured out how to "securitize" millions of mortgages, investors found a new way to put savings to work.

4. *Bonds from issuers outside the United States.* These represent an increasingly large share of PIMCO's portfolio. One component of this market, bonds issued by companies in emerging markets, chalked up higher returns in 1996 than the red-hot U.S. stock market.

The new species of bonds created fresh risks as well as opportunities. In such a melee, even professionals lost sight of proper tradeoffs. A top-notch bond manager, according to Bill Gross, must now be one-third economist, who knows—or thinks he or she knows—when interest rates are going up or down; one-third mathematician, because bonds are mathematical creatures; and one-third horse trader, because there is a buyer and a seller in every transaction, and there are always people at the other end of the telephone line who want to take your money.

BOARDING-HOUSE REACH

The worst mistake investors make nowadays, Gross warns, is overreaching for yield. That's always a pitfall. Like bears who find honey, he says, investors reach for the goods without sufficient attention to the dangers. Yield-hungry investors have only to consider financial fiascoes like the Washington State Public Power Authority bankruptcy (WPPS, but known as "Whoops") in 1982, Orange County's catastrophic flirtation with leverage and derivatives in 1995, and the failures of numerous companies that seemed like sound investments at the time. "My business is to inject enough risk in order to provide attractive returns to clients," Gross says, "but not that much risk that they'll have to sell the farm. Perhaps the outhouse, but never the farm."

Gross measures success on total return, not on yield alone. Total return weighs price changes along with yield. He is extremely wary of yield-driven derivatives when credit quality is less than pristine. "We don't use what they call 'kitchen sink' derivatives, the bottom-of-the-barrel type of derivatives. We basically employ longer-term strategies, conservative strategies that seek to outperform the market over time. That's been our secret."

Gross avoids leveraged bond investments, where investors supply a small portion of an investment and borrow the rest. If everything goes right, the returns can be handsome; but if the market goes against you, a wipeout is possible. That's a harsh lesson he learned early in his career. In 1968, he borrowed $45,000 to buy $50,000 worth of bonds, in the expectation that interest rates were headed down and prices up. Had it worked out, he'd have doubled his money. Instead, interest rates went up, prices fell, and Gross saw his $5,000 stake evaporate in less than a month. The stakes are higher now; a misguided investment could gobble up $50 million in an instant.

In such waters, Gross steers PIMCO toward a modest-sounding objective: beating key bond-market benchmarks by one percentage point, year after year. Actually, that's a home run in the bond business. A one-percentage-point advantage over 10 to 15 years, Gross observes, produces total returns in the range of 15 to 20 percent more than the competition. For an institution the size of PIMCO, beating the market by 20 percent over the next ten years—a performance comparable to PIMCO's returns from 1986 to 1996—would fetch billions of dollars for investors, over and above tough competition.

THE WORLD ACCORDING TO GROSS

Monthly newsletters to PIMCO's customers describe Gross's view of factors that drive bond markets. In November 1996, he wrote:

> There are all sorts of rules in the bond market, a few of which are as follows: (1) watch out for economic growth, (2) beware of inflation, and (3) keep an eye on foreign investors. It's that latter commandment that has caused a stir lately, at least among the financial press, and it's a topic that usually produces a rush of adrenaline through my veins. . . . The current argument goes that the stability of US interest rates at these presumably low levels has been aided significantly by the buying of Treasury securities by foreign investors. Not only do foreigners own 30 percent of all US Government debt outstanding, but during the past two years, they have funded nearly 100 percent of the federal government's deficit. "Where would we be without them?" the skeptics ask, and the implied answer is probably somewhere between 7–8 percent yields on the long [30-year US Treasury] bond. Could this be so? Do our interest rates depend only on the kindness of strangers?
>
> I think not. They depend more on our own domestic resolve, and I'd like to show you why. The fact is that our annual budget deficit is really a mirror image of our trade deficit (at least in the United States) and the latter plays the perpetual role of funding much of the former. The simplified explanation reads as follows: Trade deficit pays for budget deficit. This is primarily so because foreigners almost *have* to invest in US Treasuries. Every day, every month, every year [that] the US consumers buy more than our corporations sell to foreign countries, there are dollars that necessarily have to be reinvested in our money markets. Our trade deficit, in other words, must necessarily come back home like salmon swimming upstream to spawn, and these surplus dollars almost invariably take the form of purchases of Treasury Bills or Bonds.[1]

In his newsletters, Gross also reveals another, more introspective side of himself. He is apt to muse about books and movies, or men and women, as to predict which way inflation is heading. In May 1996, when filmgoers were flocking to *Twister,* a disaster movie with a plot centering on tornado chasers, Gross wrote:

> This whole business of meteorology and tornado chasing . . . is a strange phenomenon to me. My personal experience with a cold front clashing with a warm front is distinctly different from what you may have seen at the movies. It typically occurs on a cold February evening when I crawl into bed 15 minutes after my wife. My frigid toes' touching her toasty ones produces more thunder and lightning than anything the Midwestern plains have ever experienced. After the screams die down and relative calm is restored, she'll reiterate for the umpteenth time that nowhere in her wedding vows did she promise to serve as a human heating pad. It's at this point when I know I'll never figure out meteorology—or women, for that matter.[2]

Such personal observations often connect to topics investors expect Bill Gross to explore. In this case, it was funnel clouds on the bond horizon following a sharp fall in prices during the preceding Spring. Gross forecast blue skies ahead, however, and it turned out he was right.

NO SUBSTITUTE FOR DISCIPLINE

Sometimes, however, Bill Gross just wants to speak his mind. Often, he stresses the need for discipline—a hallmark of his personality and his investment style. A passage in his April 1996 newsletter displayed, in visceral terms, his aversion to people who cannot control their appetites—a reaction to the untimely death of baseball umpire John McSherry during the Opening Day game in Cincinnati. Gross contrasted the tragedy with Franz Kafka's "A Hunger Artist," a tale about a professional faster, and then commented:

> Well, well—one man who couldn't stop and another one who couldn't start—eating, that is. Their stories, though, are really not about food, but [about] life itself—what compels us to do what we do, what forces us to act or not to act, what makes us who we are. Is personal behavior, though, really beyond our control? Shakespeare would retort that the fault lies not in our stars, but in ourselves, and I applaud that—strong-willed 175-pound guy that I am. But, on the other hand, who are we other than the amorphous, gelatinous blob of moving flesh and

bone that's been molded primarily without our input, first by genes, and then by environment into the living person we know as ourselves? Are we all just walking Cuisinarts, or, better yet, mobile computers with a consciousness? *TIME* magazine in [a] cover story in March [1996] asked, "Can machines think?" and if they can, it might well have asked the corollary, "Are people machines?" The fact is that sophisticated modern machines can do just about anything a human being can do. Several months ago, one of them even defeated the grandmaster of chess in a best-of-seven match. *TIME* suggested that the difference between "us" and "them" was a human being's consciousness. We are "aware" whereas they are not. But even if that is true, to me it's not enough. Who wants to be a machine that simply knows it's a machine? Who wants to walk the Earth as a preprogrammed robot with no input as to his final fate? To my mind, free will is the key to our unique position among life's animals. Without it, this business of living is reduced to a meaningless game. Unless the John McSherrys of the world can *stop* eating and the hunger artists can *start,* we might as well turn out the lights.[3]

For his part, Gross intends to live to be 100 years old. "I turned 50 a year ago," he said in 1995, "and at that point I determined I wanted to double it." He jogs, bicycles, never eats more than half a sandwich for lunch. "I've been jogging for 20 years," he says, "and it's not something I enjoy but something I take the time to do—from 12 noon to 1:00—in order to ensure that (1) I'm healthy and can keep up with my family and (2) I can continue to manage money for as long as I like to. Too often, people with poor health have to resign or simply die. I'd like to stick around for the next 30 or 40 years and see how this bond market turns out in the 21st century."

Gross is a creature of habit, according to his wife, Sue. He eats the same breakfast Monday through Friday, never deviating: raisin bran, bananas, juice, and coffee. He never drinks a beer before 6:00 P.M., and then he'll have two. "But at 5:59 we don't have beer," she says. He exercises every day to keep the stress under control.

RACE TO THE FINISH

Discipline comes naturally to Gross. He claims he fasted for four straight months when he was 16 years old, to slip below maximum weight limits for a high school "B"-level basketball squad. Thin to start, at 5' 10" and

139 pounds, he wound up weighing in at a "skeletal" 109 pounds. This was not anorexia, he insists, but "brainless willpower." He displayed similar resolve more recently, when he ran the equivalent of six marathons in six days. "Breath upon breath, stride after stride, it all turned into an apparently inexplicable journey of self-abuse, culminating with the hemorrhaging of my kidneys on the last two miles," was how he described it. "Brainless willpower Part II, but not masochism. My objective was to run from the Golden Gate Bridge, 150 miles down the coast to Carmel in six days, and I made it by 'just saying no' to the pain."

Long-term success in the bond market requires unbending discipline also, but the pain, though often in evidence, is less visceral. "Discipline suggests following through with a long-term philosophy. Not that you don't change or bend. Discipline means not caving in to psychological whims of the moment that can force an investor to either sell at the bottom or buy at the top."

Every second requires discipline. Each time the Federal Reserve adjusts the interest rates it charges its borrowers—chiefly banks—bond prices fluctuate. Usually the range is far less than 1 percentage point. In extreme circumstances though, bond prices can gain or lose 3 percent in a day, according to Gross. That's equivalent to a 200-point move when the Dow Jones Industrial Average was 6,500.

UNEASY MOMENTS

A couple of occasions have rattled Gross, one for a few days and another for the better part of a year. When the stock market crashed in October 1987, Gross lost focus. "I was mesmerized by the tape," he recalls, "transfixed by the action of the stock market. So much so that I failed to realize that a crash of that magnitude would foster a wonderful environment for bonds." He overlooked at first the very likely prospect of the Fed's coming to the market's rescue with bags of cash. "The next day, the bond market rallied, but for one day I was anesthetized by the tape and lost my perspective."

More recently, Gross suffered doubts during the prolonged bear market of 1994, the worst bond market in 70 years, when interest rates on the 30-year bond climbed from 6 percent to 8 percent over twelve months, causing the price of those bonds to fall by 25 percent. It was a year-long jolt, Gross says, a sobering experience. "I would wake up at three or four in the morning asking what would go wrong the next day, and it almost assuredly did." Though challenged, he did not abandon his bullish conviction that yields would recede and prices would come back. He kept PIMCO on that course, and the market ultimately vindicated him.

His confidence stems in part from a reading of demographic trends. "You know if, as an investor, I had to know one thing—if I was sequestered on a jury for the next twelve months and couldn't read anything else—I'd want to know about demographics. I'd want to know how many households are going to be formed in the next twelve to twenty-four months, what the demand for housing was going to be, what the pressure on the labor market was going to be from new job entrants. All those combine in terms of influencing inflation and influencing fiscal and monetary deficits and influencing supply and demand and, in turn, influencing the bond market as well."

A NOTE ON CREDIT QUALITY

Two factors govern a bond's sensitivity to interest rates: (1) credit quality and (2) maturity. Credit quality is a measure of the borrower's capacity to pay investors on time. Maturity governs how long investors must wait to get their money back.

Today, the U.S. Government is the world's most reliable borrower. The full faith and credit of the U.S. Government bestows risk-free status on the bonds it issues. (Pessimists note, however, that the safest bonds in the world 100 years ago were issued by the Habsburg Empire.) If all else fails, Uncle Sam can print money, ensuring timely payment of interest and principal. But risk-free status extends only to the risk of default. Investors with long-term Treasury securities, like any bondholders, suffer the inroads of inflation when prevailing interest rates outstrip the yields they are receiving, causing bond prices to fall. Only short-term Treasury bills, maturing in less than a year, are safe from inflation risk, simply because investors will recoup their full investment within 12 months.

In the corporate world, "investment grade" bonds issued, for example, by General Electric have excellent credit quality, but they're not risk-free. GE builds jet engines and refrigerators, but it cannot operate for long at a loss, nor can it print money to stave off default.

A bond's maturity governs volatility. Short-term bonds mature in one year or less. Short-term bonds issued by the U.S. Government are called *bills.* Treasury *notes* mature in 1 to 6 years, *bonds* in seven years or more. Bonds maturing in 20 or 30 years are not uncommon, and in the recent past a handful of corporations have issued bonds maturing in 100 years. Perpetual bonds—with their roots in Holland—also appear from time to time. Needless to say, they suffer more than shorter term bonds when inflation begins to appear. Ordinarily, however, market yields slope upward more gradually as maturities lengthen. The impact of inflation is less pronounced between bonds with 15-year and 30-year maturities than between bonds maturing in less than 10 years.

HUGGING THE YIELD CURVE

For bonds of a given credit quality, investors can identify the market yields at various maturities. The exercise isn't different from plotting points on a graph, with time on the horizontal axis and interest rate yields on the vertical axis. Even though the graph shows yield for bonds that mature in, say, 20 years, it doesn't predict the future. It simply shows how much General Motors, or the U.S. Government, or any other borrower, must pay in the current market to borrow money for one year, three years, ten years, or twenty years. The result of plotting these points is a slope widely known as the *yield curve.*

The demand for bonds at various maturities shapes the yield curve, which normally slopes upward sharply in early years and more gradually afterward. When bond experts talk about "the yield curve," they're normally referring to the curve based on yields for risk-free Treasury securities.

Experts draw conclusions about the current state of the bond market from the yield curve. If the yield curve were a crystal ball, all economists would be billionaires. As a practical matter, an investor who has owned a bond that matures in five years (which at that point is effectively a five-year bond) can judge from the yield curve whether the initial rate of interest, or the "coupon," is above or below yields in the market for bonds of equivalent risk.

If the coupon says that the bond was issued with a yield lower than the going yield, then the investor should expect to sell the bond for less than bond's face value, or par value. If the coupon says that the bond was issued with a yield higher than the going yield, the investor can expect to sell the bond for more than its face value. When such a self-adjusting mechanism prevails, and computer-aided traders can spot inefficiencies in seconds, bonds these days do not stay mispriced for long.

Bonds almost always trade at premiums or discounts to *par value*—the amount equal to the face value of a bond, which is usually $1,000. Prices are quoted in relation to 100 percent of par value. A price of 102 reported in newspaper bond columns means the bond's price is 2 percent above par or $1,020. A price of 98 means the price is 2 percent below par or $980.

MIDDLE OF THE ROAD

PIMCO has been successful, Gross reports, by staying close to the middle of the market—the region of the yield curve with maturities usually ranging from three years to seven years. Bonds in this intermediate range provide total returns comparable to bonds that mature in ten or fifteen years, without entailing as much risk.

When inflation appears to be on the rise, PIMCO shortens maturities to limit possible price deterioration. When interest rates are high and appear to be on the verge of descending, PIMCO extends maturities in a portion of the portfolio, to capture long-term rates and increase exposure to potential price improvements.

Because bond prices adjust instantly to every sign of inflation, bargains are extremely rare and are seldom dramatic. Unlike the stock market, where prices of forgotten stocks can increase fivefold by the time investors wake up, the bond market is generally more efficient—with the noteworthy exception of bonds on the verge of default or bankruptcy. Bonds issued by companies that have become distressed often sell for prices well below values that can be realized in bankruptcy settlements. On these, investors can chalk up equitylike gains. The same is true of bonds issued by nations when their economies are stumbling. In 1995, when Mexico was on the verge of default, Gross took a measured gamble on distressed Mexican government bonds, which were selling for a fraction of their face value. He concluded that the problem was not Mexico's inability to meet its debts, but the fact that so much of its debt was coming due at one time. By rescheduling debt payments, Mexico could restore its financial condition. As history has recorded, that's what happened, thanks to a big bailout from Uncle Sam. A year later, bonds that PIMCO had scooped up for 30 cents and 40 cents on the dollar fetched twice as much. The same sort of bargain can be had in the corporate bond market when investors overreact to bad news.

BEAT THE DEALER

Gross declares that five months of playing blackjack for seventeen hours a day taught him the skills and discipline needed to succeed in the bond business. "The biggest link between Middletown, Ohio, and Butler Creek and what I do now occurred in Las Vegas, after I was graduated from Duke." He credits Edwin Thorpe, the author of *Beat the Dealer,* with introducing him to diversification. "I was investing, as opposed to gambling," he says, "because there are times in blackjack when the odds favor the player. Those are the times when you want to bet a lot of money, but not so much that you ruin your chances if you lose. What I learned there, on the table, was that you have to diversify." He adhered to the principle of "Gambler's ruin": Never bet more than one-fiftieth of your stake, so a losing streak won't wipe you out.

Important differences exist between blackjack and the bond market. Not least, there are only 52 cards in a deck and every card that is visible affects the likelihood of another turning up, if you can keep count. That's a far cry from the bond market, where a single move up or down, or even a pattern, conveys no information about subsequent moves. But Blackjack, Gross insists, taught him to exercise patience and to employ money on a constant and consistent basis. At times, he'd leave the table to escape a run of bad luck. "But what I didn't realize," he says, "was that based upon the [card counting] methodology I was using, it was to my advantage to be at the table all the time."

In five months, Gross claims, he turned a $200 stake into $10,000. The payoff was not as spectacular as it sounds. Considering all the time spent at the tables, he figures he earned $3 an hour, or about the minimum wage at the time. But he says he was never in it for the money. "To me, it was a goal to be conquered, as opposed to an end in itself." Lessons for PIMCO are in evidence daily. "Playing blackjack in 1966 was a question of using a methodology or philosophy over a long term. Counting cards as an attempt to put the odds in my favor. The same thing happens in the bond market today. By playing long enough and looking at it on a long-term basis, we've put the probabilities in our favor."

At a blackjack table or in the bond market, a long-term objective must precede single trades or sweeping strategies. Good bond management or good investment management, Gross says, is a long-term race. It's a marathon, not a sprint.

Gross has not returned to blackjack. These days, he visits Las Vegas because his wife's family lives there; the closest he has been to the tables recently was while watching animal tamers Sigfried and Roy. Trading bonds supplies both the satisfaction and the fun he gleaned from betting on playing cards.

"It's a game," Gross says of bond trading. "Every day you wake up and it's a different story. It's a different set of circumstances and a different set of facts to sift and focus on. But when you really get down to it, it's the game playing of the markets, the fact of winning or losing and the reinitiation of the battle every morning. It's so exciting and keeps me young. It's kept me going for twenty years and hopefully will keep me going for twenty more. It's just fascinating work."

7

Asset Allocation

NINETY PERCENT OF THE GAME

The world's top investment managers typically make money in only two ways. They put their chips either on individual securities or on whole classes of assets. Guess: Which way produces the vast majority of investment gains, year in and year out?

Hint: High flyers and market timing explain only a small fraction of long-term investment performance.

Do not confuse the task of finding individual stocks and bonds with the separate task of deciding which asset categories are the most desirable. It matters far more to investment returns whether money is invested in, say, baskets of U.S. Treasury securities, German stocks, Japanese real estate, or emerging market debt—rather than in a single five-year Treasury note, a lens maker in Düsseldorf, an office building in Yokohama, or a high-interest loan to a low-cost cotton grower in Nigeria, no matter how promising such individual investments appear.

And here's the big payoff: By exploiting differences in the ways asset classes fluctuate, asset allocation defies the law of gravity that normally contrains investment performance. Forget the usual tradeoff that links higher returns to greater risk. Global asset allocation models focus on aggregate portfolio risk, rather than on the riskiness of individual components. A sound allocation combines diverse asset classes in ways that boost

returns without an equal increase in risk—or reduce risk without sacrificing returns.

CLASS DISTINCTIONS

"Investment decisions should focus first and foremost on markets or asset
classes. Over time, that's going to explain roughly 90 percent of investment returns," declares Gary Brinson, the CEO of Brinson Partners, in
Chicago. Brinson Partners, a U.S. unit of Swiss Bank Corporation,
manages $120 billion for a blue-chip roster of institutional investors who
seek optimal returns across a global gamut of asset classes. It's a bold assertion not universally accepted by asset allocators who insist that an investor's choice of asset classes accounts for much less than Brinson's
calculation. But even his sharpest critics concede that investors who ignore differences among asset classes cripple their long-term investment
performance.

A planet brimming with asset categories yields innumerable combinations of assets, each bearing its own risks and rewards. All told, some $43
trillion of investable assets comprise a gigantic banquet table, with dishes
ranging from low-risk, low-return bonds issued by the United States Treasury, to high-return, high-risk private equity issued by fledgling companies making one product in remote parts of the world. In terms of
markets, asset allocators understand that the choices and sizes of portions
matter far more to investment results than do the particular ingredients in
each dish.

THE WHOLE GAME

Growing ranks of global asset allocators select the safest mix of possibilities, subject to a client's required returns and appetite for risk. Because of
his pioneering role in understanding, articulating, and applying this investment style, beginning in the late 1970s, Brinson was named, in 1995,
"The Father of Global Asset Allocation" by *Fortune* Magazine.[1] Other
prominent voices have joined the chorus. To heavy-hitting investment
strategist Barton Biggs, of Morgan Stanley, choosing asset classes takes a
front seat. "For big money," Biggs told *The Business Times* in February
1996, "stock picking is irrelevant. Asset allocation is the whole game."[2] As
retirement portfolios grow, as mutual funds proliferate, and as informa-

tion about remote markets becomes accessible, global asset allocation is fast becoming critical to all investors.

SKYWARD BOUND

Brinson, the future father of global asset allocation, entered college in 1966 with no interest in, much less exposure to, securities markets. "I was going to be an aeronautical engineer," says Brinson, the son of a Seattle bus driver, "because I grew up in the Pacific Northwest and Boeing was there."

By his junior year at Seattle University, his plans had changed. For reasons he can't pinpoint, Brinson became intrigued with financial markets. "Some food appeals to you and other foods don't. The more I was exposed to them, the more I became interested in trying to puzzle through what makes markets work."

His first investment, ten shares of Eastern Airlines, emptied his pockets of nearly all that was left after paying tuition with the wages he had earned from an Italian sausage factory. It also reflected Brinson's instinct for seeing business developments according to a market perspective. In the mid-1960s, prop jets were on the way out and jets were on the way in. "You had this whole new era that was going to develop," Brinson recalls. He made a few bucks in the end—not a whole lot, but, more important, the outcome fanned confidence in his grasp of financial markets.

Initially, the academic world suited his interest in unraveling the puzzle of securities markets. Master's degree in hand, he was teaching finance at Washington State University and preparing to enter the PhD program at Stanford University when an offer from The Travelers Insurance Co. distracted him. He put Stanford on ice and, in 1970, headed for the real world in search of practical experience at a multiple-line insurance company that had a growing investment management business.

NEW THEORIES TO THE TEST

At Travelers, Brinson flourished in a setting where the reality of financial markets put new theories of financial markets to the test. "I certainly found myself much more engrossed in that and decided that maybe the best path for me was in the real world," says Brinson.

In those days, investors were getting a first taste of modern portfolio theory, a powerful tool for measuring and controlling investment risk. It wasn't easy to swallow. Modern portfolio theory—MPT for short—was a new and strange language to most investors. Brinson, already fluent in MPT, was well equipped to provide translation, and, at Travelers, a group of unorthodox managers welcomed new ideas.

"The evolution of modern portfolio theory gave us more quantitative tools to understand the risk characteristics of a portfolio," says Elliot Williams, who had joined Travelers' investment operation a couple of years before Brinson. "That fed right into Gary's understanding of markets and the investment tools he needed."

Instead of independent portfolio managers commanding cadres of securities analysts, authority at Travelers rested with sector managers who routinely collaborated on all portfolios. "Gary was attracted to that," says Williams, "because as much as anybody I know, he understood the distinctiveness of different disciplines that may be needed in the investment process."

EARLY BLUEPRINT

Along the way to becoming head of portfolio construction at Travelers, Brinson made his mark quickly. "It was early on," says Williams, "that he had a vision even for Travelers that astounded me. But it's exactly what he built at First Chicago and Brinson Partners." The blueprint sounds simple enough: Create an organization with skill sets in each asset class, then look to the people within those asset classes to figure out where to find exceptional returns—what experts call "alpha."

Consistent with this outlook, Travelers became one of the first customers of the risk-analysis tools developed by Barr Rosenberg, whose quantitative approach to investing is the subject of Chapter 3.

Brinson's notions about asset allocation did not develop all at once. Travelers at the time had no meaningful exposure to markets outside the United States. But adverse market developments in 1974—to cite one instance—bolstered Brinson's conviction that the prevailing means of diversification fell short. He watched a portfolio of very solid, small, and intermediate-size companies take a beating over a period of nine or ten months. The experience underscored the limits of diversification in a single asset class: Even companies that ultimately deliver expected financial performance can leave investors in the lurch for extended stretches of time. When that happens, Brinson observes, "nine or ten months can seem like a lifetime." Meanwhile, Travelers made him president of its portfolio management operation.

THOROUGHLY GLOBAL GARY

Brinson says that his current approach to asset allocation began to gel in the late 1970s, when investment ideas centered on the best stock and bond portfolios. "Just by casual observation you could see two things," Brinson says. "A lot of U.S. companies were doing business around the world and a lot of companies around the world were doing business in the U.S. I got to thinking, well, why should we think about the U.S. stock market or the U.S. bond market as being the portfolio or the market definition? Why not think about the market as one big, thoroughly global phenomenon?"

Drawn by the prospects of running his own investment shop on these global principles, Brinson left Travelers in 1981. He launched First Chicago Investment Advisors, the forerunner of Brinson Partners, under the aegis of First Chicago Corporation, a large commercial bank. But his first efforts to peddle global asset allocation under the new banner met mainly with yawns. At the firm's first seminar on the virtues of asset allocation, Brinson and his colleagues outnumbered the audience. But Brinson, whose tenacity is famous, never wavered. He kept sounding the alarm while investment managers gradually awoke from their slumber to a global marketplace they could not afford to ignore.

A LITTLE COMMON SENSE

Long before Nobel Prize-winning economists explained diversification in mathematical terms and applied it to investing, folk wisdom expressed the danger of too many eggs in one basket. Astute farmers coped with risk by growing more than one crop—in case prices for one collapsed. Likewise, wary merchant shipowners, concerned about the variability that was endemic to sea travel in wooden sailing ships, dispatched goods in more than one vessel to more than one port. In his book, *Against The Gods: The Remarkable Story of Risk,*[3] Peter Bernstein reminds readers that William Shakespeare's Merchant of Venice entertained a healthy respect for risk:

My ventures are not in one bottom trusted,
Nor to one place; nor is my whole estate
Upon the fortune of this present year;
Therefore, my merchandise makes me not sad.[4]

Building and preparing a merchant sailing ship crudely prefigured modern investment management. Architects designed ships to make the most of favorable and unfavorable winds that alternated without warning. At sea, captains kept the sails trim and monitored the course, making adjustments when the seas or winds changed. Icebergs, squalls, rocks loomed. Every mariner knew that the sturdiest craft faced perilous conditions amid forty-foot waves. Short of a calamity, the ship might reach port only to find that the price of its cargo had collapsed or the price of goods sought had skyrocketed, wiping out expected profits. Information traveled only as fast as ships under sail. In the time it took to sail from Genoa to Amsterdam in 1637, at the height of Holland's manic infatuation with tulip bulbs, the price of the most precious bulbs doubled in price—or lost half their value just as fast. So much for putting too many bulbs in one basket.

MISSING THE BOAT TO DIVERSIFICATION

As it turns out, the Merchant of Venice—like many investors today—missed the boat on diversification. "It's a fallacy to believe, and many people believe it," Professor Paul Samuelson observes, "that if you add more and more ships, that itself reduces the variability. Actually, four ships [instead of two] doubles the variability." The analogy to investing is clear. "If I double the number of stocks in my portfolio and I want to reduce my variability, my riskiness," Samuelson warns, "I don't want those stocks all to be alike."

The Great Crash should have silenced critics of diversification. But prominent investors continued to argue for concentrating assets where they were likely to spawn the highest returns. The well-known investor Gerald Loeb railed against diversification in 1935, when Black Monday 1929 and the Dow Jones Industrials' ensuing 90 percent decline to 41, in July 1932, were still fresh memories. "Once you obtain confidence, diversification is undesirable," Loeb declared. "[Diversification] is an admission of not knowing what to do in an effort to strike the average."[5]

In all fairness to Loeb, investors in the 1930s had far fewer investment options to choose from than their counterparts today. Stocks and bonds constituted most of the securities available to individual investors. But as the investment spectrum widens, investors who restrict themselves to the same asset classes that existed sixty years ago forgo returns and expose assets to needless risk. Following Loeb's advice is riskier today than ever before.

"It is very important to think about one's portfolio as a mix of assets, and the more robust that mix of assets can be, the historical evidence suggests that the better the investor is going to do," Brinson says. "Now, obviously, somebody can win with a lottery ticket. Somebody can bet on a single stock and have a big victory. But if we look at investment circumstances, what we'll find is that a diversified portfolio, a mix of assets, is [an essential ingredient]."

BAD NEWS FOR STOCK PICKERS AND MARKET TIMERS

In the post-World War II era, Harry Markowitz, Bill Sharpe, and other academic pioneers first described how diversification affects investment risks and returns. They supplied the foundation on which asset allocation is built. Credit for showing exactly how global asset allocation ultimately governs investment performance, however, belongs chiefly to Brinson and two coauthors, L. Randolph Hood and Gilbert Beebower. Their study, published in July 1986 in the *Financial Analysts Journal,* tallied investment results chalked up by 91 large U.S. pension plans from 1974 through 1983.[6]

Couched in the methodical language of a doctoral thesis, "Determinants of Portfolio Performance" distinguished investment strategy (picking individual stocks and bonds) from asset allocation (picking whole asset categories). The conclusion lobbed a hand grenade into a community that loves stock pickers and market timers. "Although investment strategy can result in significant returns," the authors observed, "these are dwarfed by the return contribution from investment policy—the selection of asset classes and their normal weights."

Five years after the first article cast a new light on investing, Brinson, Beebower, and Brian Singer confirmed that picking individual stocks and market-timing decisions add only marginal gains to investment results. At eighty-two large pension funds from 1977 through 1987, asset allocations supplied the lion's share of returns.[7] This research earned the trio of authors the coveted Graham and Dodd Scroll award in 1991.

FOUR SIMPLE PRINCIPLES

Academics typically mull evidence for years without advancing the cause of investors, and money managers dismiss academics' conclusions as ivory-tower nonsense. Brinson's ability to straddle both worlds is exceptional. He can grasp an abstract theory *and* put it to work to reshape practical investment solutions. The upshot is a global asset allocation strategy resting on four basic principles:

1. Think globally.
2. The value of asset classes should not rise and fall together.
3. Focus on the long term.
4. Monitor and adjust allocations to accommodate changed investment climates.

THINK GLOBALLY

For a glimpse of the world as Brinson sees it, investors should study a map of the globe that looks very different from the famous Mercator projection published by *National Geographic*. The asset allocation world is represented by a patchwork of more or less rectangular shapes, showing the stages of economic development and the sizes of capital markets. On this computer generated map, Russia and China together amounted only to about one-third the size of Japan in 1992.[8] Japan and Western Europe, with highly developed markets, were about equal in size, and the United Kingdom looked bigger than all of South America. At the same time, the map opened an investor's eyes to thriving capital markets in nations like Singapore, Brazil, Spain, Norway, Chile, Australia, Malaysia, and South Africa, and to fledgling markets like Indonesia, Greece, Turkey, Trinidad, Jordan, and Zimbabwe.

Each country features a distinctive population, economy, currency, regulatory structure, and natural resources, and, consequently, an investment climate that poses unique combinations of risks and rewards. Stock exchanges abound in most industrialized countries, and they are sprouting up in many third-world countries as well. In the United States, shares of stock worth trillions of dollars change hands annually, principally on the New York Stock Exchange, NASDAQ, and more than a dozen regional stock exchanges. In Europe, more than 40 stock exchanges handled a growing number of shares. Former Soviet bloc countries, where capitalism flourished briefly prior to communism, have awakened capital markets after several

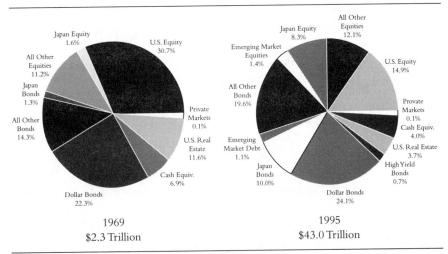

Figure 7.1 The Big Banquet 1969 vs. 1995. (*Source:* Brinson Partners, Inc.)

dormant decades. Latin America has its share of stock exchanges in Brazil, Chile, and Mexico, for example. Tiny exchanges are emerging in countries like Botswana, where a handful of stocks are listed today.

Vast economic changes have enlarged the world's investment opportunities almost twenty-fold since 1969. In the year Richard Nixon was inaugurated U.S. president the first time, all the stocks, bonds, and non-residential real estate in the world—i.e., the world's total investable assets—comprised a $2.3 trillion investment portfolio dominated by the United States (Figure 7.1).

In 1995, the world's investment portfolio looked very different, and the United States had a much less commanding role. Not that the United States is a has-been, by any stretch of the imagination; the market value of our slice of the pie grew 646 percent in 26 years, to $12.9 trillion. No country or region of the world matches North American industrial output today. But growth of the global marketplace is also way up after growing at a faster clip than the United States in recent decades, often by significant margins. As a result, 30 percent of the world's equity capital resided in the United States in 1990, according to Brinson and Roger Ibbotson, coauthors of *Global Investing: The Professional's Guide to the World Capital Markets.*[9] Their observation marks a 180-degree reversal. In 1960, only 30 percent of the world's equity capital resided outside the United States.

The United States represented less than one-third of the world's investment pie in 1995, versus three-fourths of it in 1969. But far from reading such developments as signs that the United States has been eclipsed, asset allocators contend that investment opportunities have multiplied. Thanks to advances in technology and the opening up of capital markets to foreigners, an investor in Dubuque is as close to investment action in Singapore as are most Singaporeans.

Self-Defeating Poppycock

In this robust global investment environment, the investment spectrum is limited only by an investor's required rate of return and appetite for risk. However, the news may be more than some investors think they can take; putting hard-earned dollars to work in places that seem so remote sounds like more risk than run-of-the-mill risk aversion can bear. To Brinson, this conventional assessment is not only poppycock, it is self-defeating for the risk-averse investor. Ignoring global asset allocation hampers investment performance by investors with access to mutual funds and exposes them to the market catastrophes they fear most.

With investment horizons so plentiful, Brinson warns, it is wrong to settle for a few stocks in unrelated industries and a few investment-grade bonds thrown in as life preservers. It is even wrong to assume that U.S. multinational companies like Coca-Cola, which rings up 80 percent of its revenues elsewhere in the world, substitute for more direct participation in the global economy. "If you just stop there and omit important companies that operate in other parts of the globe," Brinson advises, "you'll wind up with a portfolio that is too limited."

To Brinson, simple logic dictates a global course. He lives in Chicago, which supplies a vantage point on global markets equal to the view from anywhere consumers drive cars, watch television, and wear clothes imported from abroad. "You look at a city like Chicago," says Brinson, "and it has a great deal to offer in terms of local companies and industries and investments. But if we look around, we also find that people are participating in the global economy."

Global Village

Why shouldn't consumers of goods produced around the globe become consumers of global securities? Indeed they should, insists Brinson, whose Native American roots run deep (he is the great-grandson of a Cherokee Indian). "For people to say just because I'm a resident of the United States that I'm going to restrict my investments to the United

States is terribly myopic, and numerous studies have shown that it really [curtails] investment opportunities. The more one thinks about global investment opportunities, the greater the chances of success."

A few square blocks in downtown Chicago show Brinson how the most powerful and most fragile economies are linked. Chicagoans, like fellow Americans from San Juan to Anchorage, drive cars made in Germany, using fuel pumped in Saudi Arabia. They watch TV programs emanating from England on TV sets manufactured in Japan, wear clothes made in Pakistan, and sip coffee from Kenya and hot chocolate from Switzerland. These products would not exist without a manufacturing base, and a vibrant manufacturing base relies on capital markets to finance global growth and expansion. As this process accelerates, so will demand for global asset allocation.

Dizzying Possibilities

Embracing the concept of asset allocation raises a thorny problem on the practical level. Where in the world do you start? Where do you end? A prolific array of choices spawns dizzying possibilities.

In theory, asset classes can be carved in dozens of ways to suit any preference. Commercial real estate is an asset class, residential real estate is another. These asset classes in turn consist of sub-classes. Commercial real estate can be divided into office towers or strip malls and residential real estate into apartment buildings and suburban tract houses, among other components. German stocks form one class, so do German bonds. Ditto for any country with capital markets big enough to produce reliable statistics. Stocks and bonds in fledgling economies form emerging markets. Countries issue sovereign bonds. So-called "Brady bonds" bailed U.S. banks out of disastrous loans to Latin American nations unable to repay their debts in the 1980s; they now form an asset class—and one of Brinson Partners' most lucrative investments. Capital markets in the United States are big enough to slice up several ways: large stocks, small stocks, high tech stocks, value stocks, and Treasury securities due in one year, five years, or twenty years, to name but a handful of asset categories. Add to this list bonds derived from residential mortgages, derivatives, futures, and options, depending on appetites for risk.

In practice, it pays to narrow the number of asset classes. "At any one point in time," Brinson explains, "we may be working with fifteen to twenty distinctly different asset classes or markets around the world." The Global Securities Portfolio, one of eleven institutional portfolios that Brinson Partners manages, held eight broad asset classes in December 1996:

1. **U.S. Equity**
2. **Non-U.S. Equities**
   - Japan Equity
   - All Other Equities
3. **Emerging Markets Equity**
4. **Dollar Bonds**
   - U.S. Bonds
   - International Dollar Bonds
5. **High-Yield Bonds**
6. **Non-U.S. Bonds**
   - Japan Bonds
   - All Other Bonds
7. **Emerging Markets Debt**
8. **Cash Equivalents**

Returns on Investment

Each broad asset class can be described by its historical levels of risks and returns, which ultimately direct asset allocation strategies.

Start with returns, a language most investors understand. Who hasn't chatted about a stock on the way up or a hot mutual fund? Simple returns express the percentage increase (or decrease) in a portfolio's value over time. ("My shares of Intel have gone up 25 percent so far this year.") Compound returns extend the concept somewhat, by expressing the annual return required to get from the beginning value to the ending value—taking into consideration that there is more money in the pot at the end of each year. ("Since I bought them five years ago, my shares of Intel have gone up by 22 percent a year.")

"It is instructive to look at the history of returns," Brinson observes, "not because history will repeat itself—it surely won't. But it is helpful to look at the history of returns to understand how characteristics can change. Because that nature of changing investment circumstances has always been with us and will always be with us."

Data compiled by Ibbotson & Associates provide annualized returns for most leading asset classes. The following five asset classes supply handy and familiar benchmarks to professional investors, who use them to judge the relative attractiveness of less familiar asset classes:

Type of Asset	Annual Returns 1926–1996
U.S. Treasury bills	3.7%
Intermediate-term Treasury notes	5.2
Long-term Treasury bonds	5.1
Large company stocks	10.7
Small company stocks	12.6

Source: Used with permission. © 1998 Ibbotson Associates, Inc. All rights reserved. (Certain portions of this work were derived from copyrighted works of Roger G. Ibbotson and Rex Sinquefeld.)

"Primarily, the asset allocation process is all about gaining a comprehensive understanding of these characteristics of these asset classes," Brinson says. "By *characteristics,* I don't mean what is going to happen tomorrow to U.S. real estate, versus what's going to happen tomorrow to interest rates in France."Instead, Brinson means the long-term investment performance characteristics that differentiate the German stock market from the Australian stock market, or the Russian bond market from the U.S real estate market. An asset allocater assembles those different asset classes together into one unified portfolio that attempts to maximize this relationship between return on the one hand, and minimizing risk on the other.

Risks on Investment

Hand-in-hand with return on investment goes risk on investment, a less congenial concept. Everyone relishes a fresh tip on a hot stock poised to gain 25 percent, but who drools over a market performer with half the risk of the S&P 500? It sounds like a rather dull way to nurture net assets. Risk in the absence of a measurable return sounds sexy if it entails mountain climbing or downhill skiing, but, in the stock market, risk is generally something most investors ignore. Asset allocation teaches a different lesson: investors can take risk to the bank. Over time, managing risk with care builds far more wealth than groping blindly for lofty returns.

Risk and Volatility.   Experts equate risk with volatility. An investment is more volatile or less volatile to the extent that its price jumps around. A handy way to measure volatility suffers from an imposing but now familiar name: standard deviation.

When encountering investment terminology that sounds sophisticated, always remember that Wall Street, as a wordsmith, is literal-minded and not very imaginative. As a practical matter, standard deviation merely describes the way actual price changes deviate from an imaginary line between the starting price and the ending price. When the stock price jumps around a lot, that's high standard deviation, or relatively high risk. When the stock price follows a fairly predictable, smooth path, that's low standard deviation, or relatively low risk. Think of standard deviation, perhaps, as the measure of a wayward teenager's tendency to stray from a straight and narrow path.

"The return dimension is relatively easy to handle because people are familiar with it," Brinson observes. "Where things sometimes get a little sticky is in the volatility." The easiest way to express risk to an average investor, Brinson finds, is to talk about how rough was the road on the way to the return. "So statistically there is a technique called standard deviation," says Brinson. "It just measures the degree of bumpiness in the road." If two returns are identical, a rational investor would prefer the road that is less bumpy.

Ordinarily, a blue-chip stock like Ford or Merck hits few potholes. Blue-chip status means a company has a smooth year-to-year record of substantial earnings and reliable growth. Because the price of a stock represents a claim on future earnings, the price of the stock should reflect the company's steady growth in earnings. But not always. Matters can get out of hand, and do.

Convinced in the early 1970s that some fifty blue-chip stocks would increase earnings forever at 20 percent a year, while the number of shares would remain limited, wide-eyed investors drove their valuations sky high. When earnings faltered, however, investors fled, ending the so-called Nifty Fifty phenomenon. The collapse of prices for the best stocks the New York Stock Exchange offered highlights the hazards that asset allocation, with a far wider array of investments, is designed to avoid.

Five Benchmarks for Serious Investors

Just like return on investment, standard deviation (a.k.a. risk on investment) is expressed as a percentage. It applies to U.S. stocks, Japanese stocks, Indonesian stocks, or any other stocks; it applies also to U.S. Treasury bonds or bonds issued by Zimbabwe or the Russian Republic, provided there is a sufficient series of historical data on the asset class if not on the individual security. Morningstar Inc. publishes standard deviations for most mutual funds. A new company going public doesn't have a sufficient track record to compute its standard deviation, but investors can compute the standard deviation for initial public offerings as an asset class. Most computer spreadsheets can calculate a standard deviation from a series of stock prices, but a history of fewer than five years may not produce a meaningful result and longer histories are preferable. In any event, standard deviations for major asset classes are widely available. These five categories supply professionals with valuable benchmarks, as shown by the accompanying table:

Type of Asset	Risk on Investment (Standard Deviation) 1926–1996
U.S. Treasury bills	3.3%
Intermediate-term Treasury notes	5.8
Long-term Treasury bonds	9.2
Large company stocks	20.3
Small company stocks	34.1

Checking unit prices in a supermarket enables grocery shoppers to learn the price of food per gram. In much the same fashion, investment shoppers can price the return they expect to take home per unit of risk. Instead of vague appreciation of the celebrated risk–reward continuum, asset allocators deduce precise values on which to base asset allocation decisions. Then it's up to an investor to decide, in an informed way, how much risk he or she can take.

With an understanding of risk and the ability to measure it, skilled asset allocators can survey investment horizons for asset classes likely to deliver juicier returns than alternatives with comparable risk. Positive excess returns are the brass rings of asset allocation; negative excess returns are to be avoided.

A Word to Remember

Increasingly, risk is becoming part of the average investor's vocabulary. "As financial advisers," says Nobel laureate William Sharpe, "our job is to make investors happy by taking into account both the return on the asset mix that we expect in the future and also the risk—*and how willing that investor is to bear risk in order to get a higher return.* That's basically the job of an asset allocator, whether it's a machine or a human being or a combination."

THE VALUE OF ASSET CLASSES SHOULD NOT RISE AND FALL TOGETHER

Asset allocation begins where asset classes interact. It's not just a matter of picking classes with optimal risk–reward profiles. It's also a matter of matching asset classes so that investors can reduce risk in portfolios without sacrificing returns, or boost returns without a commensurate increase in risk.

"While it may sound counterintuitive," Brinson says, "innumerable studies have shown that if you can combine those assets, each one of which might be volatile in and of itself, you wind up with a portfolio that is less volatile."

Financial Alchemy and Covariance

The key to this financial alchemy lies in one more concept that takes getting used to: covariance. It's actually nothing more than a way to measure the degree to which different asset classes behave relative to one another. Think of a mother duck and her ducklings. If the ducklings follow behind her in a straight line, that's high covariance. Ducklings who zig when siblings zag exhibit low covariance. And the duckling that goes south instead of north displays negative covariance.

In the financial world, this notion of covariance, particularly the notion of low covariance, becomes profoundly important. Finding investments with attractive returns but low covariance shows investors the best way to diversify portfolios with an eye to containing risk.

"Covariance is really just a fancy statistical term for diversification," Brinson explains, using diversification to capture the notion that volatility or risk endemic to one stock or asset class can offset the volatility of another. "Covariance really means the degree to which things move together. If something has a lot of covariance, then it means that it moves in the direction similar to other things."

Shares of large U.S. companies and small U.S. companies don't behave identically, but covariance is high. Investors have only to recall 1987 for evidence that both are vulnerable to a loss of confidence in the U.S. stock market.

Price changes in sovereign bonds issued by the U.S. and Australian governments display low covariance historically, the International Monetary Fund reports. When bond prices surge or collapse in the United States, Australian bonds show minimal correlation. Some classes mirror each other. When Switzerland's bond market goes up, for example, it's more than likely that bonds in Canada are going down. When inflation in the United States approached 20 percent in the late 1970s, fixed-income investments suffered mightily while real estate assets enjoyed the ride.

In financial markets, experts compute precise covariances for many asset classes. Using these data, they can determine how various mixes will affect the total portfolio. Take, for example, U.S. stocks and foreign stocks. Each class displayed characteristic risks and returns over the time period from 1969 through 1996, a 27-year stretch that includes both bull and bear markets. Foreign stocks, to no one's surprise, are considerably riskier.

Brinson's Comet

Because non-U.S. stocks march to the beats of different drummers, risk and return statistics differ. In that same 27-year stretch, 1969 through 1996, owning foreign stocks produced a heftier return than U.S. stocks, but with greater risk.

One might expect the blending effect to follow a more or less straight line from U.S. stocks to non-U.S. stocks. That's not what happens. Because of covariance, adding riskier foreign stocks to a domestic portfolio exerts an expected boost on returns, but the combined risk gets lower as risks of individual asset classes offset each other. Points showing progressive mixes of one stock or another follow a long, curved path that resembles a comet traveling around the sun. Experts can do the math, but an investor can see the startling result: returns increase while risk decreases. The lower the covariance, the sharper the curve (Figure 7.2).

Goldilocks and Global Risk

Every combination of two or more asset classes can form a curved line similar to the curve that blends stocks of U.S. companies and foreign companies. The curves illustrate maximum return at the various levels of risk that an investor is willing to assume. Investments above the curve have too much risk. Below the curve, the returns are too low. Goldilocks would say that the risk along the curve is not too hot and not too cold; it's just right.

Similar curves called the *efficient frontier* can describe the optimal blend of, say, U.S. and South African stocks, where covariance is minimal. They can also describe the returns investors can expect from bonds. Looking at the world's bond markets, Brinson says, people are typically surprised to learn the difference in returns between bonds issued in the United States

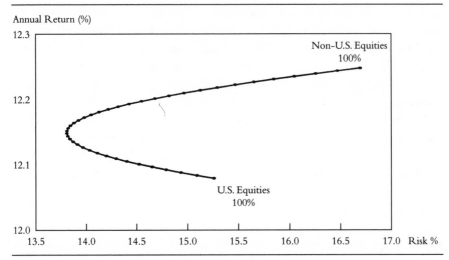

Annual Return (%)

Figure 7.2 Brinson's Comet. Effect of diversification. S&P 500 Index and MSCI non-U.S. equity index (in U.S. dollars). (*Source:* Brinson Partners, Inc.)

and bonds issued elsewhere. By starting with a strictly domestic bond port-folio and then changing it so the mix includes 15 percent non-U.S. bonds, Brinson can lower overall risk while bumping the annual return up by a half percentage point.

Asset allocation cannot erase individual risks, but it shifts them to a larger arena—the total portfolio—where they can be managed to an in-vestor's advantage. "Investors are faced inevitably with the tradeoff be-tween seeking higher return and lower risk," Brinson concedes. "And there is no way to escape that tradeoff. You can seek higher return, but you have to be willing to trade that off against higher risk. The asset allocation focus really enables the individual to think about that tradeoff at the aggregate portfolio level."

FOCUS ON THE LONG TERM

"Anybody can be lucky," Brinson concedes, "and of course you're always going to find stories, as you would expect, of random occasions where people on a hunch or a whim make a lot of money." But hope is gener-ally a poor guide for investing. Asset allocation emphasizes expectations based on historical track records and a long-term outlook. That's less alluring, but, all told, a more reliable investment strategy than one based on hope.

"We really believe that when you do this over a period of fifteen years," Brinson says, "there is more at work than just luck or randomness. Our process is built on very rigorous, old-fashioned analysis of companies and industries."

No Shortcuts

A realistic asset allocation should not be rushed; it's a long-term undertaking. The acquisition of information and knowledge is time-consuming and arduous; there are no shortcuts, no silver bullets. "I've been at this for twenty-five years," Brinson observes. "Every time I've tried to find a shortcut, I wind up cutting myself or cutting the investment return."

Embarking on a long-term asset allocation strategy requires more than passing effort. "In the institutional setting where we work, the nature of the work begins at the company level or the industry level," says Brinson. "We try to examine all underlying characteristics, then we build and build on that base of knowledge, until we've encompassed the entire asset class."

Hopes versus Expectation

Thoughtful asset allocation boils down to the difference between what an investor hopes will happen and what an investor can realistically expect will happen. "The individual investor really does need [to] appreciate the depth and degree of work that goes into any successful investment program," Brinson warns. Analyzing companies or industries, both of which are pivotally important to overall investment return, consumes large amounts of time and attention on the part of the investor or the managers hired to oversee the allocation—at the mutual fund level or the private level. "They need to be people," Brinson says, "who share the work ethic and the determination for success."

Bucking the Crowd

Because of the long-term orientation, asset allocation constitutes an anchor against the tide of crowd psychology, which is very hard to resist. One of the great hurdles for individual investors, says Brinson, is a relentless appetite for flavor-of-the-month type investments. They get all the head-lines and become seductive for investors who figure that that's where op-portunities lie or disaster lurks. Most people don't think about risk carefully and strategically. Instead, Brinson observes, when they happen to see the dark side of the market they change their minds—usually at just the wrong time. "Frankly, we found our best performance to be in areas that tend to be obscure," says Brinson, "and we found performance enhance-ments oftentimes when avoiding those areas which are receiving the atten-tion of the day."

MONITOR AND ADJUST ALLOCATIONS TO ACCOMMODATE CHANGED INVESTMENT CLIMATES

Brinson Partners seldom tampers with asset allocations. That's not to say, though, that causes for adjustment never surface. An asset class might war-rant a shift in weighting owing to extreme overvaluation or undervalua-tion, or a specific asset within an asset class might grow more or less attractive. At other times, a client's investment objectives may change.

Within asset classes, new investment opportunities often arise that in-vestors should take advantage of. By Brinson's calculation, this activity or-dinarily accounts for about 2 percent of actual returns. Another 2 percent of actual returns comes from interim adjustments to the weights of asset classes aimed at capturing excess returns from short-term fluctuations in asset class prices.

"Our approach is, we don't think one needs to really turn these port-folios a great deal," Brinson says, "unless circumstances change." Circum-stances may pertain specifically to one client, if the client shifts his or her investment goals or risk profile. College tuition, medical costs, retire-ment, or other needs for added liquidity might dictate an adjustment in an individual's asset allocation.

"You can certainly sit back and monitor this without feeling the need or the anxious expectation of frequent change," says Brinson. On the other hand, asset allocations can drift just because some assets perform better than others. Such drift thwarts the discipline needed to allocate as-sets in the first place.

Say the asset allocation starts with just 80 percent large, New York Stock Exchange-type stocks, and 20 percent bonds that mature in five years. If stocks gain 20 percent and bonds gain 8 percent, at the end of the year the portfolio will consist of 18.4 percent bonds and 81.6 percent stock. A more tumultuous year might dislodge the asset allocation in a more dramatic way. Even when changes are small, over time they can distort the disciplined goals and risk profile set out at the beginning. "You wouldn't want to fall asleep for so long that you fall out of line with the mix and weight of asset classes that you desired," says Brinson.

Replacing assets enjoying good performance with assets that are not doing so well takes exceptional discipline, but in Brinson's eyes that's the key to long-term success. Professional investors call this "rebalancing" the portfolio. "It's actually easier to say than to do," Brinson concedes. Rebalancing often defies the natural inclination to place more bets on the hot asset classes that have run their course.

Asset Allocation versus Market Timing

"Asset allocation and market timing are distinctly different concepts," Brinson asserts. They are easy to confuse because a decision to lighten up on U.S. equities and add weight to emerging markets, for example, sounds like market timing to most investors.

"Market timing is saying, 'I bought this stock, it's trading for $10, and I think I can find somebody to buy it for $12,'" explains Diana Cohen, a Brinson Partners principal. "Market timing is making forecasts of future price movements, saying, 'In two weeks, the price is going to be Y, so I will either buy more or sell more.'" An adjustment to an asset allocation recognizes an underlying shift away from the conditions that warranted the initial allocation, or the "policy weighting."

A Level Playing Field

For instance, Brinson Partners began backing away from U.S. equities early in 1997. As an asset class, stocks were assuming different characteristics.

Says Cohen: "It is saying we think the U.S. equity market is really overvalued. If we think the market is overvalued, the implicit thought is: ultimately, it's going to come down; it's going to decline back to where it should be. Therefore, we don't want to own as much of this asset class. We would prefer to be in an asset class we think is fairly valued or we think that is maybe undervalued. We will take a look not only at the excess return expectations we had for an asset class, but also look at the risk component. So what we are doing is making relative value judgments. We put all these asset classes on a level playing field and then take a look at where we expect positive excess return or negative excess return."

Dislocations

Adjustments usually amount to trimming a slice of one asset class and making incremental additions to another. Major dislocations are few and far between, but they do occur. Since launching his firm in 1981, Brinson has navigated a handful:

1. Overvaluation of domestic small capitalization stocks in 1983.
2. Undervaluation in international fixed income markets in 1985.
3. Overvaluation of some sectors of the real estate market in 1985.
4. Extreme overvaluation of the U.S. stock market in the summer of 1987.
5. Extreme overvaluation of the Japanese stock market in 1988.

The reason for easing up on U.S. stocks early in 1997 was not Brinson's way of predicting imminent collapse. Brinson trimmed the weighting for U.S. stocks because that asset class had exhausted the expectations that warranted an allocation in the first place. "We're not saying necessarily that there will be a decline in the market," Cohen insists. "You can get to the same [target] value with a return of 2 percent a year. As your price essentially flattens out over time, you're still estimating a positive return from this point forward but it may increase in a different path and a different pattern. So you can get to the [target] value in a number of different ways. You can get to it through a decline in price, or you can get to it sort of standing still over time." Either way, in the judgment of Brinson Partners, U.S. stocks were not expected to deliver their share of total returns, warranting a shift in the asset allocation.

Avoid Monitor Mania

So long as frequent monitoring doesn't prompt overreaction, Brinson favors it. But he also urges caution. "In general, the flow of information helps educate investors and certainly provides them with at least the same information, in most cases, that professionals are getting. If, however, individuals misinterpret the usefulness of that information and start thinking that because they are getting it frequently they should trade their portfolios frequently, that would be a grave error. It would be a big mistake if investors all of a sudden started thinking that frequency of information somehow meant that they had to engage in high-frequency trading of their portfolios." Besides running the risk of poor investments, transaction costs can take huge hunks out of returns.

A formal review of asset allocations once a year makes a great deal of sense to Brinson, but these reviews shouldn't automatically warrant changes to the portfolio, he warns. The principal benefit is an opportunity for an individual or a family to reconsider their circumstances.

Three Sample Asset Allocations

Designing a long-term asset allocation entails five key steps:

1. Decide which asset classes to include and which to exclude.
2. Consider long-term expected returns, risks, and covariances among classes.
3. Decide what portion of the portfolio each class should take up (the "normal weight").
4. As circumstances change, adjust normal weights in order to capture returns that short-term fluctuations produce.
5. Select individual securities within each asset class to boost returns within that asset class.

All of the following sample portfolios recognize that asset allocation does not bear fruit overnight. Different individual objectives suggest different strategies that often vary more in *relative weights of asset classes* than in their character. Common threads are a long investment horizon, a global outlook, and an emphasis on aggregate risk.

A Conservative Asset Allocation.   This portfolio is for investors who don't want a fear of loss to keep them awake at night. A conservative asset allocation exhibits the overall risk characteristics of a portfolio that consists exclusively of U.S. government bonds—meaning very low risk to income. Thanks to covariance, however, one-fourth of the portfolio can be invested in securities other than bonds.

What's more, the bonds included in the conservative mix can be widely diversified among short-term, medium-term, and long-term securities issued by corporations and by the U.S. government. About one-tenth of the portfolio can reside in non-U.S. bonds. This robust definition of all the fixed-income alternatives that exist along the bond spectrum also would include securities that derive value from thousands of home mortgage payments—all told, a representative sample of all fixed-income alternatives that exist within the U.S. bond spectrum.

A smaller proportion, around 11 percent, belongs in equity markets, and a slimmer amount, around 5 percent, should remain in short-term securities, or "cash equivalents," that are readily convertible into cash at face value, called cash equivalents. About 6 percent of the portfolio belongs in U.S. real estate (other than a home mortgage), with about 3 percent apportioned to high-yield bonds—a class of securities that might sound risky to conservative investors. "If we can add some assets that on their own might be somewhat risky, but in the aggregate don't increase the risk of the portfolio, then that's a way of enhancing the return and the characteristics of future performance."

This advice reiterates the dominant theme of asset allocation. "The notion of overall risk is what we care about," says Brinson. "We want to look at the aggregate portfolio. We want to understand whether the riskiness of that aggregate portfolio is at the conservative end of the spectrum" (Figure 7.3).

This conservative asset allocation is designed to cushion an investor against inflation, which can be cataclysmic for bondholders if interest rates rise and bond prices decline. In the late 1970s and early 1980s, investors who sold long-term bonds they had bought a few years earlier had to settle for far less than each dollar they had plunked down originally. To some

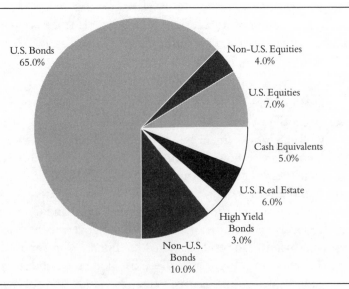

Figure 7.3 A Sample Conservative Asset Allocation. (*Source:* Brinson Partners, Inc.)

investors, the prospect of inflation makes bonds seem awfully risky. Real estate, for example, sounds like a better deal than bonds because, under the influence of inflation, rents increase and so does the underlying asset value. All of this begs the question: Why should anyone, including conservative investors, own bonds?

Risk, Brinson says, has two dimensions. In the 1970s, when interest rates headed skyward, real estate did very well and bonds tanked. But the 1980s and the early 1990s told the opposite story: Bonds flourished while real estate sagged. "That just illustrates the point that these underlying asset markets can offset each other in response to changed economic circumstances," Brinson declares. The two asset classes normally display negative covariance; inflation helps one and punishes the other. In other words, the benefits still accrue while the risks tend to cancel each other out. "Overall," Brinson says, "what we're looking at here is a mix of assets for somebody who views the future in a conservative mode. There would not be a great deal of volatility and change in this portfolio."

A Moderate-Risk Asset Allocation. This portfolio would typically have a smaller component of fixed-income investments than the conservative portfolio, and a wider assortment of asset classes with more aggressive characteristics, including emerging market securities emanating from companies in exotic places like Russia, China, and Uganda. Another piece of the pie is devoted to private market or venture capital investing, which assumes that investors won't need their cash back on short notice. For these investments in real estate and fledgling companies, investors should not count on collecting a return on investment in less than five years. But if they finally collect, which is not a sure thing, lucrative payoffs ordinarily reward the early confidence and the prolonged uncertainty.

These markets tend to offer, over time, higher potential rewards to investors who are willing to travel a bumpier road than their conservative counterparts can tolerate. But the aim of asset allocation is to embrace these risks without putting the whole pie at risk. Even though venture capital is a very risky asset in and of itself, the choice of other assets offsets somewhat the risks without ruling out the big potential rewards that well-heeled investors enjoy (Figure 7.4).

Once strictly the province of the rich who can afford to take losses, risky assets are increasingly within the means of typical investors with $20,000 to $50,000 saved toward retirement. They too can afford to diversify assets sufficiently to assume the kinds of risk that produce big rewards. Their alternatives might not be as expansive as for investors with

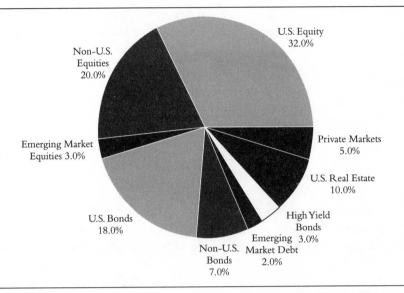

U.S. Equity
32.0%

Non-U.S.
Equities
20.0%

Private Markets
5.0%

Emerging Market
Equities 3.0%

U.S. Real Estate
10.0%

U.S. Bonds
18.0%

High Yield
Bonds
3.0%

Emerging
Market Debt
2.0%

Non-U.S.
Bonds
7.0%

Figure 7.4   A Sample Asset Allocation with Moderate Risk. (*Source:* Brinson Partners, Inc.)

more capital, Brinson warns. Nonetheless, if they are willing to think about the investment process, opportunities multiply.

An Aggressive Asset Allocation.   This portfolio is for the investor who can sleep nights while perfectly aware that investments are guaranteed to fluctuate. From the standpoint of its risk profile, this asset allocation resembles a portfolio consisting strictly of U.S. stocks. But instead of 100 percent exposure to a single class, U.S. stocks make up only 41 percent of the mix. Much riskier stocks and bonds issued by companies in emerging markets take up 8 percent, and bonds constitute a much smaller portion than in the other two more risk-averse portfolios (Figure 7.5).

What identifies an investor as conservative, middle-of-the-road, or aggressive? The answer is critical when building a portfolio from scratch, but it also should guide a choice of mutual funds for investors who prefer that route. Without it, there is no use mimicking another investor's pie chart.

"Clearly, different investors have different objectives, and rightfully so," Brinson says. Age is a key factor. Younger people can afford to take greater risk, because they have time in their favor. Shorter time frames usually warrant more conservative approaches. These parameters must be

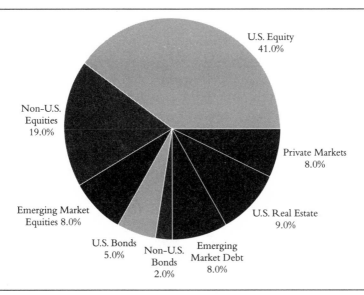

U.S. Equity
41.0%

Non-U.S.
Equities
19.0%

Private Markets
8.0%

Emerging Market
Equities 8.0%

U.S. Real Estate
9.0%

U.S. Bonds
5.0%

Non-U.S.
Bonds
2.0%

Emerging
Market Debt
8.0%

Figure 7.5   A Sample Aggressive Asset Allocation. (*Source:* Brinson Partners, Inc.)

balanced, however, with expected cash requirements, tax status, and the kinds of loss an investor can stomach while waiting for the long-term benefits to materialize.

Because taxes are a very important economic consideration, individual investors should assemble their asset mix not just from the perspective of its being conservative or aggressive, but in accordance with the tax circumstances they are in. That clearly will tilt the types of investment to areas that minimize adverse tax consequences. That may mean tilting the portfolio toward municipal bonds or other areas of the bond market that have better tax consequences.

A large audience of institutional investors cared about global asset allocation when Brinson and his associates bought their firm from First Chicago and launched Brinson Partners. But independence didn't last long before Swiss Banking Corp. swooped in and snapped up Brinson Partners. Not bad for a fellow who almost settled for ivy-covered walls and a swivel chair with a campus view. Others would have leaped at the chance to earn a doctorate from Stanford University, but not Brinson. He's pleased to have the world on a computer screen, if not on a string. Says Brinson, in his laconic way, "I like what I do."

8

Risk and Investor Psychology

WORTH THE RISK

I have a strong interest in history, and it talks to me," says author and investment adviser Peter L. Bernstein. Ever since an introductory course in economics awakened him, as a young Harvard student, to a field then absorbing the stunning impact of *The General Theory of Employment, Interest and Money* by John Maynard Keynes, Bernstein has paid close attention to the way financial systems work.

Bernstein's career path after Harvard led him to the New York Federal Reserve, the wartime Office of Strategic Services, a teaching post at Williams College, the Amalgamated Bank of New York (where he managed the bond portfolio and, later, foreign exchange), his father's old-style investment management firm, and, eventually, his own consulting firm, providing high-level investment advice to major foundations, large personal trusts and money management firms. In 1974, he launched *The Journal of Portfolio Management,* a forum for new ideas about investment that has helped shape financial markets and investment practices. Bernstein is also the author of many articles and books that chronicle the progress of risk measurement and analysis from ancient times through the latest developments in modern portfolio theory and behavioral finance. In 1997, Bernstein joined Sir John Templeton, Warren Buffett, and John Neff by becoming the fourth recipient of the prestigious Award for Professional Excellence, the highest accolade conferred by the Association for Investment Management and Research, the professional organization of securities analysts and portfolio managers.

"Risk is the chance of loss, and for most of history it was viewed as that," Bernstein observes. "There is a chance I'm going to lose. But in the capitalist system, risk is also opportunity. Nothing ventured, nothing gained is as important to keep in mind as the fear that if I don't manage my affairs, I can get wiped out."

Contrast risk in America's history, says Bernstein, with the history of any other country to see how risk fosters opportunity in an open society unencumbered by narrow rules and stuffy traditions. "The Spanish Empire, with all that gold they found in Peru and all the gold in Mexico, such tremendous wealth, whatever happened to the Spanish Empire? Nothing. The Dutch, in a tiny little country, went all over the world accumulating masses of wealth; and the English, too. These were open societies. And America comes from that tradition, only much stronger. The Spaniards had a heavy-handed monarchy, very tightly organized, no freedom of thought. They had adventure but they didn't know how to capitalize on it. America is an adventure all the way and seems particularly so today when our economy and society seem so much more flexible even than [those] in Europe. Freedom is risk. Democracy, when you think of where this country started—what a risk that was."

THE BIG QUESTION

The unprecedented economic boom of recent decades has made the United States an exceptional haven for risk taking. Tens of millions of Americans now invest in stocks either directly or through mutual funds and retirement plans. Still others are tuned into bond markets, where inflationary jitters drive interest rates up or down. Reacting to this climate, investment gurus and would-be gurus have turned out how-to books by the truckload, purporting to yield the secrets of success. But the most compelling question of all still goes unanswered: Will stock prices go up tomorrow? Or will they go down? Unless investors can predict the future with certainty, investing will always involve risk—a word derived from the Latin verb *recicare*, which means *to dare.*

Risk affects much more than financial markets. It is ingrained in our everyday life. Every decision that favors one choice over another entails risk, whether it's choosing a meal at a restaurant (you might not like the chef's seasonings), taking your car downtown rather than public transportation (you might get stuck in traffic or dent a fender), confessing your true affection for someone (you might be rebuffed), or bungee jumping (the cord might snap). Conversely, the outcomes might all be favorable.

The nature of risk changes very little. Consider this passage from *The Psychology of Speculation,* written by Henry Howard Harper and published three years before the 1929 stock market crash: "All speculations, and even the most conservative investments, have some slight element of risk. All lines of business are more or less a gamble; marriage is a gamble; political preferment is a gamble; in fact nearly everything in life, including our very existence, is an uncertainty; yet people are not thereby discouraged from entering into any and all of these ventures. Those who look only for certainties have far to search and little to find in this world."[1]

Risk means that more than one thing *may* happen in the future, and what *will* happen is unpredictable. People do not know and cannot know what the future holds. "Risk is about life; life is about time and tomorrow, which we don't know," Bernstein observes. "Risk is really about life, because life is about moving into an unknown future and making choices and decisions all the way. We make choices about human relationships, about our health care, about whether to cross the street against the light, just as much as picking General Motors or selling General Electric. Every minute we are concerned with the future and never know what it is going to be."

Each move of the ticker tape is an unsentimental reminder of the consequences of faith and folly. Sometimes the printouts are exhilarating, but, much as investors would like to believe otherwise, being wrong at times also goes with the territory. Bernstein finds such risks scary and exciting at the same time. In a culture that tends to applaud success, however, wrong decisions are hard for most investors to accept. Losses gnaw at egos and destroy confidence. When money is lost, investors may suffer excruciating misgivings, even if they keep the news to themselves. Many losses seem irretrievable. When assets are earmarked for retirement, the future seems to dwindle away with every market downtick.

"The big risk in investing is not buying something that goes down, not being wrong, not finding out that the future is different from what you expect," Bernstein says. "It's knowing how to manage yourself when you are wrong, because [at times] you are going to be wrong." Failing to heed this lesson can lead even well-informed investors, along with the rest of us, to seek dubious risks in good times and to shun prudent risks in bad times. Bernstein recalls his own father's futile efforts to convince his beleaguered investment partners to remain in the stock market in 1931, when it was scraping bottom. Discouraged by reversals, they voted to dissolve the firm and get out—just when they had the least to lose and the most to gain.

No matter what advice experts offer, however, willingness to tolerate risk is strictly a personal matter. "There is no way any professor of economics or minister of the church can tell you what your risk tolerance should be," warns no less an expert than Paul Samuelson, the U.S. economist who won the second Nobel Prize for economics, in 1970. Reason and experience provide little consolation when results are disappointing, as Samuelson discovered for himself after buying a cocoa contract for his mother. "It went down 30 percent," he recalls, "and she was not a happy camper."

TALKING TURKEYS

In the face of risk, identical handicaps afflict the most and the least experienced investors alike. "Every natural human impulse seems to be a foe to success in stocks. And that is why success is so difficult," Fred C. Kelley observed in 1930 in *Why You Win Or Lose*. Investing is not a spectator sport. Someone who follows the accounts of his baseball team every day doesn't expect to join the major leagues. Investors, though, march blithely onto the playing field with only the skimpiest understanding of markets and their own inadequacies. "Many a man or woman," Kelley wrote, "who would not expect to be successful as a circus clown, opera singer, or grocer, without some kind of preparation or talent, nevertheless expects to be successful right off in the stock market—probably the most intricate and difficult game on earth. The reason for this faith in success without any special qualification is doubtless the most universal belief in luck."[2]

Why, for instance, do investors often hold onto a stock hoping to catch the last uptick? Seeking to explain his own tendency to follow this self-defeating practice, Kelley recalled the behavior of a turkey trapper he had once known.

> I learned that men win or lose not so much because of economic conditions as because of human psychology. Certain mental traits that we nearly all have are barriers to success. Why, when I had a profit on a certain stock, didn't I sell it? Why did I stand by and see my profit reduced as prices went lower and lower without ever offering to sell?

It dawned on me that my behavior was almost exactly the same as that of an old man I knew in boyhood. He had a turkey trap, a crude contrivance consisting of a big box with the door hinged at the top. This door was kept open by a prop to which was tied a piece of twine leading back a hundred feet or more to the operator. . . . When enough turkeys had wandered inside the box, my friend would jerk away the prop and let the door fall shut. Having once shut the door, he couldn't open it again without going up to the box, and this would scare away any turkeys lurking outside. The time to pull away the prop was when as many turkeys were inside as one could expect.[3]

On one occasion, the trapper had a dozen turkeys in the trap. But one of them wandered out before he closed the door. One might have expected him to settle for eleven turkeys, but instead he resolved to wait for the twelfth to find its way back. Meantime, others walked out until eventually only one remained. "I'll wait until he walks out or another goes in, and then I'll quit," the trapper told Kelley. In the end, the solitary turkey joined the others, and Kelley reports that the trapper went home empty-handed.

Wise investors make mistakes, but they rarely underestimate the stock market's capacity to disappoint, especially when the market is rising. The late Henry Goldberg, a leading Big Board specialist who began selling stocks on the New York Curb Exchange in the first decade of the twentieth century, was once asked to describe the stock market in a single word. His answer after a moment's reflection: "Treacherous." In an instant, the market can reclaim gains that took an investor weeks, months, or even years to accumulate. Witness upheavals in October 1987 and October 1997, to say nothing of October 1929.

Although it may seem unthinkable to many investors today, the market can stall for long periods of time. The Dow Jones Industrial Average flirted with the 1,000 mark in January 1966 but fell to 631.16 in May 1970—a 37 percent decline—before closing above the 1,000 mark for the first time in November 1972. Thereupon it slipped back again by 42 percent and didn't cross 1,000 to stay until October 1982—ending a 16-year stretch without a meaningful gain, notwithstanding wild fluctuations along the way. (In contemporary terms for investors in early 1998, imagine the Dow Jones Average plunging from 8,200 to less than 5,000 before permanently crossing the 8,200 mark in the year 2013.)

Investors who ignore such barren stretches and behave as if markets always go up expose themselves to serious financial and emotional reversals. To shun risk altogether, Bernstein warns, is just as foolhardy. Such a course means forgoing opportunity, and it subjects an investor to harsh consequences later in life, when the time comes to start living on one's investment assets.

OUT OF SIGHT, OUT OF MIND

Insights into investment risk were still primitive when Bernstein entered Harvard as a freshman in the fall of 1936. Economics luminaries in Cambridge took scant notice of Benjamin Graham and David Dodd, whose 1932 edition of *Securities Analysis* is considered the bible of fundamental securities analysis today. Still less thought was given to the great issues of investment risk and efficient markets that would garner a slew of Nobel prizes for financial economists in subsequent decades. The introductory textbook drew largely on the pioneering work of Alfred Marshall, first published in 1890. "There was nothing about stock market investment," recalls the distinguished economist Robert Heilbroner, Bernstein's long-time friend, Harvard classmate, and fellow alumnus of the Horace Mann preparatory school in New York City. In the senior-year competition for top honors in economics, Heilbroner barely nosed out Bernstein for the summa cum laude. Bernstein had to settle for magna cum laude even though Heilbroner concedes that his rival's thesis was "in many ways more analytically interesting" but less sexy. Both he and Bernstein recall studying economics under the great Russian émigré economist and 1973 Nobel laureate Wassily Leontief, whose brilliant insights suffered in translation because his accent garbled the pronunciation of key terms.[4]

Keynes's views dominated the discipline in those days. "The received wisdom in pre-1929 economics was that there could be no such thing as the depression," Bernstein remembers. "If it happened, it was simply due to frictions in the system, but the depression was not an inherent part of the system. Keynes came out and said, 'Yes it is,' that you could have unemployment equilibrium. So it was a complete discard of the classical economic ideas. It gave a theoretical structure to what we saw around us."

After graduation, Bernstein accepted an invitation to join the New York Federal Reserve's research department. A year later, just as the United States was entering World War II, he landed in the Fed's foreign department. His research covered a wide spectrum, he says, from ideas introduced by Keynes, to the means by which Germany and the Axis financed the war, and the role of the U.S. Central banking system during wartime. The Federal Reserve was not in command of the U.S. banking system then as it is today. Owing to an influx of foreign gold during the Great Depression and the near-standstill in lending, Bernstein says, commercial banks were holding billions of dollars in excess reserves largely outside the Fed's reach.

Seeking a more direct role in the war effort, Bernstein signed up to join a ground-crew unit in the Army Air Corps, but the combination of his poor eyesight and superior analytical skills led instead to Washington, DC and the Office of Strategic Services (OSS), the forerunner of the Central Intelligence Agency. There he made a study of the supply of strategic materials, especially ferro-alloys, available within Germany. Still restive so far from the front, he finally secured a posting with the Air Corps, which sent him to North Carolina for three months of basic training and then to Yale University[5] for five months of preparation as a communications officer. He made it to Europe as a captain in the Air Corps, but was assigned to the OSS for the duration.

In September 1946, the stock market suffered its first severe postwar decline, triggering widespread fears of another crash. By that time, Bernstein was teaching economics at Williams College and was happily oblivious to events on Wall Street. But with academic promotion dependent on his earning a graduate degree, Bernstein spent just one year on the Williams campus and then joined the Amalgamated Bank of New York, the banking arm of the Amalgamated Clothing Workers Union. After starting out as economist and manager of the bond portfolio, he soon moved over to the foreign desk, which was becoming a hub of commercial activity between the United States and the newly declared State of Israel.

Bernstein's banking career lasted five years. In 1951 he joined Bernstein-Macauley, established by his father in 1934. "We were social workers to the rich: nice, wealthy people," he recalls with both faint sarcasm and nostalgia. The words of one wealthy client, whose company had just gone public, still ring Bernstein's ears: "Listen, young man, you don't have to make me rich. I am rich." This attitude was far removed from today's performance driven mutual-fund climate. "Ours was not performance-oriented, it was a hand-holding kind of business," says Bernstein. "We were involved in every aspect of their lives. Once people have told you how much money they have, they've told you the most important thing." He became head of Bernstein-Macauley in 1965.

Less eager than his younger associates to tackle new, riskier ventures, like building a pension fund clientele, particularly since his own investment represented most of the firm's capital, Bernstein sold a controlling interest in Bernstein-Macauley, in 1967, to Carter, Berlind, and Weill, a hot new brokerage firm that was well suited to a wider array of investment risks.[6] Bernstein's new partners were a team of eager young investment bankers, including Arthur Levitt, who later became Securities and Exchange Commission Chairman. The ringleader was Sanford ("Sandy") Weill, who engineered a string of mergers that would ultimately swallow up Hayden Stone, Shearson-Hamill, and Lehman Brothers, some of the most illustrious names in investment banking. Bernstein enjoys recalling that the purchase of Bernstein-Macauly was Sandy Weill's first deal.

Carter, Berlind flourished during Bernstein's tenure. But in 1973, Bernstein exchanged the nail-biting rigors of managing clients' money for a less hectic existence. He and his wife, Barbara, launched a new firm, under his name, to provide high-level investment advice to major foundations, money managers, and large personal trusts.

"DO YOU BEAT THE MARKET?"

Unlike professional investment advisers in the late 1960s and early 1970s, who belittled academic theories, Bernstein sought out top thinkers in the growing field of financial economics. The list included Bill Sharpe, who brought Bernstein up short one day in 1968 by asking whether he could beat the stock market. "It just never occurred to me if we were or weren't beating the market," says Bernstein. "I assumed that we were. I suspect the first ten years or so I was in the business that we did, because the market was much less sophisticated, and with a systematic approach you probably did beat the great unwashed public."

Adroit investment could still beat the market more often in those heady days, Bernstein says. "We had some big winners," he recalls. "We bought the puberty boom. We bought the demographics. We bought Tampax and Gillette—big, big positions in Tampax and Gillette." These were two of the best stocks to own for much of the next three decades. Tampax was eventually part of a merger, but, in 1997, Gillette was still a highly desirable stock to own.

The main reason why it is harder to beat the market today, Bernstein notes, is that institutions routinely own at least half of a company's stock, as compared with slim fractions of outstanding shares in the 1950s and early 1960s. Many pension funds were barred from owning any stock on behalf of beneficiaries—a legacy of the 1929 Crash that the most conservative institutions continued to observe until the 1970s. Most shares of stock had been bought during the Great Depression, so sellers were often subject to enormous capital gains taxes. Consequently, not much stock was traded. When individuals did buy and sell, they were susceptible to frequent overreactions.

Bernstein attributes his comfort level with academics to his long involvement with academia. He had taught introductory courses on economics and on money and banking at the New School for Social Research in New York City, and his Random House, 1965 book, *A Primer on Money, Banking and Gold,* sold thousands of copies and remains a basic text in many college-level economics programs today.

A two-year bear market created interest in what academics were saying about risk. In 1974, a dismal S&P 500 logged a total return of minus 40 percent. Persuaded that the investment profession needed new ways to manage risk, Bernstein became the first editor of *The Journal of Portfolio Management* under the aegis of *Institutional Investor Magazine.*

BARN DOORS AND JOLLY CONFERENCES

In the first issue of his new journal, Bernstein chided investment professionals for their miserable performance, academics for their pathetic efforts to communicate their arcane messages, clients for their flimsy grasp of securities markets, and regulators for excelling at closing barn doors after the horses had been stolen. Bernstein outlined the *Journal's* mission with relaxed eloquence:

> The maiden issue of this journal appears at a critical time for our profession. The dismal record of portfolio management over the past five years needs no elaboration. The causes of this record, however, are far more obscure than its painful visibility. With all the research input, the sophisticated economic analysis, the jolly conferences, the attention to decision making structures, and the increased understanding of risk and reward, how could so many have failed to see that all the known parameters were bursting apart?
>
> The objective of this journal is to provide a platform where practitioner, academic, regulator and client can communicate with one another, can clarify the areas of agreement and disagreement, and can provide fresh viewpoints of the perennial problems of risk-adjustment, security selection, and timing.[7]

Under Bernstein's editorial direction, *The Journal of Portfolio Management* rapidly emerged as a prestigious forum for the latest thinking in investment. That first issue, published in autumn 1974, carried articles about efficient markets, random walks of stock prices, and myths about beta. Authors included the 1970 Nobel laureate Paul Samuelson; the contrarian chairman of Batterymarch Financial Management Corporation, Dean LeBaron, an early proponent of index funds; and the late Fisher Black, coauthor (with 1997 Nobel laureate Myron Scholes) of the Black–Scholes Options Pricing model that is widely used today. For subsequent issues, William Sharpe wrote about adjusting for risk in portfolio management, John Kenneth Galbraith shared reminiscences of the Great Crash, and Henry C. Wallich, a governor of the Federal Reserve, discussed innovation and vitality in a bond market subject to inflation. The Spring 1975 issue carried a trail-blazing collection of papers on fixed-income portfolio management, just as that discipline was experiencing the upheaval that gave rise to active bond traders like Bill Gross, the founder of PIMCO and the subject of Chapter 6.

Wreckage left by the 1973–1974 bear market prepared the investment community for a message that had been long in coming. Notions about the risk–reward tradeoff had been abroad long before *The Journal of Portfolio Management*'s maiden issue; it predated even the writings of Alfred Marshall that had introduced Bernstein and Heilbroner to economics at Harvard. From the era of seventeenth-century shipowners to the time of modern spacecraft engineers, generations of investors have believed it possible to tip risk in their favor. In *Extraordinary Popular Delusions and the Madness of Crowds,* published in 1841, Charles Mackay described early financial follies in England, France, and Holland that drove thousands of investors to ruin, and nearly bankrupted their countries in the process. Many investment books published since Mackay's time have drawn on his lucid accounts of Tulip-mania, the South Sea Bubble, and the Mississippi Scheme to illustrate the dangerous combination of crowd psychology and investment risk. Those events are seen as precursors to investment fads in our own time, including passions for any stock that sounded "electronic" in the late 1950s, so-called "story stocks" in the 1960s, the "Nifty Fifty" big-growth stocks in the 1970s, oil and real estate in the 1980s, and who knows what—perhaps technology stocks again—in the 1990s and beyond.

A half-century after Mackay's book was published, Gustave Le Bon, in a book titled *The Crowd: A Study of the Popular Mind,* examined the mind-numbing power that crowds exert. When crowd psychology takes hold, Le Bon observed, judgment vanishes and the individual's ability to keep risk in proper perspective is imperiled. "So far as the majority of their acts are considered," he wrote in 1895, "crowds display a singularly inferior mentality."

> When studying the fundamental characteristics of a crowd we stated that it is guided almost exclusively by unconscious motives. Its acts are far more under the influence of the spinal cord than of the brain. In this respect a crowd is closely akin to quite primitive beings. The acts performed may be perfect so far as their execution is concerned, but as they are not directed by the brain, the individual conducts himself . . . as the exciting causes to which he is submitted may happen to decide. A crowd is at the mercy of all external exciting causes, and reflects their incessant variations. It is the slave of the impulses which it receives. The isolated individual may be submitted to the same exciting causes as a man in a crowd, but as his brain shows him the inadvisability of yielding to them, he refrains from yielding. This truth may be physiologically expressed by saying that the isolated individual possesses the capacity of dominating his reflex actions, while a crowd is devoid of this capacity.[8]

In the years preceding the 1929 Crash, economists and stock market enthusiasts in this country began to articulate the connection among psychology, the economy, and market risks. In an essay in the *Journal of Political Economy* titled "Economics and Modern Psychology," economist John Maurice Clark challenged his fellow economists to face the facts. "If the economist borrows his conception of man from the psychologist, his constructive work may have some chance of remaining purely economic in character," Clark declared. "But if he does not, he will not thereby avoid psychology. Rather, he will force himself to make his own, and it will be bad psychology."[9]

Three years before the Crash, Henry Howard Harper had described a climate primed for financial catastrophe. Gripped by crowd psychology, individual investors had lost sight of customary curbs on risk taking. "Hysterical 'bulls' care nothing whatever about the earnings or dividend returns on a stock," Harper had warned. "The only note to which they attune their actions is the optimistic slogan, 'It's going up!' and the higher it goes, the more they buy, and the more their ranks are swelled by new recruits."[10]

Education has not curbed the worst tendencies of investors, unfortunately. Under clouds of self-deception that defy the laws of probability—if not plain common sense—investors routinely buy hot mutual funds too late, for example, and sell promising funds too soon. Little seems to prevent them from following the crowd as it rushes ahead or shies away.

THE FATHER OF CONTRARY OPINION

No one has crusaded against the crowd's fatal attraction with more cantankerous determination than Humphrey Neill, "the father of contrary opinion"—a moniker that *Life* magazine bestowed on him in 1949. For 25 years, from 1949 until 1974, shortly before he died, Neill published the *Contrary Opinion Newsletter* from his barn in Saxton's River, Vermont. His small but devoted audience included Edward C. Johnson II, the man who built Fidelity Investments into a mutual fund powerhouse; personal finance maven Sylvia Porter; actor Marlon Brando, who once sought Neill's opinion on the price of gold; and Peter L. Bernstein, who recalls that Neill was quick to encourage his critics. "The angrier you made him by your arguments, the more he wanted to hear what you had to say," Bernstein says.

"The stock market is always going lower (when it is headed down) and always is going higher (when it is headed up)," Neill reminded *Newsletter* subscribers in June 1962. "Sounds stupid, doesn't it? But that about expresses the public psychology. The crowd rides the trend and never gets off until they're bumped off."[11] Neill was reacting to a six-month market slide led by investors who were deserting the mad rush to hot growth stocks. Their infectious change of sentiment caused the Dow Jones Industrials to tumble 27 percent between November 1961 and June 1962. Neill summed up his assessment of crowd psychology with this aphorism: If everyone thinks alike, then everyone is likely to be wrong. (For the Winter 1975 edition of *The Journal of Portfolio Management,* Neill wrote "I Was There," his firsthand account of the Great Crash.)

As a publication designed to make theory accessible to investment professionals, *The Journal of Portfolio Management* plowed new territory. Although bits and pieces of modern portfolio theory had already reached stockbrokers, a place to air them more fully was still needed four decades after Harry Markowitz realized there was no point in thinking about returns without thinking about the level of risk required to produce them.

What was needed was a valuation model to incorporate the risk that future earnings and dividends might never materialize.

The way to control investment risk, Markowitz reasoned, is to diversify the risk over a broad class of securities. His theory rests on the fact that all securities do not trade alike; some go up while others go down in response to market stimuli. This interaction of securities, called covariance, offsets overall risk without a commensurate sacrifice of return. In contrast with prevailing wisdom, which held that the way to get rich was to concentrate investments where the expected payoff was highest, Markowitz had delivered a bombshell. His conclusions about covariance and diversification, buttressed by sound theory and market data, inaugurated the era of modern portfolio theory.

Markowitz's bombshell triggered a debate that was confined largely to academic circles. For example, James Tobin, in a breakthrough 1958 paper, contended that a portfolio consisting of all stocks represents the optimal tradeoff of risk and reward. But it took more than a decade for someone to take diversification to a level that professional investors could understand and apply. The person who did that was Bill Sharpe, who found a way around the chore of sorting out multitudinous relationships among individual stocks. Instead of calculating the covariance of every stock in relation to every other stock, Sharpe demonstrated that what's important is the relationship between a single stock and the rest of the market as a whole. His single-index model, later called the single-factor model, introduced the world to *beta,* which measures the sensitivity of a stock or a group of stocks to underlying movements in the stock market. This insight, along with refinements, secured Sharpe's place alongside Markowitz and the economist, Merton Miller, who shared with him the 1990 Nobel Prize for economics.

Since beta's arrival, financial economists have produced successive refinements of diversification techniques. Sharpe's own improvements include the "reward-to-variance" ratio, now known as the Sharpe ratio, and the capital asset pricing model (CAPM), a means of determining the values of risky securities. Those advances supplied the underpinning for index funds, which rest on the evidence that an average investor cannot possibly outperform the stock market consistently in the absence of nonpublic information. The Black–Scholes Option Pricing formula soon followed. A so-called Arbitrage Pricing Model, credited to Stephen A. Ross, Sterling Professor of Economics and Finance at Yale University, and Richard Roll of the University of California at Los Angeles, further enlarged the dimensions of diversification and risk management.

NEW RECIPES FOR RISK

As economists were perfecting ways to manage risk, Wall Street was busy cooking up new kinds of risk. Today, the vast spectrum of risk opens up more gradations of risk and return than ever before. It stretches from the comparative safety of principal in bank accounts, certificates of deposit, and U.S. Treasury bills all the way to exotic debt and equity securities issued by entities in every part of the world, including startup companies in nations where one or two banks, a couple of utilities, and perhaps a few businesses that export raw materials make up most of the economy. Meanwhile, whole classes of derivative securities have emerged whose values hinge on the changes in price of underlying securities. Derivatives' returns over time that are commensurate with additional risk, but using them in conjunction with securities with different risk profiles can create opportunities to reduce overall risk in an investment portfolio.

Yet, with so many sophisticated tools at hand, and with the sobering record of market panics to instruct investors, something still was missing to explain common investment mistakes. "It seems that a descriptive theory of portfolio construction, based on Markowitz, does not hold," Meir Statman declared in a paper titled "How Many Stocks Make a Diversified Portfolio?"[12] People ignore opportunities for properly designed diversification, according to Statman, and efforts to reduce transaction costs do not supply a satisfactory explanation.

The search for answers to Statman's question forms the discipline of behavioral finance. Its principal task is to reveal the myriad inconsistencies of investment decision making and point out sensible ways to behave. To describe how investors cope with risk, pioneers of behavioral finance have developed a new language that features concepts like loss aversion, framing, and mental accounting—sources of the psychological foibles that constantly trip up both professional and amateur investors. In contrast with cadres of quantitative analysts who build artificial intelligence models of stock market behavior, says one behavioral finance expert, only half-jokingly, "What we do more is study natural stupidity."

Behavioral finance won legitimacy as an academic pursuit in the mid-1970s. "The merger of psychology and economics began on the fringes of academia two decades ago," Newsweek reported in 1995. "Two Israeli-born psychologists—Daniel Kahneman of Princeton and [the late] Amos Tversky of Stanford—challenged the notion that economics is nothing more than the study of people trying to make as much money as they can. Through patient explanations and personal friendships, the two men started getting economists to pay attention to things like herd instincts, irrational fears and poor self control. If you ignore psychology, they reckon, you can't predict how people will act."[13] (Shades of John Maurice Clark, in 1919.)

UPS AND DOWNS ARE NOT ALIKE

Kahneman and Tversky helped win credibility for behavioral finance by demonstrating that individuals suffer twice as much pain from a loss as they enjoy a gain of the same magnitude. Imagine a market for coffee mugs with a college emblem—popular items on college campuses. In this exercise, half the participants receive a mug with the option to keep it or to sell it. Other participants bid for the mugs. Repeatedly, researchers found, mug owners were willing to part with a mug only for twice as much as mug buyers were willing to pay for one. That two-to-one ratio holds up in repeated tests of behavioral finance. A bird in the hand *is* worth two in the bush, observes psychiatrist John Schott of the Harvard School of Medicine, who counsels patients with gambling problems.

Behavioral finance experts use a specialized term—loss aversion—to describe the unequal sensitivity of investors to losses and gains. Loss aversion differs from risk aversion, a more familiar term that expresses the generalized fear of any risk. Much of the credit for articulating the concept of loss aversion and exploring its implications goes to Richard Thaler, the Robert P. Gwinn Professor of Economics and Behavioral Science at the University of Chicago's Graduate School of Business. Thaler first observed the phenomenon of loss aversion as an unintended consequence of his dissertation on the value of human life. "I was trying to estimate how much you had to pay people to get them to take risky jobs," Thaler says. "The economist's approach is to study a lot of statistics and estimate how much more people get paid in risky jobs." Instead of building a model based on voluminous statistics, Thaler started asking people questions—an approach his thesis adviser had frowned on.

According to statistical estimates, the value of saving one life would be somewhere in the range of one million to two million dollars. But Thaler asked two questions, not one. First he asked, "Suppose you were exposed to some risk, a one-in-a-thousand chance of dying next week. How much would you pay to avoid that risk?" A typical person gave one thousand dollars as the answer.

Then Thaler turned the question around. "How much would you require to accept a risk with a one-in-a-thousand chance of dying?" he asked.

"According to economics," Thaler explains, "those two questions should be more or less the same." Both ask the value of a life in the face of one chance in a thousand of dying. "But people don't think of those questions as the same," he says. "The very same persons who would say they'd only be willing to pay a thousand dollars to get rid of a risk would have to be paid fifty thousand or two hundred thousand to take a little bit more risk."

These inconsistent responses puzzled Thaler. Although economic theory seemed to preclude them, every inquiry produced similar results. "It's a part of life that isn't explained or understood by the standard economic theories," Thaler says.

In the stock market, loss aversion tends to cloud investment decisions. "When people are thinking about investing, they focus on losses because losses loom so large in their minds," Thaler says. "They think more about losses than they do about potential gains. So whenever I talk to investors about how they should be investing, say, for retirement, if they take a very cautious attitude and say, 'This is my retirement savings, I can't afford to lose,'" Thaler then asks, "Have you thought about how much you are losing by *not* investing that money in the stock market?"

INVISIBLE RED INK

People who put their savings into certificates of deposit during 1995–1997, for example, sacrificed an opportunity to pocket returns in excess of 60 percent. That's clearly a loss, Thaler says, but people don't think of it as a loss. Fear of losing money outweighs the potential for making money because investors attach too much weight to consequences and too little weight to probability. They suffer, says Thaler, from loss aversion and myopia, or myopic loss aversion, a term illustrated by a famous coin-toss wager that Paul Samuelson once offered a colleague. If heads, Samuelson promised to pay his colleague $200. If tails, Samuelson would collect $100. The colleague, savvy about statistics, offered to take the bet with a twist: they would flip the coin 100 times. Although it sounds odd to refuse a bet once but accept it 100 times, it makes good sense to anyone with faith in probability. If Samuelson's colleague were to win only 40 percent of the time, safely within the statistical range of probable outcomes, he would pocket $2,000—the difference between winning $200 forty times and losing $100 sixty times. Professor Samuelson, no fool, turned him down.

Typical investors tend to worry about each flip of the coin—or its stock market equivalent, each price movement. Paying less attention to all the ups and downs and letting probability work in the long run is a much more lucrative course, besides being easier on the stomach lining. Since 1926, common stocks have produced a real return, net of inflation, of about 7 percent, and bonds have produced a 1 percent real return. An investor who opted for safety in 1926 by putting $10,000 into medium-term government bonds would have had $250,000 in 1996. Despite periods of time when bonds outperformed the stock market, the investor who invested the same amount in stocks matching the return of the Standard & Poor's 500 would have had $7.5 million. The difference is less dramatic for shorter stretches, but still significant. Which course sounds riskier? Yet investors saving for retirement stubbornly behave as if bonds were safer than stocks, whereas history at least demonstrates that on a long-term basis the opposite appears true. To Thaler and his colleagues in behavioral finance, the tendency of investors to give up extra returns for an illusion of safety constitutes "the equity premium puzzle."

Investors would do well to think about retirement assets much as they think about the value of their homes, where value matters only when it is time to move. Imagine the anxiety homeowners would undergo if CNN were to report the value of every home on a day-to-day basis, to say nothing of a moment-to-moment basis. "People have a comfort level with their home investments precisely because they don't get any information about it," Thaler says. "When people ask me how to invest for retirement, I tell them to put the bulk of their investment in stock and then forget about it. Don't open the mail from the mutual fund company. I tell people to put their screensavers on ESPN and get the sports scores. That's much better than getting the stock scores." Investors can offset their bad instincts, Thaler suggests, by evaluating their portfolios no more often than once every eleven or twelve months.

Warren Buffett's long-time friend and partner, Charles Munger of Wesco Financial, warns that too much attention to price fluctuation all but guarantees financial suicide. What is it, he asks, that a handful of successful horseplayers have in common? They bet very seldom and bet big. "It is not given to human beings to have such talent that they can just know everything about everything all the time," Munger proclaimed in a 1994 lecture to students at the University of Southern California School of Business. "But it is given to human beings who work hard at it—who look and sift the world for a mispriced bet—that they can *occasionally* find one. And the wise ones bet heavily when the world offers them that opportunity. They bet big when they have odds. And the rest of the time, they don't. It's just that simple."[14] It needs to be said, however, that

Munger and Buffett are not passive investors. If they don't like what they see in their portfolio companies, they can change it.

Besides preventing people from buying stocks in the first place, myopic loss aversion muddies the decision to sell a stock they own. "Suppose that I have several stocks in my portfolio," Thaler says, "and I need to sell one of them to buy a new car. I have some stocks that I've made money on and some that I've lost money on, and I have to pick one to get rid of. What we find is that people seem to be reluctant to sell one of their losers. They're more willing to sell one of the stocks that's gone up than one of the stocks that's gone down."

Why? Even in handling their taxable accounts, investors tend to part with winners before losers, evidence that loss aversion triumphs over rational judgment. Thanks to tax-advantaged write-offs, Uncle Sam shares an investor's losses. When a stock goes up, however, the Internal Revenue Service trims an investor's gains. Even when a stock produces no taxable proceeds, human nature often trumps logic. "When you sell a stock that is down," Thaler observes, "you have to admit that you made a mistake. Whereas if the stock is just sitting there, you can tell yourself a story that it may go up." Not unlike the stubborn turkey trapper, who hoped in vain for the twelfth turkey to wander back into his trap.

"If you have a stock that has gone down," Thaler says, "you don't have to enter it into your mental books until you actually sell it." In behavioral finance, such self-delusions illustrate a concept called "mental accounting," the method investors use to justify poor decisions.

Gamblers routinely indulge in mental accounting. Thaler calls a common technique the "two-pocket" theory of gambling. "If you go to a casino and you observe somebody who won some money early in the evening, what they tend to do is take the money they've won and put it in one pocket. They take the money they brought with them, put it in another pocket, and then they treat the two pockets as different. The money they've recently won they call the casino's money, and that money is easy-come, easy-go. The money they brought with them, that's *their* money, real money, and they're not happy about losing some of it—while they don't really feel bad about losing the house money."

Actual cases of two-pocket mental accounting are common. One of the patients psychiatrist John Schott treats for gambling went to a casino with $1,000 and returned with $247. "He triumphantly announced to his family, when asked how he did, that he had won $247," says Schott. "Now most of us would treat that as having lost $753. But by his form of accounting, that was a win."

CASINO NIGHT FEVER

Another of Schott's patients went to a casino in Connecticut with a plan to double his bets at the craps table until he had won a sufficient sum, or until his stake was exhausted. Among gamblers, Schott says, this kind of bravado is not unusual. "Their belief is that at some point they're going to hit a hot streak and then that series of doubles will get them rich. I had one client who did indeed go and get into a hot streak, and after a series of wins had gotten up to seventy-five thousand dollars of winnings. At that point he debated with himself whether to stop or not, and decided to go for one more roll of the dice. As luck would have it, he lost the seventy-five thousand. But when he got home and his wife asked him how he did, he said, "I had a wonderful time. I broke even.""

Professional traders in the stock market exhibit similar behavior, says Schott. They remember their wins but not their losses—a reminder of the adage that success on Wall Street has two components: a rising market and a short memory. "If they sit down to do a real accounting of what they have done, their actual return, especially after costs of trading, it turns out to be not very good," Schott explains. "But they've believed in themselves all this time. They kidded themselves because of the excitement they get from playing the game."

Investors fool themselves in other ways. "I've had people come to me for advice about their investments and bring records for the past three or four years. And I'll ask them how they did," Schott says. "They'll tell me, 'Well, I made 15 percent compounded per year.' We'll go over the records and we'll discover that the stocks they had did indeed compound at that rate. But stocks they had that had lost money were not included in the accounting." Nor do they count the stocks they sold that afterwards went up.

Even market veterans are swayed by overconfidence and bet too heavily on long shots. Securities analysts, Schott finds, forecast corporate earnings with a very high level of certainty. Yet studies show that their forecasts are commonly wrong. "They attempt to systematically overbelieve in what they do," says Schott. This seems to be a built-in human condition. Most drivers, for example, say they are better-than-average drivers. Thaler likes to ask his students at the beginning of the year how many expect to exceed average performance, and most of them always do.

Overconfident investors habitually overestimate their risk tolerance— quite often by a factor of two-to-one. An investor who is asked the degree of financial loss he or she is willing to risk in hope of a certain gain will almost always reply with a number that subsequently turns out to be too large. Offered, say, prospects of a 50 percent gain over a three-year period, investors typically report that they can tolerate a 20 to 25 percent loss along the way. "But in fact," Schott reports, "if the investment goes sour they begin to panic at 10 percent, and a lot of people will want to get out then."

Although investors should guard against overconfidence, the most successful investors rely heavily on huge doses of self-confidence. A line between the two is hard to draw, but the latter usually entails broad knowledge about markets, strict discipline, and comfort with risk. "It's self-confidence that goes beyond what we normally think of as self-confidence," Schott says. "It is an absolute belief in themselves and their system. They've had the ability to work out an investment plan that is an excellent one that makes sense. That allows them to completely deal with any issues of anxiety they have about investing. They have very few doubts about what they are doing. Some of them are people who also carry that to a high level of belief in religion or God or some system that is very important to them." Barr Rosenberg's deeply felt Buddhism comes to mind, as does Foster Friess's devout view of Christianity.

THE SUBCONSCIOUS INVESTOR

At the root of an investor's attitudes toward risk lie powerful subconscious attitudes toward money itself, according to Schott. "We're not only talking about the actual loss of money and the actual loss of its purchasing power," he says. "We're also talking about all the psychological meanings of money. And we're talking about the self-esteem that is involved with doing a good job investing. So risk is really a very broad psychological concept. And at this time there really isn't a good quantifiable way to look at that." Conclusion: What's a risk for one person is not a risk for someone else.

In a psychological sense, money has a couple of meanings. Insofar as money relates to self-esteem, everybody seeks more of it. Success as a provider reflects mastery of the game. Schott also contends that attitudes toward money are related to toilet training. "People who have neurotic conflicts in that area have to struggle with intense feelings of shame if they make an error in investing, or if the market starts to go down," Schott says. "They want to hide their losses from their families. So they develop all kinds of not-too-functional defense mechanisms." Likewise, investors tend to develop emotional relationships with an investment that prospers, and their self-esteem becomes linked to it. Ultimately, such investors often take negative information about a stock personally, and reject views that might alter their opinion. Before they come to terms with reality, the wonderful stock is in the dumpster.

Loss aversion, mental accounting, and other notions that behavioral finance has produced over two decades lend credence to the case for value investing, according to Bernstein. "Value investing is a direct application of those ideas," he says. "Because people are simple-minded in how they try to understand what goes on in the market, they like to own what is comfortable instead of what's uncomfortable. They make big errors in valuation. Therefore, if you really understand this, you can make money as a value investor."

In one of history's most famous wagers, the seventeenth-century French intellectual, Blaise Pascal, engaged a form of mental accounting to confirm the existence of God. Weighing the risk of believing in God against the risk of not believing, he concluded that belief in God, if wrong, had no consequences. But nonbelief, if wrong, would exact a cost of eternal damnation. So he believed. According to this logic, says Bernstein, Pascal would probably prefer value investing to growth investing. "If you buy something that is in trouble with the stock depressed, and you are wrong, the bad news is already in the stock," Bernstein says. "Whereas if you are right, you're going to have a big winner. If you think about a growth company, it's the other way around. The good news is in the stock price, so if you're wrong you get killed. I think Pascal would have been a value investor."

A healthy way to think about risk now and in the twenty-first century, says Bernstein, sounds simple-minded enough: It's silly to take a risk unless there is a reward. This advice is less satisfying than a tip on a stock primed to skyrocket, but investors who dismiss it almost always pay a stiff penalty. "You don't make a decision whose outcome is uncertain just for the hell of it," says Bernstein. "You have to expect something at the other end. And so the degree of risk that you take has to have some kind of relationship to what you expect to earn on it, and vice versa. You don't put money in a certificate of deposit and expect to get 15 percent return a year for the next 30 years, but if you put money in a small, high-tech stock, it's a risky thing to do. That company could disappear tomorrow. Its fancy, complicated technology you probably don't really understand. You should risk only a small amount of your money in something like that because the chances of winning may not be very big and you won't know how to make the wise decision if the stock's price falls."

BEAUTY CONTEST AND MR. MARKET

We can think of the stock market as a scale that registers the weight of investors' beliefs. "The stock market is not an abstract animal," says Bernstein. "It's a lot of people out there making decisions. And whenever you make one or don't make one, you're making a bet against what all those other people are doing."

Wittingly or unwittingly, all investors participate in a competition that John Maynard Keynes once compared to a beauty contest popular in London during the 1930s.

> Professional investment may be likened to those newspaper competitions in which the competitors have to pick out the six prettiest faces from a hundred photographs, the prize being awarded to the competitor whose choice most nearly corresponds to the average preferences of the competitors as a whole: so that each competitor has to pick, not those faces which he himself finds prettiest, but those which he thinks likeliest to catch the fancy of the other competitors, all of whom are looking at the problem from the same point of view. It is not a case of choosing those which, to the best of one's judgment, are really the prettiest, nor even those which average opinion genuinely thinks the prettiest. We have reached the third degree where we devote our intelligences to anticipating what average opinion expect the average opinion to be. And there are some, I believe, who practice the fourth, fifth and higher degrees.[15]

To move to the third degree, to say nothing of higher degrees, is far from instinctive to investors, and it's not clear that practice can help. "It's a different level of judgment," Bernstein explains. "Investors are always dealing with other investors. That's why it's such a complex game. You might be right. The girl is absolutely beautiful, but everybody else likes redheads this year and for some reason they don't react to your choice."

The legendary investor Benjamin Graham used a different analogy to portray risk in a capricious stock market outside of an investor's control. He likened the stock market to coping with a partner who changes his mind about the business without warning from day to day.

> Imagine that in some private business you own a small share that cost you $1,000. One of your partners, named Mr. Market, is very obliging indeed. Every day he tells you what he thinks your interest is worth

and, furthermore, offers either to buy you out or to sell you an additional interest on that basis. Sometimes his idea of value appears plausible and justified by business developments and prospects as you know them. Often, on the other hand, Mr. Market lets his enthusiasm or his fears run away with him, and the value he proposes seems to you a little short of silly.

If you are a prudent investor or a sensible businessman, will you let Mr. Market's daily communication determine your view of a $1,000 interest in the enterprise? Only in case you agree with him, or in case you want to trade with him. You may be happy to sell out to him when he quotes you a ridiculously high price, and equally happy to buy from him when his price is low. But the rest of the time you will be wiser to form your own ideas of the value of your holdings, based on full reports from the company about its operations and financial position.[16]

At the same time, choice is a luxury that allows the system to work. "Decisions that are difficult to reverse are much riskier," Bernstein observes. Putting up a new factory, for instance, is risky because once the factory is up, it may be hard to sell. But in the stock market, an investor can buy a share of stock in the company that built the factory and then sell it if the factory turns out to be a mistake.

"In any risk that you take or any decision that you make," Bernstein says, "the degree to which you can reverse [your decision] is critical. This is a point that has a lot to do with why the stock market is such an important place, and such an important institution, and why countries that have given up socialism, the first thing they do is establish the stock market. Putting up a factory, investing in a new technology, building an oil rig, are decisions that are hard to reverse without incurring stiff consequences.

"The stock market gives you an opportunity to change your mind after you've made the investment," says Bernstein. "So it makes people willing to invest in those irreversible things. I buy a stock in a high-tech company where the company can't reverse its decisions, but I can reverse mine if I want to." Companies can raise capital because investors are not locked in if the risks become unacceptable. "People will buy," Bernstein says, "because if things aren't going well, they can get out."

Notes

CHAPTER 1: GROWTH

1. Superstar Funds, *Smart Money,* Vol. V, Number IV, June 1996, p. 101.

2. Carla Fried, "11 Superior Funds to Buy Now," *Money Magazine,* February 1997, p. 54.

3. Jerome B. Cohen et al., *Investment Analysis and Portfolio Management,* 5th ed., (Homewood IL: Irwin, 1987) p. 21.

4. Peter L. Bernstein, "Growth Companies v. Growth Stocks," *The Harvard Business Review,* September–October 1956, Vol. XXIV, No. V pp. 87–98.

5. Benjamin Graham, *The Intelligent Investor,* 4th ed., rev. (New York: Harper & Row, 1973) p. 55.

6. Jeremy J. Siegel, *Stocks for the Long Run,* (Chicago: Irwin Professional Publishing, 1994) p. 89.

7. Graham, p. 56.

8. John Kenneth Galbraith, *The Great Crash* (Boston: Mariner Books, 1997) p. 47.

9. Donaldson, Lufkin & Jenrette, Inc., *Common Stock and Common Sense* (New York: Author, 1958) pp. 9–10 (excerpted).

10. Burton Malkiel, *A Random Walk Down Wall Street,* 4th ed., rev. (New York: W.W. Norton & Co., 1985) p. 50.

11. The Dow Jones Averages 1885–1990, Phyllis S. Pierce, (Ed.) (Homewood, IL: Business One Irwin, 1991).

12. Fred W. Frailey, "Foster Friess: Insider Interview," *Kiplinger's Personal Finance Magazine,* August 1994, p. 94.

13. Peter J. Tannous, *Investment Gurus* (New York: New York Institute of Finance, 1997) pp. 232–233.

CHAPTER 2: VALUE

1. Benjamin Graham, *The Intelligent Investor,* 4th ed., rev. (New York: Harper & Row, 1973) p. 79.

2. Graham, p. 79.

3. When a company earns $2 a share and its PE is 25, the stock price is $50. When it earns $1.90 a share (off by 10 cents, or 5 percent) and the PE is 20, then its price is $38 a share, a difference in price of 24 percent. See also the "Magical Multiples" chart on page 9.

4. One company that conformed to this description in 1997 was Chrysler Corporation. Suitably enough, Neff sits on its board of directors.

5. John Neff, "How I Multiplied Investors' Wealth 45 Times," *Money,* 1994, p. 18.

6. *Barron's,* December 14, 1987.

7. Kathryn M. Welling, "Canny Contrarian: Old Pro John Neff Is Not Afraid to Fight the Tape," *Barron's,* July 19, 1982, p. 6.

8. Memo to Windsor Board of Directors, February, 1974.

9. Memo to Windsor Board of Directors, February, 1976.

10. Jed Horowitz, and Barbara A. Rehm, "Dingle Slams Bank Bill Calls Citicorp 'Insolvent,'" *American Banker,* August 1, 1991, p. 1.

11. John Meehan and William Glasgall, "Citi's Nightmares Just Keep Getting Worse," *Business Week,* October 28, 1991, pp. 124–125.

12. John Milligan and Ida Picker, "The Collapse of Citibank's Credit Culture," *Institutional Investor,* December 1991, pp. 53–65.

13. Michael Quint, "Citicorp's Burden," *New York Times,* October 18, 1991, p. D1.

14. Steven Lipin, "Is Beleaguered Citcorp's Stock Finally a Buy?" *The Wall Street Journal,* December 26, 1991, p. C1.

15. Fred W. Frailey, "John Neff: Insider Interview," *Kiplinger's Personal Finance Magazine,* February 1994, p. 80.

CHAPTER 3: QUANTITATIVE

1. Chris Welles, "Who Is Barr Rosenberg and What the Hell Is He Talking About?" *Institutional Investor,* May 1978, p. 59.

2. Peter L. Bernstein, *Capital Ideas: The Improbable Origins of Wall Street* (New York: Free Press, 1992).

3. Ibid., p. 259.

4. From a personal experience: Even an old refrigerator can have alpha. A playwright in New York City moved into a Greenwich Village apartment once occupied by John Lennon. When it came time to replace his worn-out refrigerator, he left it out on the street to be picked up. Only afterwards did friends chastize him for ignoring its value as a John Lennon relic. Value beyond the expected value for worn-out refrigerators meant this one had alpha. But no one exploited it.

5. Kathleen Pender, "Automated Money Managers," *San Francisco Chronicle,* August 14, 1989, p. C9.

6. Barr, a vegetarian, raises chickens for eggs. When the chickens are too old to produce eggs, he gives them to a woman who cares for them until death do them part. To Barr's other credentials, add hero to the chickens of the world.

Chapter 4: Index Funds

1. Warren Buffett does not quite fit the same mold. He is an active investor who can influence management when he does not like the direction in which the business is headed.

2. After he arrived at RAND in 1956, Sharpe flourished. "You could spend one day out of five on any subject you wanted," Sharpe recalls. "And you could use the company's resources for it." One paper published internally suggested a smog tax on vehicles in Los Angeles. Word leaked out. "Local papers wrote it up as a couple of mad scientists in this top secret facility trying to meddle with our right to buy gasoline, but we thought it was a great idea."

3. Charles D. Ellis, with James R. Vertin, *Classics: An Investor's Anthology* (Homewood, IL: Dow Jones Irwin, 1989) p. 412.

4. Peter L. Bernstein, *Capital Ideas: The Improbable Origins of Modern Wall Street* (New York: Free Press, 1992) p. 87.

5. *The Dow Jones Averages 1885–1990,* Phyllis S. Pierce, (Ed.) (Homewood, IL: Business One Irwin, 1991) The Dow Jones Industrial Average did not close above the 1,000 mark until November 1972. Then it tumbled again to 631.16 before closing above the 1,000 mark to stay, in October 1982. An investor who hitched his or her wagon to the Dow in January 1966 would have waited 16 painful years for a meaningful gain.

6. Bernstein, pp. 87, 192.

7. For a brief discussion of beta's sibling, alpha, see Chapter 3 on Barr Rosenberg.

8. Charles D. Ellis, "The Loser's Game," *The Financial Analysts Journal,* July/August 1975, p. 19.

9. A.F. Ehrbar, "Some Kinds of Mutual Funds Make Sense," *Fortune,* July 1975, p. 57.

10. A.F. Ehrbar, "Index Funds—An Idea Whose Time Is Coming," *Fortune,* June 1976, p. 146.

11. David Dreman, "An Inefficient Market," *Forbes,* March 28, 1994, p. 146.

12. George M. Frankfurter, "The End of Modern Finance?" *The Journal of Investing,* Winter 1993, p. 9.

13. Peter Lynch, with John Rothchild, *One Up On Wall Street* (New York: Penguin Books USA, 1989) p. 34.

14. Bernstein, *Capital Ideas,* p. 201.
15. William F. Sharpe's Home Page; www.sharpe.com.

CHAPTER 5: EMERGING MARKETS

1. Marcus W. Brauchli, "Southeast Asia's Monetary Chiefs Thrust into Spotlight" *The Wall Street Journal,* Monday, August 25, 1997, p. A15.
2. Power Brokers, *Smart Money,* September 1997, p. 146.
3. Russ Wiles, "Manager's Forum: Knowing His Places," *Los Angeles Times,* May 13, 1997, p. D4.
4. "Buy When Blood Is Running in the Streets," *Fortune,* October 31, 1994, p. 54.
5. James Cox, "The King of Emerging-Markets Funds," *USA Today,* November 27, 1995, p. 5B.
6. Jeff Prestridge, "Mobius Leaves Nothing to Chance," *The Sunday Telegraph,* January 17, 1993, p. 41.
7. Mark Mobius, *Mobius on Emerging Markets,* (London: Pitman Publishing, 1996) p. 348.
8. Rebecca Blumenstein, "GM Expands Overseas Push for Capacity," *The Wall Street Journal,* September 11, 1997, p. A3.
9. Jim Levi, "Optimist in the Temple of Doom," *Evening Standard,*(London) February 7, 1994, p. 31 (edition A).
10. A cynical investor might say that such an appetite for American TV dooms emerging markets from the get-go.
11. "How Templeton's Mark Mobius Finds the Big Opportunities in Emerging Markets," *Bottom Line,* March 1, 1997, pp. 3–4.
12. Bill Griffeth, *The Mutual Fund Masters* (Chicago: Probus Publishing, 1995) p. 161.
13. Stanley Reed, "Hop a Plane, Buy a Stock," *Business Week,* December 30, 1991, p. 127.
14. "Selecting Stocks in Japan," Pacific Rim Analyst Interview, *The Wall Street Transcript,* April 27, 1992, p. 105.
15. "Waving, Not Drowning," *Global Investment Management,* July 1992.
16. Peter C. Du Bois, "Global Spectator Eyes Brazil, Hong Kong, and Turkey," *Barrons,* November 7, 1994, p. MW7.
17. Kerry Capell, "Emerging Markets," *Financial Planning on Wall Street,* Summer 1992.
18. Aaron Driver, "Goldfinger," *Super Review,* April 1997.
19. Alison Warner, "Top Marks for Mobius," *Equity International,* (UK) February 1992.
20. "The Money Manager," *The Wall Street Transcript,* March 2, 1992.
21. "Emerging Market Makers," *Equity International,* (UK) March 1989.

22. Margaret Price, "Picking Stocks Where Data Is Scarce," *Global Finance,* January 1988, p. 44.

23. Cox, p. 5B.

24. Peter Waldman and Paul M. Sherer, "High-Tech Trauma: A Company's Travails Show Why Economy in Thailand Is Shot," *The Wall Street Journal,* September 8, 1997, p. A1.

25. Matthew Montagu-Pollock, "A Determined Hunter of Value," *Asian Business,* Hong Kong, July 1992.

26. Scott McQuade, "An Intrepid Adventurer," *Financial Adviser,* (UK) November 1991.

27. Montagu-Pollock, *A Determined Hunter . . . ,* July 1992.

28. "EIU Country Profile 1996," *Thailand,* Economist Intelligence Unit.

29. Jonathan Guthrie, "The World Turned Upside Down," *Professional Investor,* November 1992.

30. Mobius, pp. 321–322.

31. "The Money Manager," *The Wall Street Transcript,* March 1992.

32. Griffith, p. 158.

33. Lawrence Minard, "The Principle of Maximum Pessimism," *Forbes,* January 16, 1995, p. 67.

34. For most investors, contrarian investing is much easier said than done. "Investors always say they are contrarians, but we only know a handful of them," observes Mark Faber, another talented emerging markets investor. "If you wish to test your propensity to contrarian reasoning, see whether you have the guts to short the Yen as your own Christmas gift." Marc Faber, *The Great Money Illusion,* (Hong Kong: Longman Group Ltd., 1988) p. 150.

CHAPTER 6: FIXED INCOME

1. *Pacific Investment Management company newsletter,* The Rules, November 1996. [This is not one of Gross's catchier titles, of which there are many: The Final Whimper (after T.S. Eliot), March 1997; Classical Gas, December 1995; Mantle in Wonderland, November 1995; Dale Carnegie in Bondland, April 1995; Men Behaving Badly, October 1996; Gone Fishing, October 1995, to name a few.]

2. PIMCO newsletter, *Twister,* May 1996.

3. PIMCO newsletter, *Bon Appetit,* April 1996.

CHAPTER 7: ASSET ALLOCATION

1. John Wyatt, "Hot Tips from Three Investing Superstars," *Fortune,* December 25, 1995, p. 90.

2. "Investing: The Greatest Game in the World," *The Business Times* (London), February 2, 1996.

3. Peter Bernstein, *Against the Gods: The Remarkable Story of Risk* (New York: John Wiley & Sons, 1996) p. 93.

4. William Shakespeare, *The Merchant of Venice,* Act I Scene I.

5. Gerald M. Loeb, *The Battle for Investment Survival* (Burlington, VT: Fraser Publishing, 1995) p. 119.

6. Gary P. Brinson, L. Randolph Hood, and Gilbert L. Beebower, "Determinants of Portfolio Performance," *Financial Analysts Journal,* July–August 1986, pp. 39–44.

7. Gary P. Brinson, Brian D. Singer, and Gilbert L. Beebower, "Determinants of Portfolio Performance II: An Update," *Financial Analysts Journal,* May–June 1991, pp. 40–48.

8. Roger G. Ibbotson and Gary P. Brinson, *Global Investing: The Professional's Guide to the World Capital Markets* (New York: McGraw-Hill, 1993) p. 7. (Source: Ibbotson Associates, Inc., using data from World Development Report 1992: The challenge of Development, © 1992 by the International Bank for Reconstruction and Development/The World Bank.)

9. Ibbotson and Brinson, p. 14.

Chapter 8: Risk and Investor Psychology

1. Henry Howard Harper, *The Psychology of Speculation* (Burlington, VT: Fraser Publishing, 1926/1966) p. 106.

2. Fred C. Kelley, *Why You Win or Lose* (Burlington, VT: Fraser Publishing, 1930/1991) p. vii.

3. Kelley, pp. 22–24.

4. Both Heilbroner and Bernstein found it difficult to discern "ncrizzes" (increases) from "ndcrizzes" (decreases)—a rather important distinction in Leontief's line of work.

5. "I have no roots at Yale," says the Harvard graduate, "I have roots in the Army Air Force."

6. After adding Arthur Levitt to the firm's shingle, Carter Berlind Weill & Levitt acquired Hayden Stone, a venerable firm with a tarnished reputation but a more recognizable name. The new firm assumed the new name CBWL-Hayden Stone, a half-way measure in case Hayden Stone proved to be more of a liability than an asset. But the initials prodded Wall Street to bestow an altogether different moniker on the upstart firm: Corned Beef with Lettuce.

7. Peter L. Bernstein, "What This Journal Is About," *Journal of Portfolio Management,* Fall 1974, p. 50.

8. Gustave Le Bon, *The Crowd: A Study of the Popular Mind* (Marietta, GA: Cherokee Publishing, 1982) pp. 16–17.

9. John Maurice Clark, "Economics and Modern Psychology," *Journal of Political Economy,* 1918, Vol. 26, p. 4.

10. Harper, p. 83.

11. Humphrey B. Neill, *Contrary Opinion Newsletter,* June 1962, p. 1.

12. Meir Statman, "How Many Stocks Make a Diversified Portfolio?" In *Frontiers of Finance: The Batterymarch Fellowship Papers* (Cambridge, MA: Basil Blackwell, 1990) p. 466.

13. Marc Levinson, "Dismal Science Grabs a Couch," *Newsweek,* April 10, 1995, p. 41.

14. Charles Munger, "A Lesson on Elementary, Worldly Wisdom as It Relates to Investment Management and Business," In *Outstanding Investor Digest,* May 5, 1995, p. 58.

15. John Maynard Keynes, "The General Theory of Employment, Interest and Money," Chapter 12.

16. Benjamin Graham, *The Intelligent Investor,* 4th ed., rev. (New York: Harper & Row, 1973) p. 108.

Bibliography

Benartzi, Shlomo, and Richard H. Thaler, "Myopic Loss Aversion and the Equity Premium Puzzle," *Quarterly Journal of Economics,* February 1995, pp. 73–92.

Bernstein, Peter L., "Growth Companies v. Growth Stocks," *The Harvard Business Review,* September-October 1956, pp. 87–98.

Bernstein, Peter L., "What This Journal Is About," *Journal of Portfolio Management,* Fall 1974.

Bernstein, Peter L., *Capital Ideas: The Improbable Origins of Modern Wall Street* (New York: Free Press, 1992).

Bernstein, Peter L., *Against the Gods: The Remarkable Story of Risk* (New York: John Wiley & Sons, 1996).

Blumenstein, Rebecca, "GM Expands Overseas Push for Capacity," *The Wall Street Journal,* September 11, 1997, p. A3.

Bogle, John C., *The First Index Mutual Fund,* Monograph published by The Vanguard Group, July 1997.

Brauchli, Marcus W., "Southeast Asia's Monetary Chiefs Thrust into Spotlight," *The Wall Street Journal,* Monday, August 25, 1997, p. A15.

Brinson, Gary P., L. Randolph Hood, and Gilbert L. Beebower, "Determinants of Portfolio Performance," *Financial Analysts Journal,* July-August 1986, pp. 39–44.

Brinson, Gary P., Brian D. Singer, and Gilbert L. Beebower, "Determinants of Portfolio Performance II: An Update," *Financial Analysts Journal,* May-June 1991, pp. 40–48.

Brown, Ken et al., "Power Brokers," *Smart Money,* September 1997, p. 146.

Capell, Kerry, "Emerging Markets," *Financial Planning on Wall Street,* Summer 1992.

Clark, John Maurice, "Economics and Modern Psychology," *Journal of Political Economy,* Vol. 26, 1918, p. 4.

Cohen, Jerome B., Edward D. Zinbarg, and Arthur Zeikel, *Investment Analysis and Portfolio Management,* 5th ed. (Homewood IL: Irwin, 1987).

Cox, James, "The King of Emerging Markets Funds," *USA Today,* November 26, 1995.

De Bondt, Werner F.M., and Richard H. Thaler, "Financial Decision-Making in Markets and Firms: A Behavioral Perspective," In R. Jarrow et al., (Eds.), *Handbooks in OR & MS,* Vol. 9, 1995, pp. 385–410.

Donaldson, Lufkin & Jenrette, Inc., *Common Stock and Common Sense* (New York: Author, 1958), pp. 9–10.

The Dow Jones Averages 1885–1990, Phyllis S. Pierce, (Ed.), (Homewood, IL: Business One Irwin, 1991).

Dreman, David, "An inefficient market," *Forbes,* March 28, 1994, p. 146.

Ellis, Charles D., and James R. Vertin, (Eds.), *Classics: An Investor's Anthology,* (Homewood, IL: Dow Jones Irwin, 1989).

Faber, Marc, *The Great Money Illusion* (Hong Kong: Longman Group Ltd., 1988).

Frailey, Fred W., "John Neff: Insider Interview," *Kiplinger's Personal Finance Magazine,* February 1994.

Frankfurter, George M., "The End of Modern Finance?" *The Journal of Investing,* Winter 1993, p. 9.

Fried, Carla, "11 Superior Funds to Buy Now," *Money,* February 1997.

Driver, Aaron, "Goldfinger," *Super Review,* April 1997.

Du Bois, Peter C., "Global Spectator Eyes Brazil, Hong Kong, and Turkey," *Barrons,* November 7, 1994.

Ehrbar, A.F., "Index Funds—An Idea Whose Time Is Coming," *Fortune,* June 1976 p. 146.

Ehrbar, A.F., "Some Kinds of Mutual Funds Make Sense," *Fortune,* July 1995.

Galbraith, John Kenneth, *The Great Crash,* (Boston: Mariner Books, 1997).

Graham, Benjamin, *The Intelligent Investor,* rev. ed., (New York: Harper & Row, 1973).

Graham, Benjamin and David Dodd, *Security Analysis* (Reprint), (New York: McGraw-Hill, 1934).

Griffeth, Bill, *The Mutual Fund Masters* (Chicago: Probus Publishing, 1995).

Gross, William H., *Everything You've Heard about Investing Is Wrong!* (New York: Times Books, 1997).

Guthrie, Jonathan, "The World Turned Upside Down," *Professional Investor,* November 1992.

Harper, Henry Howard, *The Psychology of Speculation,* (Burlington, VT: Fraser Publishing, 1966).

Horowitz, Jed and Barbara A. Rehm, "Dingle Slams Bank Bill, Calls Citicorp 'Insolvent,'" *American Banker,* August 1, 1991, p. 1.

Ibbotson Associates, *Stocks, Bonds, Bills, and Inflation: 1997 Yearbook* (Chicago IL: Ibbotson Associates, 1997).

Johnson, Paul, *The Birth of the Modern* (New York: HarperCollins, 1991).

Kelley, Fred C., *Why You Win or Lose: The Psychology of Speculation* (Burlington, VT: Fraser Publishing, 1991).

Keynes, John Maynard, *The General Theory of Employment, Interest and Money,* (New York: Harcourt Brace, 1936).

Le Bon, Gustave, (Ed.) *The Crowd: A Study of the Popular Mind,* (Reprint) Marietta, GA: Cherokee Publishing, 1982).

Levi, Jim, "Optimist in the Temple of Doom," *Evening Standard,* February 7, 1994.

Levinson, Marc, "Dismal Science Grabs a Couch," *Newsweek,* April 10, 1995, p. 41.

Lipin, Steven, "Is Beleaguered Citcorp's Stock Finally a Buy?" *The Wall Street Journal,* December 26, 1991, p. C1.

Loeb, Gerald, *The Battle for Investment Survival* (Burlington, VT: Fraser Publishing, 1988).

Lynch, Peter, with John Rothchild, *One Up on Wall Street* (New York: Penguin Books USA, 1989).

Mackay, Charles, *Extraordinary Popular Delusions and the Madness of Crowds* (New York: Farrar, Straus & Giroux, 1841).

Malkiel, Burton, *A Random Walk Down Wall Street,* 4th ed. (New York: W.W. Norton & Co., 1985).

McQuade, Scott, "An Intrepid Adventurer," *Financial Adviser,* November 1991.

Meehan, John and William Glasgall, "Citi's Nightmares Just Keep Getting Worse," *Business Week,* October 28, 1991, pp. 124–125.

Milligan, John and Ida Picker, "The Collapse of Citibank's Credit Culture," *Institutional Investor Magazine,* December 1991, pp. 53–65.

Minard, Lawrence, "The Principle of Maximum Pessimism," *Forbes,* January 16, 1995.

Mintz, Steven L., *Five Eminent Contrarians: Careers, Perspectives & Investment Tactics* (Burlington, VT: Fraser Publishing, 1994).

Mobius, Mark, *Mobius on Emerging Markets,* (London: Pitman Publishing, 1996).

Montagu-Pollock, Matthew, "The Prince of Emerging Markets," *Asian Business,* February 1989.

Montagu-Pollock, Matthew, "A Determined Hunter of Value," *Asian Business,* Hong Kong, July 1992.

Munger, Charles, "A Lesson on Elementary, Worldly Wisdom as It Relates to Investment Management and Business," *Outstanding Investor Digest,* May 5, 1995, p. 58.

Neff, John, "How I Multiplied Investors' Wealth 45 Times," *Money Guide,* 1994, p. 18.

Neill, Humphrey B., *Contrary Opinion Newsletter,* June 1962.

Prestridge, Jeff, *Mobius Leaves Nothing to Chance,* January 17, 1993.

Price, Margaret, "Picking Stocks Where Data Is Scarce," *Global finance,* January 1989.

Reed, Stanley, "Hop a Plane, Buy a Stock," *Business Week,* December 30, 1991.

Quint, Michael, "Citicorp's Burden," *The New York Times,* October 18, 1991, p. D1.

Sharpe, William F., "Capital Asset Prices: A Theory of Market Equilibrium Under Conditions of Risk," *The Journal of Finance,* Vol. 19, No. 3, September 1964, pp. 425–442.

Sharpe, William F., William, F. Sharpe's Home Page, Version: January 24, 1997, (http://www.sharpe.stanford.edu).

Siegel, Jeremy J., *Stocks for the Long Run,* (Chicago: Irwin Professional Publishing, 1994) p. 89.

Statman, Meir, "How Many Stocks Make a Diversified Portfolio?" In Deborah H. Miller and Stewart C. Myers (Eds.) *Frontiers of Finance: The Batterymarch Fellowship Papers,* (Cambridge, MA: Basil Blackwell, 1990) pp. 465–480.

Tannous, Peter J., *Investment Gurus* (New York: New York Institute of Finance, 1997).

Thaler, Richard H., "The Psychology of Decision Making with Applications to Financial Markets," April 10, 1995, Sloan School of Management, MIT.

Warner, Alison, "Top Marks for Mobius," *Equity International,* February 1992.

Welles, Chris, "Who Is Barr Rosenberg and What the Hell Is He Talking About?" *Institutional Investor,* May 1978.

Welling, Kathryn M., "Canny Contrarian: Old Pro John Neff Is Not Afraid to Fight the Tape," *Barron's,* July 19, 1982, p. 6.

Wiles, Russ, "Manager's Forum: Knowing His Places," *Los Angeles Times,* May 13, 1997, p. 4.

Williams, John Burr, *The Theory of Investment Value* (Reprint of 1938 edition, Harvard University Press) (Burlington, VT: Fraser Publishing, 1997).

Wyatt, John, "Hot Tips from Three Investing Superstars," *Fortune,* December 25, 1995.

Index